The SECRET of the SOUL

Also by William Buhlman

ADVENTURES BEYOND THE BODY

Using Out-of-Body Experiences
to Understand Our True Nature

The SECRET
of the SOUL

WILLIAM BUHLMAN

HarperSanFrancisco
A Division of HarperCollins*Publishers*

For permissions see page 272.

HarperCollins books may be purchased for educational, business, or sales promotional use. For information please write: Special Markets Department, HarperCollins Publishers, Inc., 10 East 53rd Street, New York, NY 10022.

HarperCollins Web site: http://www.harpercollins.com

HarperCollins®, 🔖 ®, and HarperSanFrancisco™ are trademarks of HarperCollins Publishers, Inc.

FIRST EDITION

Library of Congress Cataloging-in-Publication Data
Buhlman, William.
The Secret of the Soul : using out-of-body experiences to understand our true nature / William Buhlman.—1st ed.
p.   cm.
Includes index.
ISBN 0–06–251671–X (pbk.)
1. Astral projection.   I. Title.
BF1389.A7   B845   2001
133.9'5—dc21   00–054485

01 02 03 04 05 ❖ RRD(H) 10 9 8 7 6 5 4 3 2 1

To my wife, Susan,
and all those who seek the truth of our existence

Contents

Illustrations

Fig. 1. Soul Journey

MARIE CARLSON

To All on the Spiritual Path

Today many of us are awakening to the realization that we possess the natural ability to separate from our bodies and have a profound spiritual experience. When we examine the core of all religions and spiritual paths, we find a common theme of revelations and experiences beyond the physical body. No matter what we believe or don't believe, we will eventually separate from the chrysalis of our flesh in order to experience our spiritual essence. There is simply no escaping the fact that our consciousness must transcend the limits of the body in order to have an authentic spiritual experience. Eventually we must master the ability to explore beyond our dense limits, for transcending these limits is at the very heart of our spiritual evolution. This is why out-of-body exploration and the information we derive from it are so important to all of us. This is the true purpose of this book.

AUTHOR'S NOTE: *The experiences recorded here have been edited for content and clarity. The names and locations of the participants have been changed to preserve their privacy. Many of the common elements and recurring themes of these experiences are explored from various perspectives throughout this book.*

The Out-of-Body Experience

Out-of-body experiences are the most common paranormal experience known.

Melvin Morse, *Transformed by the Light*

Since the publication of my first book, *Adventures Beyond the Body*, in 1996, I have conducted an ongoing international survey of out-of-body experiences. To date, I have received over sixteen thousand responses from over thirty countries, making this the largest survey of its kind ever conducted. The number of participants alone makes the survey significant, and some of its most enlightening results are the multitude of compelling testimonies from people all over the world—people just like you and me.

One of the primary goals of the survey was to gather information about the commonly reported phenomena associated with the out-of-body experience, or OBE. My intention was to examine the reported vibrations, sounds, and sensations that occur immediately before, during, and after an OBE; today these phenomena are widely referred to as the *vibrational state*. Information and insights obtained from this survey are presented throughout this book.

One of the most surprising by-products of the survey was the large number of letters I received from parents struggling to understand the panic attacks and paralysis that their children experienced during sleep. I believe that children by their very nature are less conditioned by their physical surroundings and are more open to spontaneous out-of-body experiences than are adults. They consistently report a high incidence of the vibrations, sounds, and phenomena associated with the vibrational state; many experience these on a recurring basis.

I was also surprised by the early age at which children reported having their first out-of-body experience: The first reported journey occurred at an average age of four to twelve. In addition, the number of out-of-body experiences appears to decline dramatically during the early teen years. This may be due to the intense physical indoctrination and conditioning, so inherent in our society, that teenagers undergo. Often children are educated in our modern culture to identify completely with their physical bodies instead of being taught that they are unlimited spiritual beings free to explore beyond their physical surroundings. Clearly, there is much more to be learned regarding the link between children and out-of-body experiences, and research in this area may one day yield exciting answers to the true nature of the soul.

The survey results also provide evidence of a connection between OBEs and near-death and after-death experiences, as well as between OBEs and extraterrestrial contact and abduction experiences. Further research into the OBE phenomenon may shed light on those mysterious events as well. Are they connected, and if so, how? It is my hope that this book will begin to answer these questions.

The key to understanding some of these mysteries may be the vibrational state—the universal prelude to out-of-body states of consciousness and spiritual experiences. In a sense, this state is nature's way of preparing us for the ultimate adventure beyond the confines of the physical body.

Throughout human history yogis, saints, and mystics have referred to sounds and vibrations as important elements of their spiritual experiences. It is my belief that they were describing various vibrational-state phenomena.

Research tells us that the vibrational state is a normal occurrence that can be self-initiated and expanded into a fully conscious out-of-body experience. When we become experienced and effective at responding to the vibrational state, we are one step closer to personal and spiritual empowerment. It is now clear that the out-of-body experience is an important if not essential ally in our spiritual exploration. The more knowledge we obtain about these experiences, the better prepared we will be to explore beyond our physical limits and discover our true spiritual essence.

There is so much to learn, so much to discover. The answers lie somewhere beyond the boundaries of what most of us have come to think of as everyday reality. This book is for those of us who desire to take that brave first step into the unknown, beyond the boundaries of physical reality. This book is for those of us who are ready to unlock the secret of the soul.

PART 1

THE
TESTIMONIES

1

Meetings and Messages
Beyond the Body

I couldn't believe it when I saw him. He was healthy and energetic, full of life. This was the father I remembered—not the thin, frail man who had lain for weeks in a hospital bed.

BARB G., NEW YORK, NEW YORK

One of the most amazing out-of-body experiences is a fully conscious meeting with a loved one who has passed on. This personal contact can provide startling insight into our spiritual natures and the unseen dimensions around us, and a powerful verification of our own immortality. It also provides an excellent opportunity for us to reunite and communicate with a friend or loved one whom we feared lost to us forever. It is common for people to report personal encounters with departed loved ones during out-of-body and near-death experiences. What I have found especially interesting is the diversity of these meetings. The reported contact can take almost any form: a child, a recently passed wife or husband, a cloud or sphere of intelligence, or a gentle grandparent. Sometimes the contact is with someone known; at other times it may be with someone who appears as a guide or teacher.

In the OBE survey I conducted, 24 percent of the respondents' experiences involved contact with a departed loved one. In addition, 22 percent of the respondents saw or felt the presence of a nonphysical being. Increasing evidence suggests that most contact is with individuals we have known at some point in our past. Often spirits are attracted to us because there is a connection to our soul group, a past life, or because there is an emotional or spiritual relationship that we are unaware of.

CONSCIOUSLY MEETING DEPARTED LOVED ONES

One of the great benefits of out-of-body exploration is the self-empowerment that it offers. It provides us with abilities and perceptions extending far beyond the limits of matter. For many it opens up a new world of possibilities that our society is only beginning to examine and understand. For example, our current concepts of death and dying are a based on some very old assumptions. Many of us still look upon death as the end of life. Our vocabulary is filled with statements indicating the finality of death: "the last breath," "the final moments," on so on. Out-of-body experiences provide substantial evidence that when someone dies, that person has in fact only changed their vibratory rate and the density of their body. The person is still very much alive and well.

I was living in Michigan when my mother called from Maryland at about 1 A.M. to tell me that after a long illness, my father had passed away. After packing a bag and making airline reservations, I decided to lie down on my living-room sofa to rest for about an hour or so before my flight. Suddenly there was a sense of motion or vibration, and I found myself sitting in my parents' basement on a Danish-style couch that they had for years. There was a voice from around a corner— it sounded very much like my deceased mother-in-law's—that said, "Susie, your daddy's here." In an instant I saw my father standing in front of me, a pipe in his mouth, dressed in a flannel shirt and brown Levi's. I said, "What are you doing here? You are supposed to be dead. But you look great." He opened his arms to me and said, "Everything is good here. I feel great. I just wanted you to know." I stood and embraced him—he seemed solid—and in an instant I came back to my sofa in

Michigan. It was that experience that convinced me beyond anything I had been told during my Catholic upbringing that there is existence beyond this life. I am certain that we will meet again. —SUSAN W., BEL AIR, CALIFORNIA

It is common for people who have died to remain relatively close to the physical world for several days after death. During this period they often visit their loved ones and express their good-byes. We often receive this communication during sleep. Many are unaware that during sleep we move slightly out of sync with our biological bodies. This provides a potential window of direct communication with our minds. How we perceive and remember this communication is based on our awareness. Some have no recollection of the visitation, while others perceive the contact as a dream ranging from a vague memory to an incredibly vivid interactive experience. Those who are trained and comfortable with out-of-body exploration possess an enormous advantage because their consciousness is far more open and prepared for this multidimensional contact and communication. In other words, they are far more likely to experience spiritual visitations in full awareness. Those who are fearful of spiritual contact remain largely unaware of the contact or interpret it as a fleeting dream.

One of the reasons people learn self-initiated out-of-body exploration is to consciously meet and communicate with their deceased loved ones. This kind of meeting is far more common than many believe. Research indicates that a large percentage of parents who have lost a child will have some kind of contact with that child within a year of the loss and that more than 50 percent of people experience a reunion with their departed spouse.

My wife had passed after a long illness, and the first few days afterward passed like a blur. Even though her death relieved her from pain, I was numb with grief. Most of the time I had friends and family with me, but one evening when I was alone I relaxed on the sofa, recalling the lifetime we had spent together. As I closed my eyes to rest, I felt my body start to tingle and vibrate, and then I became very, very light. I was almost

dizzy. Then suddenly I felt like I was in a painting. It was sur-real: It was my house, but different; the colors were vibrant, and there were soft edges around everything. And that's when I saw her. She had never looked more beautiful; there was even a glow around her. She was wearing the dress from our wed-ding, but had no shoes on her feet. She did not speak, but from the peaceful expression on her face I knew she was okay. I could feel her thoughts tell me that we would be together again when the time was right. With an unearthly grace, she moved out of my sight. When I opened my eyes, my body was like a lead weight. It was several minutes before I could move. That was six years ago, and it started the healing process for me.
—LES D., RALEIGH, NORTH CAROLINA

When we develop our natural abilities to consciously per-ceive and explore beyond the limits of our body, we are no longer limited to dreams and visions in order to communicate with our deceased loved ones. Our ability to experience per-sonal communication beyond the physical is profoundly self-empowering. As we grow in this ability, we are better able to expand the ways we perceive and communicate with the unseen worlds around us. Eventually we will reach a point where we become a spiritual explorer who is fully aware of and consciously interacting with the other dimensions of reali-ty. I believe the increasing number of people around the world who are beginning to explore and cultivate this ability repre-sents a major leap in the development and evolution of human consciousness.

SELF-INITIATED MEETINGS WITH DEPARTED LOVED ONES

Many people wish to meet or communicate with their departed loved ones, either to send a message or to be assured that they are in a good place. This desire has contributed to the popularity of psychics and mediums. Today a large number of people pursue out-of-body exploration as an alternate means of consciously meeting their loved ones. The following examples show how valuable this experience can be.

For a month I did an OBE technique as I fell asleep. I woke up at 6 A.M. lying on my left side. I felt strange—tingling and light. There was a light humming sound. I realized I was floating about one to two inches above my body base. I was really excited—not scared at all. I thought about my living room, thinking I would—bam!—be there, but nothing happened. When I thought about myself, I seemed to drift back into my body. When I thought about my living room again, I vibrated more and drifted back up, but I didn't separate. Finally I just decided to sit up, and did. Just like that, I was out of my body.

Thinking that I didn't have long, I walked out of my room, down my hall, and I called out for my departed brother: "Andy?" I missed him badly and wanted to see him. Alive with excitement, I saw a dark image standing at the entrance to the kitchen. I yelled out, "Who is it?" The image jumped back, like someone was playing with me. I was startled but not scared. I said again, more demanding, "Who's there?" The image stood up and walked in front of me. It was Andy. I ran down the stairs and put my arms around him. He was solid. I said, "Andy, where are you? Are you okay?"

And he said, "Would you believe it, I'm on the other side of the mountains." When he said this, a picture of the mountains, with a cabin and stream, appeared in my head. I also felt his feelings of peace and happiness. Also his feelings of fun, like he was living it up. He said to me, "You should do what you want to do now, because I wish I would have when I was alive." Then he gave me another picture—of a duplex in the slums, with a beat-up truck, and a wife that he felt no love for. I felt his emotions of sadness and despair. He said, "This is what my life was. I always wanted to live on the other side of the mountain, but I had to wait till I died before I went." And I said, "Well, you should have done that when you were alive." Then Andy said, "I know, but I didn't. When you are alive, you worry about people too much. Sometimes it's hard to be dead, because you want to come back and tell people that they can have the other side of the mountain while they're still alive." He also told me, "Stop listening to other people, and have your other side of the mountain." Instantly, I snapped back into my body.

My brother Andy had died several years before. He was twenty-eight years old. —LAURIE K., WARREN, MICHIGAN

Andy is giving his sister a personal message about self-empowerment. He is reminding her to follow her intuition and pursue her dreams in this life. It's important for us to be open to receiving messages from loved ones; often their personal knowledge of us can provide a valuable source of guidance or information.

My experiences were brought about by the death of my father and grandmother. The first one was spontaneous. During the experience, I traveled to view my grandmother and was greeted by all her friends and family who had died before her. She was incredibly happy. I fell back into my body in a spiral drop and woke with a start. I knew without a doubt that I had been out of my body and that I had seen my grandmother. I thought, "If I can do it once, I can do it again!" I bought a book on out-of-body experiences and got the idea of what to look for—the vibrations, paralysis, and such. I was very emotionally driven. My father had died suddenly, and I didn't get to say good-bye. Every night as I fell asleep I said over and over that I wanted to see my dad. Two weeks went by, and I had almost given up when it happened. I believe he was surprised to see me. I knew he was dead and he knew that I knew. I climbed on his lap, put my forehead against his, and told him I loved him, and we both cried.

It was wonderful, wonderful! —FRAN M., LOUISVILLE, KENTUCKY

SPONTANEOUS MEETINGS WITH
DEPARTED LOVED ONES

There are many variations of reported spontaneous meetings with departed loved ones. Some of these meetings, as that described in the following case, can be startling, perhaps even contributing to the reports of ghost phenomenon.

When my daughter was ten years old, she would wake up in the middle of the night due to nightmares. This would happen twice a month or so. She always told me the same story: She heard voices, felt strange and numb, and couldn't move. She said she would try to scream for me but no sound would come out. She also said that someone was in the room with her. She described the person as a young woman with very long brown hair and a long dress to her ankles. She was very tall, about six feet, with a round face. When I heard this description I was shocked. My grandmother, who had died five years earlier, was five feet, eleven inches tall, and often wore long dresses to her ankles. The description was of her. I wish I would have known about sleep paralysis and OBEs back then. I think I would have handled the situation better. —DEBBIE B., TROY, MICHIGAN

OBEs can be joyous and healing, as in the following case.

I have traveled out of body on several occasions, but there was one time when I felt totally different. I was flying through the clouds, and past the clouds into a bright white yellowish light. As I was going to the light an extreme peacefulness came over me. I felt very light . . . I also felt an overwhelming amount of love come through me. It was something I had never felt before. The light was so bright, I felt like squinting when I saw it . . . but I just kept my eyes open and looked straight at the light and saw that the light was not hurting my eyes. Looking around, I heard voices in the distance. I saw my grandparents, who had died some ten to fifteen years before. I was so very happy to see them. I felt our energies become one. I felt like I was home. I wanted to stay . . . but they told me that I was to go back, for it was not my time to be with them. Reluctantly, I came back. When I came back into my body, it felt as if I was "jump-started" like a jolt of electricity. I was gone at that time for forty-five minutes. —BOB T., MOBILE, ALABAMA

Some visits are not with those who have died, but rather with those who have yet to live, as in this next case.

During one of my experiences a feminine presence fondled my mind and whispered in my ear. I am left with the impression that she was—if I ever do have children—my future daughter. She whispered her name, urging me to get out of bed to write it down, and then she kissed me on the cheek. —RACHEL B., DENVER, COLORADO

Communication with nonphysical loved ones is often described as a form of direct knowingness or thought transference. Emotions, images, and thoughts are often communicated simultaneously.

I was opened up to these experiences in the summer of '96. I was twenty-one years old and very depressed and had been put on antidepressants. My life changed after this experience. It woke me up. It started with a lucid dream when a female voice came and told me to go with her; weirdly enough, the voice was my own. I went with her because I felt safe with her. She had me look through a window and asked me, "Do you remember this person?" On the other side was a man whistling a song in his workshop area. That side of the window was very white and bright. We floated closer past the window and then— "Yes!"—I knew that man; it was my grandpa, who had died nine years before. When he realized I was there, he looked at me and smiled. He went toward the door of his workshop that was part of a garage and walked out. I was still floating toward him, but I wasn't allowed to get too close. It was very bright now, and he looked at me and smiled and waved. I felt this peacefulness come over me, and I knew everything was going to be all right. —L. K., TARRYTOWN, NEW YORK

SELF-INITIATED MEETINGS WITH
PHYSICAL LOVED ONES

Consciously meeting and speaking with deceased friends or loved ones is an unforgettable experience. But there are also many cases of out-of-body meetings with someone still living. Many couples have reported such meetings between themselves as profound transformational experiences and sometimes have difficulty describing them in words.

In his book *The Bridge Across Forever,* the author Richard Bach describes several out-of-body episodes he and his wife, Leslie, experienced. After five months of self-initiated OBE practice, Bach and his wife found themselves together, floating above their home, able to clearly see each other's ethereal bodies. With practice, they were able to meet outside of their bodies several times a month. As a result of these shared out-of-body experiences, the Bachs found their perception of death and reality dramatically altered. He goes on to describe the personal empowerment they experienced as their awareness of themselves and their surroundings expanded with each out-of-body adventure:

> Like two warm balloons, we lifted together through the ceiling as if it were cool air . . . Like student pilots on our first solo, we moved together, no quick motions. Whatever bodies these were, they had no weight, no mass. We could glide through iron, through the center of the sun, if we felt like it.

He goes on to describe his wife's ethereal form:

> What caught my attention was a radiant form afloat, flawless sparkling silver and gold barely two feet away, exquisite living love.
>
>   Oh, my! I thought. The Leslie I've been seeing with my eyes isn't the tiniest part of who she is! She's body within body, life within life, unfolding, unfolding . . . will I ever know all of her?[1]

One of the fascinating elements of an out-of-body experience is the many reports of personal confirmation. This can have a major impact on the participant.

One of my notable OBEs took place while I was on the isle of Crete in 1971. During the experience I traveled back to my home in New York, and for some reason I was floating under the sink, which had a cabinet door, peering at the kitchen table, where my mother was talking with two friends of hers. I was enjoying my little "spy mission" when my cat, Blackie, came walking into the kitchen and stared right at me, and I'm sure he could see me. Instantly, I was swinging wildly, pendulumlike, over my body in my cheap hotel room. At which point I was completely aware and was trying not to reenter my body, but the process was by now inexorable and I woke up. I later confirmed that my mother had met with two friends that day. OBEs are real. I now have no fear of death. —QUENTIN Y., ALBANY, NEW YORK*

I was separated from the man I was going to marry, and I received a call from his mother stating that he had been in a serious auto accident. He was in intensive care and hanging on to life. I finally went to sleep, saying, "Don't die, please don't die." The next thing I remember I was literally flying through forests and found myself next to him in bed. I instantly knew he was going to be all right. Later, I also realized that I had taken the shortcut through the mountains to his place instead of going over the road. When I talked with him about this later, he told me he'd had visions of me on that same evening. —CARMEN T., BALTIMORE, MARYLAND*

INTERACTION WITH GUIDES

In addition to meeting friends or family members while out-of-body, some people report experiences with a spiritual guide or teacher, or a person or presence not known to them but who may seem familiar nonetheless. Guidance can manifest itself in many different forms, ranging from a wise being to unseen communications or visions. It's common for people to experience guidance as an unseen presence or invisible helping hands. The following is an example.

My out-of-body experiences generally take place when I am asleep in bed. The one exception occurred when I was half awake; as I lay there, I oddly began to wonder what it would feel like to fall out of an airplane from about thirty thousand feet and hit the ground. No sooner did I think of this falling motion than I felt the hands of my guides grasp my wrists and ankles, holding me alongside the plane near the right wing. As soon as I was aware of my position, I was released to fall. I could feel the wind in my hair and on my head and face as I dropped, and after what seemed to be several minutes I neared the ground. As I braced myself for impact, suddenly I did an impossible thing and reversed my fall. I did a hairpin turn and reentered my body, feeling as if I dove into water, but I was remerging with the flesh. After the experience, my analysis of the fall was that I was about six feet or less above my physical body. The return to the body took the place of crashing into the ground. —KELLY M., SIOUX FALLS, IOWA

The experience just described provides an example of one of the methods people use to initiate out-of-body adventures. By imagining the extreme motion of falling as she drifted to sleep, Kelly unknowingly performed an OBE induction technique. Inner-motion techniques provide a highly effective method of initiating conscious out-of-body experiences and contact with the unseen world around us. (An extensive variety of motion-induction methods are presented later in chapter 10, "The Art and Practice of Out-of-Body Exploration.")

My most memorable OBE involved contact with a guide. During several of my experiences I became lost in a strange environment and asked for help. On three different occasions I felt a presence and then a woman took my hand and directed me to a beautiful place. She talked to me with mind pictures, and I understood everything. I felt safe when she was with me. —MARIA T., ROME, ITALY

INTERACTION WITH SPHERES OF INTELLIGENT LIGHT

Meetings with spiritual beings can take many different forms and are sometimes described as contact with spheres of intelligent light. A wide array of colors and shapes are reported.

I lifted out of my body and floated up to the ceiling. I immediately noticed two globes of blue light in the corner. One of them spoke to my mind with pictures, and I could somehow tell that it was a familiar female presence. She told me that they loved me and that they were proud of me. I was so shocked by the event, I was speechless and then slammed back into my body. After much thought I now believe that this was my grandmother, who had died a year earlier. —JULIA B., SAN FRANCISCO, CALIFORNIA

CONTACT WITH SPIRITUAL BEINGS

Contact with radiant beings can become manifest in many different forms. In fact, a spiritual being can assume any form it deems necessary to achieve its mission or convey a message. Often a nonthreatening outer form is assumed in order to reduce our fears of the encounter, as in the following transformational experience.

About five years ago I had been living a pretty hard life but surviving. I had an experience one night where I had left my body. I have had OBEs in the past, and this was similar, but not quite like what I had experienced before. Two very large angels met me as I was looking at my body passed out in bed. They escorted me to a cemetery where my brother was buried. They took me to a service in progress, and I noticed that my whole family was there: my wife, kids, and parents . . . They were all very upset, and I couldn't understand why. The angels spoke to me, telling me that it was I who was to be buried that day. I immediately felt all the pain my family was experiencing. The angel showed me how my parents felt when my brother died and asked me if I wanted to do that to them again. It was real. I still remember to this day every moment, and every emotion involved. From that day on I have had complete sobriety, have become a vegetarian, have dropped all my ties with old acquaintances, and have been bathed in a wonderful wall of loving light. God spoke to me that day, and since then my life has been one good thing after another. I have so much to be thankful for. I feel I am truly blessed. —KEVIN H., CLEVELAND, OHIO

Kevin's experience of watching his own funeral provided him with a powerful wake-up call. He needed a message of this magnitude to get him to change his lifestyle. One of the benefits inherent in out-of-body travel is that the participant is far more conscious during the experience. If Kevin had experienced this as a dream, it would not have had the same impact on him.

It appears that the traditional concept of angels with wings is rapidly being replaced by a broader vision. Out-of-body explorers often report radiant angelic presences as powerful guidelike beings without the traditional wings. Many now believe that wings may have symbolized angels' immense interdimensional capabilities and freedom. It is now known that out-of-body travel is achieved by the power of focused will.

Spiritual contact can take many forms and often involves advice or assistance.

In adulthood, I have had more than twenty out-of-body experiences. All were spontaneous. These experiences would start with physical paralysis; then a loud roar in my ears and intense fear; then all would become quiet as I moved out through the solar plexus region of my body. During one experience, there was a glowing presence with me that was female. She expressed concern about my physical body. I was very thin at the time. She encouraged me to really look at what I was doing to my physical vehicle. —DARLA F., CHARLESTON, SOUTH CAROLINA

SEXUAL EXPERIENCES

I was somewhat surprised by the number of sexual experiences that I received in response to the survey. Some people perceived these experiences as wonderful and exhilarating, while others found them strange or even threatening. It appears that sex beyond the body is far more prevalent and diverse then expected. Males and females from various cultures reported being open and receptive to such experiences. In addition, non-physical sexual encounters commonly manifest themselves as spontaneous unions with partners we don't consciously know or remember. These are often experienced as a powerful mutual attraction that feels completely natural to the participant.

The way we perceive and experience nonphysical sex is dependent upon the energy body we are consciously using at any given time. For example, experiences that occur in the parallel and astral dimensions are perceived as very physical, while in the higher vibrational realms they are reported as more of an intense mind- and soul-melding experience. It is often described as an incredible thought embrace in which two people touch, caress, and completely melt together through the subtle energy of their thoughts. The reported orgasms are often described as global mind and emotion explosions that emanate from the soul instead of just the lower chakras. Of one thing we can be certain: Sex definitely continues beyond the body.

Form-Based or Astral-Plane Experiences

It's common for sensual experiences to occur in what is generally called the *astral plane*. During these experiences, the participants perceive themselves as possessing form-based bodies. This information is important, because it provides a clear reference point concerning our nonphysical location and our personal vibratory rate. In general, the more physical-like the experience, the denser the energy body and the dimensional reality that the person is experiencing. If you so desire, you can alter the nature of the experience by raising your internal vibratory rate. A method for doing this is described at the end of chapter 11, "Overcoming Challenges That Confront the Out-of-Body Explorer."

During one of my out-of-body experiences, I remember an encounter with a stunning young woman. I stepped through my backdoor and was in a new environment. I walked through a green field and felt the need to enter a building and saw this beautiful woman before me. She approached me, and I felt an immediate attraction to her. I felt like I knew her but could not remember where or when we had met. I could feel her thoughts caressing me, and suddenly I was sitting down and she straddled my lap. It felt like electricity was flowing through my entire being, surges of energy that I can't explain. We made love, and I felt like my entire being was going to explode. It felt somewhat like physical sex but much more expansive, like we had merged our thoughts, our minds, and our emotions. It was incredible. I didn't want it to end. —K. T., MONTEGO BAY, CALIFORNIA

After working on inducing OBEs for about a year, I have had four episodes. I believe these were my first adventures, all of which took place around my home. With each episode I was a little more aware of what to do and how to react. My last experience was as follows:

After waking in the middle of the night, I felt the vibrations coming over me. With intense desire and emotion I said to myself over and over, "Now I get out of my body." Suddenly I sensed that someone was holding my ankles, and then I was pulled off the bed. I had had similar experiences before, so I just went with it. I could feel my spirit body moving through the air to the bedroom wall, and I felt myself pass through the wall and into the next room. I could see in between the walls as I passed through them and ended up in the spare room next to mine. Standing there, I asked myself, "What now?" "Go up to the roof and look around," I answered, and I immediately shot up to the roof of the house. I looked out over the city to see what I could, but I was quickly distracted by someone at the other part of the roof. I saw a young woman of slim build standing too close to the edge of the roof to be safe. I moved toward her to encourage her to safety. I reached out my hand to help her to a safer place. She took it, and I pulled her toward me. She moved close and gave me a sensual hug, and I felt

sexually excited. We kissed a kiss as real and thrilling as any I have had in my life. My eyes were now closed, and I was kissing her deeply. I thought, "We're about to have sex." Rapidly we came to an orgasm while standing there, after which she said, "We could rule the world." I thought to myself, "I do not really have an interest in ruling the world." She seemed to respond to my thought and flew off, disappearing before me.
—LAVAR J., NEW YORK, NEW YORK

Vibrational-State Experiences

Surprisingly, over 30 percent of the sensual experiences described by respondents to my survey occurred in the vibrational state, before full separation had occurred. It is possible that nonphysical residents are attracted to the energy changes that occur when we enter the vibrational state. The very nature of this state involves a shift of consciousness from one dimension to another and presents an opportunity for various sorts of nonphysical communication or contact to occur. A substantial number of respondents reported the presence of someone close to them and also the sensation of someone in their bed or directly next to them. It is also common for people to report being sexually aroused during and immediately after an OBE. Many students of OBEs believe that this is caused by the energy stimulation that can occur within the lower chakras during an out-of-body experience. The spiritual form experienced by most people during an OBE is their astral or emotional body. This energy body is the seat of our personal desires and emotional needs, so it is only natural that sensual experiences would manifest themselves there. Whatever the reasons, it is clear that spontaneous sensual experiences are natural and are generally viewed by the participants as very pleasurable. In addition, people seem to experience more sexual freedom and openness during OBEs than they generally do in the physical world. We have to remember that as long as we are using a body for expression, even a nonphysical body, we continue to be driven by the desires and passions of our mind. It appears likely that if you enjoy your physical sex life, you will certainly enjoy the nonphysical.

I feel vibrations and sounds. My body is paralyzed, and I can feel someone softly stroking my legs. At first I am startled and scared; then I slowly calm down. After a moment I kind of enjoy the sensations as they flow through me. It's strange and sensual at the same time. —JOAN G., ROME, ITALY

The out-of-body experience I would like to relate has to do with the period of time—maybe ten to fifteen minutes—after I lay down in bed to sleep. During this time, in my most relaxed semislumber state, I have experienced the feeling of an entity slowly approaching my bed, bending over me, their face close to my face. During these experiences, I get sensations, sight through my eyelids, the sound of the floor creaking, the sound of a shape moving in front of the fan at the foot of my bed, even the sound of breathing and the feel of warm breath on my neck and in my ear. After a few minutes of these sensations, I can feel my body becoming charged with heightened sensitivity. Shortly thereafter, I can actually feel something caressing my thighs in a soft yet stimulating way. This usually leads to my arousal. These experiences began when I was about twenty-two years old, when I moved out of my parents' house and into my first apartment. These episodes were played out almost nightly for three years, until I moved back into my parents' house. The experiences stopped shortly after that. However, within the last two years they have returned, to my welcome delight, with the same interesting feelings, experiences, and sometimes with multiple visitors—two or three at a time. I am excitedly curious about this phenomenon, and do not fear it in any form. —BRAD R., HOUSTON, TEXAS

Higher-Dimensional Experiences

Higher-dimensional experiences are generally perceived to be non–form based and less physical in nature. They are often described as a spiritual mind meld without form or substance.

There is a feeling of intense movement, and I struggle to stay calm. I am fully conscious, like a globe of pure awareness without arms or legs, yet I can move and see in ways I don't understand. I can see all around me and sense the presence of someone approaching me. For some reason I am attracted to this person or being. I somehow sense and feel their warm and inviting thoughts. As we move closer to one another, I have an overwhelming need to touch and merge with this being. We seem to slowly melt into one another. Our minds or spirits touch in ways I can't even begin to describe in words. My entire mind and spirit is immersed in endless currents and levels of love. I surrender even more and feel my entire being explode with joy.

I am one! —JANET M., LONDON, ENGLAND

An intriguing question arises: Are these sexual experiences a merging with another being, or are they actually an internal reuniting with the person's higher self? Janet's strong statement "I am one" indicates that she may very well have had a reunification experience with a higher aspect of her spiritual essence. Of course, only the participant in the experience can determine the true nature of it. I believe that it's important to be open-minded to the unlimited potential that out-of-body exploration offers. We must remember that our minds are attempting to interpret ethereal experiences that are occurring beyond time, space, and form-based concepts. After many years of examination, I believe that many of these experiences are an internal reunification of our multidimensional nature. When any experience is unclear to you, simply ask for clarification and then be completely open to receiving it. This clarification can manifest itself in any number of ways, including thoughts and images.

MEETINGS WITH ANIMALS

The reports of out-of-body meetings with animals open the door to new insights into the universal spiritual nature of all life-forms. For thousands of years, a few cultures and religions in the West have assumed that animals do not possess individual souls and are instead part of a collective soul group, and therefore inferior to us. Startling new evidence collected from reports of numerous out-of-body experiences points to a radically different viewpoint.

I felt paralyzed during sleep and thought about rolling sideways out of my bed. As I gently touched the floor, I realized I was out of body. Still lying there, I looked around the room and immediately could see my cat sitting on the floor staring at me. I instinctively said hi, and to my amazement the cat seemed to speak to my mind: "Hello." This communication was very clear. It then asked why I was on the floor. I was so startled that I immediately snapped back into my body. When I opened my eyes, I noticed that my cat or its body was still asleep at the foot of the bed. —TRACY H., DALLAS, TEXAS

Many people report meetings with pets, both while the animals are physically alive and after they have died. It is not uncommon for a loyal pets, especially dogs and cats, to accompany their human friends during their out-of-body experiences.

I had one experience when I was about eight years old. My cat had died tragically, and I was devastated. One night I prayed to God/Guardian Angel to see my beloved cat one more time. The next memory I had was of myself leaving my bed and walking out the backdoor—I was watching myself from up above. I proceeded to the backyard, where my cat had been buried. I suddenly saw my cat, Tut, run toward me. I knelt down and he ran into my arms. I saw other cats, too, but I didn't know whose they were. In the morning I told my mother and she said that I had had an out-of-body experience. Now that I'm older—twenty-eight—I'm sure that it was real and an OBE. After the experience I was able to heal, because I felt reunited with my pet. —RENATA S., RICHMOND, VIRGINIA

Animals and the Silver Cord

There are numerous reports of people having seen a "silver cord" attached to their pet. The very nature of this connection points to a highly evolved spiritual component that appears similar if not identical to a human silver cord. I had such an experience in 1983. During an out-of-body experience, I saw my beagle puppy, MacGregor, walking along beside me. He appeared completely natural and solid as he wagged his tail and looked up at me. His eyes were shining, and there was a thin filament, like a spider web, stretching from his body and reaching back toward the bedroom where his physical body was sleeping. This was not something I had expected to see when out of body, and it forever changed my perception of animals.

What I have found amazing is the fact that the so-called lower life forms can communicate with surprising intelligence when they are out of body. There are many reports of animals providing companionship, advice, and assistance to out-of-body travelers.

This may explain why several ancient cultures, such as that of the Egyptians, had a deep reverence for cats—one far surpassing the status we accord mere house pets. One of the oldest and most mysterious monuments of all time is the Sphinx. This magnificent stone creation clearly portrays the body of a great and noble cat with the face of a man. Many believe that the Sphinx signified for the ancient Egyptians the inherent intelligence and advanced evolution of that animal.

Animals and Their Evolution

Not only do animals have souls; they are obviously evolving alongside us. And this appears to be true of all animals, not just domesticated pets. Many believe that animals possess consciousness and should be treated with more respect than they now receive. A growing number of people feel that we need to reappraise our beliefs concerning our relationship with the animal kingdom. To expand our vision of evolution, consciousness, and soul, we must look beyond our assumptions about other forms of life. All physical life-forms are vehicles for consciousness, used to experience the dense realms of matter. These outer vehicles of soul form an integral element in the evolution of consciousness.

We must remember that the various forms of matter are essentially tools and expressions of soul. Without this divine inner spark of consciousness, biological forms could not be animated. Is it possible that the soul of the giant redwood may be learning patience and that the soaring bird may be learning the freedom of flight? How can any soul truly learn and express these qualities except from personal experience?

Evidence suggests that some animals, such as dogs and cats, may be close to the spiritual sophistication and evolution required for them to have their first human incarnation. Many people today believe that the soul evolves through the use of increasingly more complex biological life-forms—a process generally perceived as a progression of consciousness. Let us open our minds to a much broader vision of evolution and our path to the soul.

A TECHNIQUE FOR SPIRITUAL MEETING

For years I have taught a method for directly contacting our loved ones, or any other nonphysical intelligence. It is easy to do once you are comfortable with the techniques of out-of-body exploration. The key is to focus your complete, undivided attention on the person or spirit you wish to meet.

1. After the initial separation, move away from the body and say, "Awareness now!" Repeat this request until your state of consciousness and your vision are as clear as possible.

2. Focus your complete attention upon the person you desire to meet and communicate with. Ideally, you picture this person in your mind as you announce their name or relationship and your intention—for example, "Now I meet my sister [*name*]!" or "I will meet my mother now!" Be specific, and repeat your request as often as needed.

3. Be prepared for a sense of motion or a change of environment. Also be aware that your departed loved one will often appear younger and sometimes different than they were in the physical.

4. If your vision or hearing is unclear, remember to demand an enhancement of your perceptions: "Clarity now!" or "Awareness now!" Keep all requests in the present tense, and be extremely focused.

5. Be open, and expect to receive your request.

6. If you ever doubt the validity of the contact, simply demand personal verification: "Whom or what do you represent?"

It is important for us to be open and receptive to spiritual contact and information. Self-initiated out-of-body exploration provides a highly effective method for breaking through the energy barrier or veil between the physical and nonphysical dimensions. This is particularly true in the case of a loved one who has passed over. Today many people practice out-of-body exploration methods in order to meet and communicate with their loved ones. Be aware that spiritual contact can occur at any time during an out-of-body experience and is often not requested or expected.

During contact experiences, don't become obsessed with the outer shape or form that you encounter. Remember, people may appear completely different from how you may have known them in their past, physical life. They may manifest themselves in any number of ways, including a sphere or image of light, a distinctive voice, or a younger version of the person you once knew. Often some quality that was unique to that person—their voice or thoughts—will immediately identify them for you. Pay attention to the message, however you receive it.

It was 1980. My grandfather had just passed away and I was filled with sorrow, lying on my bed. I was very close to my grandfather. I was in the U.S. Air Force at the time of his admittance into the hospital, and by the time I arrived from Sacramento, he was already in a coma. So I never got to talk to

him again. That night, while I was lying on my bed, I realized that I was in a trancelike state. I noticed that my room was getting kind of cloudy looking, and the next thing I knew I was floating near the ceiling above my bed. Then I saw a cloud off to my right and just a little above me. In the cloud was my grandfather's face. He just smiled at me. Nothing was said, and I had the comfortable feeling that he was all right.
—LANCE S., MADISON, WISCONSIN

Meetings beyond the body are normal occurrences that provide a powerful verification of our immortality and insight into our selves and the unseen dimensions around us. In general, when you experience one of these meetings, the best advice is to remain calm, focus your attention, and ask specific questions. These experiences can manifest themselves in many different forms, and the more open we are to conscious contact, the more they can and will occur. I contend that these experiences provide evidence that we are evolving into expansive multidimensional beings. We are awakening to the fact that we possess the God-given ability to consciously explore the unseen universe around and within us. As we evolve, conscious contact with the unseen dimensions and the inhabitants will become the accepted norm in our culture. Let us have the courage to embrace our unlimited spiritual potential.

1. Richard Bach, *The Bridge Across Forever* (New York: HarperCollins, 1986), 377.

2

Childhood Out-of-Body Experiences

*My mother taught me to leave my body before I
started school. It was so natural that I thought
everybody did it.*

JESSICA R., DENVER, COLORADO

We now know that many out-of-body experiences occur in childhood between the ages of four and twelve. These experiences are spontaneous and often take place in the early stages of sleep. Even though each child is an individual and perceives the experience from a unique viewpoint, some commonalties are clear. Conscious out-of-body experiences in four-to-six-year-olds are generally simple and involve flying or floating in a safe environment. As a child becomes older, the experiences become more sophisticated and may include visitations and meetings with spiritual friends and relatives who have passed on. They may then progress to spiritually meaningful events taking place in teaching environments or classrooms—some children use the term *heaven school,* a place where they encounter a "nice teacher"—which may indicate early encounters with a guide.

Those who have had a positive out-of-body experience as a child often tell me that it has had a significant influence on their spiritual outlook as an adult. They usually appear to be more inquisitive and open to alternative methods of seeking the truth of their spiritual natures.

It is important to recognize that children's out-of-body experiences are an integral part of their developing spirituality. Often they are having adventures they can't explain. They are experiencing ethereal, thought-responsive dimensions of reality beyond our linear concepts of time and space. Children commonly report walking through walls, flying, attending meetings or classes, and even communicating with people who have died. They may even develop close friendships with nonphysical beings. When such children attempt to tell their parents about their adventures, they often discover that Mom and Dad are less than receptive, if not patronizing. The common refrain they hear is "It was only a dream."

Children report a wide variety of nonphysical experiences. The key is how we, as adults, react to their concerns and how we assist these young travelers so that they may continue to explore and evolve spiritually. The out-of-body experiences of children are often misinterpreted as dreams and even nightmares by parents who are unaware of the out-of-body process. In addition, the unusual and often startling phenomena of the vibrational state, such as loud sounds and paralysis, can create an overwhelming surge of fear and anxiety—especially in a young child. The extreme fear that may arise from the vibrational state can be intense. Some adults even refer to their childhood vibrational experiences as suspected seizures.

The following is presented as an overview of the various experiences that have been reported. It is largely the result of my recent OBE survey, together with my personal contacts and interviews with thousands of people over the past ten years.

TRANSFORMATIONAL/LEARNING EXPERIENCE

One of the benefits of out-of-body travel for children is that it provides them with the opportunity to enter a unique learning environment—one that teaches them to confront their personal fears, develop relationships with their spiritual guides, and resolve karmic situations. To hear children describe this process in such a natural and honest way simply reinforces this fact.

When I was little, I would tell my mom that every night, when I was sleeping, I would leave my body and go to heaven school to learn how to be human. Almost every morning I would tell her what I learned. I would tell her things that there was no other way for me to know. I was not in school yet and did not watch TV. —LUCY R., HOUSTON, TEXAS

UNSEEN FRIENDS AND LOVED ONES

There is much more to children's OBEs than just vivid dreams or an active imagination. Reports of children's inter-actions with spiritual beings, playmates, and unseen friends are a part of every culture. I believe that many of these sto-ries are reports of real events primarily occurring on the astral plane. Children by their very nature are less indoctri-nated to the denseness of matter than adults and are more open to accepting and experiencing the unseen dimensions and their inhabitants as a reality. However, this is not to say that all children's dreams are out-of-body experiences. Each experience must be examined individually. In the end only the participant in the experience is qualified to make the determination of its objective reality. Those having the expe-rience are conscious and know beyond a doubt that they are not having a dream. They often state that the experience was definitely not a dream.

As a young child I had a friend I would play with when I was asleep. We would fly around the neighborhood and play hide-and-seek. I remember hiding in trees and on rooftops. This was very real to me, but my parents told me it was just a dream. —KEVIN L., WASHINGTON, D.C.

When I was six I visited my grandmother a day after she had died. She hugged me and told me she felt wonderful. I could feel her hug and could somehow sense her words to me. Then I was back in my body. —JUDY D., DALLAS, TEXAS

THE VIBRATIONAL STATE AND CHILDREN

The various energy sensations associated with the vibrational state are often the greatest problems encountered by both adults and children. Adults generally try to find a logical explanation for the events related to an unfamiliar experience, while children can be more frightened than curious. The unusual sounds, vibrations, and paralysis that so often occur before an out-of-body experience can become so intense that they create a panic attack or what might be considered night terrors. (See the separate section on night terrors toward the end of this chapter.) The following are just a few examples of how different children experience and react to the vibrational state.

When I first began to have OBEs I was eight years old. I didn't know what they were, so they scared me a lot. The vibrations and sleep paralysis were so intense that I was afraid I was having some kind of seizure. I can't describe the feeling of relief when I first read about OBEs and recognized what was happening to me. —MEL R., TOLEDO, OHIO

The first experience I recall occurred when I was around the age of ten. I had stayed home from school that day, and it was around noon when I was awakened by vibrations. It was so intense that it felt as if someone was shaking my bed. I sat up—or so I thought—and saw my grandmother standing at the foot of my bed. I felt a strange presence behind me, and I turned my head and saw a tall woman in dark clothes behind me, and I was immediately snapped back into my body. When I opened my eyes, there was my grandmother as I had seen her, looking over me. I asked her, "Did I just sit up?" and she told me no, I had not. I had never heard of OBEs at this age, so you can imagine how amazed I was when I found out that others had had similar experiences, including the strange vibrations. —ANDRA, VIA E-MAIL

When I was around five or six, I awoke to find myself in the hallway. As a child I would frequently sleep-walk, but there was something about this time that was different . . . I returned to my room, and, startled, found my body still in bed. Then there was a sudden burst of fear, and I experienced a jerking sensation and was suddenly looking over by my door.

Since that time, I was able to see what my father was doing even though my head would be under my pillow, or the blankets pulled over my head. —PHYLLIS H., FRANKFURT, GERMANY

THE EFFECT ON VISUAL PERCEPTION

Children report a wide spectrum of visual-perception issues during an out-of-body experience. Some experience visual distortions, while others have improved vision. There are also cases of seeing through closed eyelids, as I mentioned in the survey. The process for improving vision during an out-of-body experience is the same for both children and adults: Make a verbal or mental demand: "Clarity now!" or "I see clearly now!" Repeat this as often as needed until the desired result is achieved.

One of my best and earliest experiences when I was a kid was when I just woke up and found myself floating near the ceiling in my bedroom. I saw my alarm clock—it had glowing red numbers—and I was looking at it. I could see it, but I couldn't comprehend the numbers. Later I read that reading is extremely difficult while projecting because you are in your astral or emotional body and your mental abilities aren't all that great. Mostly I project when I am either very tired of when I'm sleeping in a strange bed. —TAMI K., JACKSONVILLE, FLORIDA

My first experience was over thirty years ago when I was twelve years old. It was late at night—3:21 A.M., to be exact. I was having trouble sleeping when all of a sudden I saw, not

with my physical eyes, the time on the clock. It was very big and clear, and I know I did not leave my bed. This strange experience frightened me a bit, and I jolted back to my body with my heart racing. The next night I did an experiment. I wear corrective lenses, so from my bed I looked at the clock across my room and behind me and found that it was only a blur unless I got up and put my face about one foot from it. I didn't talk to anyone about this for some time and then mentioned it once to my brother, who said I had had an "astral projection." —STEVE M., VIA E-MAIL

FLOATING

Floating and weightless experiences are a natural and fun part of traveling out of body. Floating sensations are universally reported by both children and adults. The following examples show how open children are to this experience.

I was probably six or seven when I flew or floated around the house the first time. The last OBE was a few nights ago. I'm seventeen now. I fell into a very deep state of consciousness. My body was quite asleep. I started drifting away, pulling away from my body. I was a little scared but tried to get over it. I then felt as though I was several feet above my bed, and I floated through the wall and into my living room. Then I floated through the wall and was outside. I started trying to fly up the street, but I guess I got scared and was jerked back into my body. —PETE K., HOPE, ARKANSAS

When I was four years old, I experienced conscious out-of-body phenomena for a period of approximately two weeks. They consisted of the feeling that I was floating up to the ceiling of my bedroom during the period prior to falling asleep. I would lie down to sleep, staring at the ceiling, and within a few minutes I would experience the sensation of floating up to the ceiling. I would be face-to-face with the ceiling, not realizing at that time that I could have gone farther. I purposely,

consciously, and willfully repeated the episodes nightly for a period of about two weeks. I have never discussed it with my family. It was my own private fun, and I enjoyed it very much.
—STEVE C., CARSON CITY, NEVADA

I was seven or eight years old when it first happened. I was dreaming that I was a nurse in a doctor's office. For some reason there was a bucket of water above the front door. I got a ladder and climbed up to take it down so no one would get hurt. While I was up there I noticed a faucet coming out of the wall just above the bucket. I thought to myself, "That's an odd place for a faucet," and that thought made me aware that I was no longer dreaming. At that point I just stared at the faucet and the dreamscape kind of melted away around it and I found myself floating in my bathroom staring at my own faucet! Then I began floating down the hall. It felt like I was being carried from beneath by two beings. I did not see them but felt their presence. When I got to my bedroom door, I felt a quick jolt and woke up in bed in my body. I never forgot that experience. It has influenced much of my spiritual curiosity as an adult. —K. B., LAKELAND, GEORGIA

FLYING

Children will often relate the joy of their flying experiences. For both children and adults this is a favorite activity. Sometimes children assume the role of a fictional flying character— most likely a subconscious creation to keep them from being frightened and to give them a position of control.

My out-of-body experiences started when I was a kid and I would fly like Superman. After awakening I would still feel that way for about ten minutes. —KEN H., SCOTTSDALE, ARIZONA

I had about six or seven OBEs. They began at the age of twelve, spontaneously for three nights in a row. Actually I

didn't remember how I got out, I only remembered the coming back into my body. I was flying in the sky just like Peter Pan. I was flying over the city at about 6:30 A.M. The sun had not risen yet and it was still gray. When I got up I was so excited that I decided to do it the following night. And it happened again . . . three times. —VIOLETTE L., GENEVA, SWITZERLAND

ELECTRICAL AND HIGH-ENERGY SENSATIONS

The feeling of electrical currents is a common high-energy sensation experienced in the vibrational state. As a child I had a lucid dream experience in which I was helping my uncle fix an electrical appliance in the kitchen. When I looked down at the tile floor, I noticed that I was standing in a puddle of water. As we worked I felt as though a surge of electricity were moving up my legs and then through my entire body and into my hands and fingers. This frightened me, and I woke up with a jolt. I was so startled by the experience that I was unable to go back to sleep. Looking back, I now believe that this vivid dream was my young mind's interpretation of the vibrational state and the beginning of an out-of-body experience. At the time I had no idea what this was or how to react to it, and I was simply shocked awake from the experience. The following experiences detail similar feelings.

I have had many out-of-body experiences. They started in my teens and continued until about one year ago. I am now twenty-nine. I do not fear these experiences—in fact, I look forward to them. The experiences were never induced. However, once the initial signs were there, I could control it and make things happen. I would lie in bed, and when I was half asleep I could still hear around me. I would hear a buzzing noise—this is the only way I can describe it. Then it felt like an electrical line with electricity running up and down my body. I could feel myself lifting out, then I could do spins and twirls. I could also see through my closed eyes. I knew that if I opened my eyes, I would snap back. I never knew when it was going to happen, but once I heard the buzzing or felt the electrical sensations, I could control it from there. Sometimes it also felt like something was touching me—which was scary at first, but then kind of nice. —VIVIENNE M., MONTREAL, CANADA

A teacher in Michigan shares her son's experiences with electrical currents:

I have never experienced the vibrations or paralysis you write about, but my son has. On a dozen different occasions he has told me about waking up with a powerful noise vibrating within him. It would scare him, because he didn't know what was happening. He says that sometimes it feels like an earthquake or an electrical current is flowing through his entire body. Sometimes he also couldn't move his body for several minutes. My son is eighteen years old now, and he says these weird vibrations started when he was about twelve. He also told me that it still happens but not as much as before . . . It's good to finally know what this really is. Now at least he's not scared of it. —SARA P., MONROE, MICHIGAN

VARIOUS PERCEPTIONS OF MOVEMENT

Movement can manifest itself as any kind of action during your experience. The following examples show the wide spectrum of reported movement.

As a preteen I had out-of-body experiences. Most common was "into the body experiences"—my name for it—rather than out of body. I would shrink smaller and smaller until I felt as if I, my body, was a gigantic airplane hangar and I was standing inside this great space. I have no fears at all about it. —JANICE J., SHREVEPORT, LOUISIANA

A very common sensation I had as a child after I went to bed at night was that I was in a swing that was suspended from way up above the clouds. I could feel myself swinging back

and forth, and it usually became an almost nauseating sensation such that I had to sit up in bed to try to alleviate it. I always felt that I flew all over the house at night. I lived in a big three-story house, so there was plenty of room. I recall being just below the ceiling usually, so I didn't hit my head, and I went from room to room and down the hall and down the stairs . . . into the basement and into the attic. I don't recall running into people often, but when I did, they couldn't see me. I am fifty-five years old now, and these experiences are still extremely vivid in my mind. —EDIE K., ST. PAUL, MINNESOTA

I've had only one such experience that I remember. It occurred when I was in the seventh or eighth grade. At the time my younger brother and I shared a two-level bunk bed in our bedroom—he in the top bunk and me in the bottom. One night I "awoke" and found myself staring at the metal mattress supports in the top bunk above me. I was looking at the metal when I realized I was only three inches from it, maybe three feet above my own mattress. I remember then looking to my side, and seeing part of my body below me. The surprise/shock instantly hit me, and the next thing I knew I was lying there as usual on the mattress, thoroughly shaken and sweating. That's the one time it ever happened, but it did make a lasting impression. —BRIAN I., PORTLAND, OREGON

Two nights in a row when I was ten, we were visiting relatives and I felt as if the couch I was sleeping on was moving. I could feel a shift in gravity each time, but heard nothing. However, the couch did appear to be in a new position in the room. It had been against the wall, but was then in the middle of the room. —BART C., KANSAS CITY, KANSAS

The first time I had an OBE I had never even heard of one. I was thirteen at the time. I was asleep one night when I woke up between wakefulness and sleep. I thought that I sure would

like a glass of water, so I got up, walked to the kitchen, and was in front of the sink. I went to grab a cup and turn the water on at the same time. Then I suddenly noticed that my hands went right through both of the objects. I think somewhere in my mind I thought I missed what I was grabbing for, because I kept trying to grab it. I noticed my hands go right through it. I became only a little concerned, to be honest. I didn't freak out. So anyway, I went back to bed and laid down and felt a strange jerk back into my body, like a loud click.
—LOU R., SEATTLE, WASHINGTON

THE FEELING OF BEING REBORN

Some children describe their experience as somehow reliving their own birth. This can be perceived as the awakening or rebirth of their consciousness.

I was taking a nap, and I don't know how long I had been asleep or whether I had been dreaming prior to this occurring. Usually I do dream during naps, but I wasn't aware of anything other than simply having been asleep. At some point, I became conscious. I don't mean I woke up; I mean I was suddenly—blink—aware. But I wasn't me; I wasn't anybody. I didn't have language or form or personality. Completely blank slate. The best way I can describe it is that there was no context and no content. Just consciousness. Period. It felt like I was out in the universe, blackness. It's what I imagine being born might be like. Before there was nothing; then suddenly, awareness. It did not feel like sleep or a dream. —SUSAN T., TORONTO, CANADA

My out-of-body experiences are not dreamlike; they are just as real as waking life. Some of my experiences are very interesting, but most people would think I am crazy. The first experience of actually leaving my body occurred when I was thirteen. From the time I was eight years old, I would hear

ringing and the whole room would start to shake. There was a whirling or shifting in space. I was very scared, and my mom took me to the doctor to see if I had something wrong with me. After that, I would just experience strange episodes of traveling down a tunnel with the ringing and shaking preceding the tunnel. That is why I thought I was sick, or that I had some kind of disease that made me come close to death while I was sleeping. When I told my father, he said I was dreaming about being born. I accepted that as a good, reasonable answer. —JOY M., SANTA BARBARA, CALIFORNIA

SELF-INITIATING AN OUT-OF-BODY EXPERIENCE

For children, as for adults, directing the focus of attention away from the body during the onset of sleep can induce an out-of-body experience. It is not important what the focal point is as long it is away from the body. For centuries, lights—such as candles, lamps, and stars—have been used as an out-of-body focusing technique.

When I was a child, seven years old or thereabouts, at night I would sit up in bed and stare at lights that would shine on the ceiling from cars passing by. Anyhow, I would just sit there; then all of a sudden I would get this feeling that I would start levitating. I'd start going up, curled in a fetal position, and I'd just be floating. Then I remember floating down the stairs in this fetal position—a real slow float. —TANIKA J., CHICAGO, ILLINOIS

One of the most popular methods to initiate out-of-body exploration is the use of visualization. Without realizing it, Satch was performing a variation of the target technique. His focus upon the worktable initiated his experience.

One night as a child of eight or so, I was in bed happily falling asleep after a long, tiring day. Suddenly I remembered some homework I had forgotten to do and tried to get up out of bed to do it, but I was just too tired and heavy to move. So I decided

to count to ten, then get up. I got to ten, but again I was just too tired and heavy to move. I tried this another time or two with no result. So I visualized myself getting up and walking over to my little worktable, kind of like a practice run. Then one more time I counted to ten, and this time I got right up and walked over, very easily. I sat down at the table and looked at my books, then noticed a lump in my bed across the room and realized that this lump was a person. Curious, I drew closer. Then I saw my own sleeping face, and with a shock I realized I was looking at myself! Suddenly there was a big bump and I was instantly back in bed looking out of my own eyes. —Satch M., Tampa, Florida

PARENTAL SUPPORT AND INVOLVEMENT

Parental support and involvement may be the most critical part of a child's spiritual development. When a child talks to a parent about an out-of-body experience or the vibrational state, the parent must decide how to assist the child. This is why parents should be aware of the phenomena associated with out-of-body experiences. In the past, most parents did not understand the natural process of out-of-body travel and attributed such experiences to dreams and nightmares. If parents want to help their children stop the experience, they need only instruct them to focus their attention on a physical part of the body, such as a finger or toe, to end the experience. To develop children's natural ability, encourage them to talk about their experience. Explain the process to them, and emphasize the naturalness of the experience. Educate children about the potential of their explorations and the spiritual aspects of out-of-body travel. If children are frightened, teach them what I call the Golden Blanket Technique, described at the end of this chapter. Many find it helpful to teach children to ask for assistance from a guardian angel, guide, or other protective being.

PARENTS AND CHILDREN

Experiences with children and adults together is often reported. How we recall and interpret the experiences will vary. Many believe that flying is our mind's interpretation of an out-of-body experience. Two or more people sharing the exact "dream" provides evidence that there may be more to this kind of experience than meets the eye.

One time when I was about seven or eight, I told my mom in the morning, "I had the weirdest dream last night: Dad and I went flying." My mom stopped whatever she was doing and said, "Wait. What did you just say?" She looked so frozen. It turns out that my dad had had the same dream! I still remember holding hands with him and going right out their bedroom window into the night. He remembers the same thing. The difference was that in his dream, his father was flying with us, too. I had never met him, because he died when my dad was young. They were really close. —GEORGE S., FRAMINGHAM, MASSACHUSETTS

I have been "flying" with my nine-year-old daughter for over two years now. I started by telling her how to "fly" in her dreams, explaining how I did it. One morning she came running in to where I was sitting and excitedly replayed her dream where she got to "really fly," just like I explained to her. She was hooked. In the following months I tried to keep relating to her that I would come and fly with her . . . One night I did, and have several times since. She would relate to me the next morning many details exactly like I saw, and things we did together, all in our "dreams." I would tell her one detail and she would tell me one, then my turn again, and so on. We go through forests, down by the ocean, and on one occasion we were inside a bubble of soap! It was really cool . . . and she liked it a whole lot, too. —SHARON D., PONTIAC, MICHIGAN

VARIOUS PERCEPTIONS OF CONTACT

The way we perceive people during an out-of-body experience can take many different forms. Some out-of-body travelers report being accompanied by glowing orbs, while others see themselves as a bright sphere of pure consciousness. The most commonly reported color is blue or white. The globes of light are one of many possible energy manifestations of consciousness.

About ten years ago, I woke up halfway out of my body and saw two large fuzzy balls of light floating in a corner up by the ceiling. I sensed they wanted me to go with them. I felt they had invaded my privacy, so I said no. They left and I fell back asleep. A week later I learned that two classmates of mine were out having OBEs on this same night. —J. T., St. Louis, Missouri

I had a floating experience when I was nine, and I clearly saw a blue ball of light move around my bed. It hovered above me for several moments and seemed to be examining me. I felt like it was talking to me in my mind. I was afraid, and the thing floated away and disappeared through the wall. —John K., via e-mail

I have had two OBEs, the first one was when I was about thirteen years old. I had been asleep, and I got out of my bed. I walked down my street to the home of an older couple I was very good friends with and went inside. I remember going right through their front door. I went to their room and saw them sleeping, and at the time I felt that something was not right. The next thing I knew, my spirit, or whatever you want to call it, went back to my room extremely fast, and I remember seeing my body lying on the bed right before I went back into it. —Larry V., Bangor, Maine

In one experience I was in the clouds on a merry-go-round with several of my childhood friends. In another I stood with my school friends in front of three doorways. I knew that I could choose any one of those doorways and take my friends along on the journey. The doors had views with far-off horizons. I would choose one and off we would go. —Tabitha K., Columbus, Ohio

Tabitha's experience shows a freedom of movement that is suggestive of a spiritually developed individual. In general, as we conquer our internal fears, our spiritual freedom becomes more evident in our experiences.

I have had perhaps ten experiences. They began when I was around twelve years old, but they rarely occur anymore. I quite enjoy the flight capability. Typically, I will find myself walking alone down a nighttime street. I will then begin to run and notice that my steps are becoming long glides at about a foot in the air, each step getting longer, until I am striding about a city block at a time. There is a mounting excitement as I recognize and remember this feeling. I never get more than about the altitude of a three-story building. I was once visited by a close friend who had died, who appeared in my bedroom and "woke" me. I noted, "You're dead," at which he laughed and replied, "So?" The visit was short—the point, I believe, having been made. —BUDDY P., LONG ISLAND, NEW YORK

FEELING THE PRESENCE OF A NONPHYSICAL BEING

As many as 40 percent of children surveyed described seeing or feeling the presence of a "nonphysical being" while out of body. There are a wide variety of reports of beings encountered—from protective "angelic spirits" and heavenly environments to dark creatures and threatening surroundings. (For a simple spiritual protection technique that children may learn, see "The Golden Blanket Technique" toward the end of this chapter.)

The first experience was when I was thirteen. I remember I couldn't sleep. I felt as if something was going to happen that I couldn't control. Finally I got to sleep. I woke up and had the classic OBE. I floated above myself and then floated through the hall. I got scared when my head got caught in the ceiling. I was looking around the attic. Then I was snapped back into my body. I told my family the next morning. They were like "yeah, yeah." How could I possibly convey my experience to them with mere words?

The episodes intensified during my teenage years and included flying around my house and fighting with many strange beings. I had to protect myself . . . as they seemed to enjoy scaring me. Sometimes I can make up songs, arrange musical pieces, and play them. That is the most beautiful time. It is so wonderful. During my last experience I met a beautiful white angelic being. It was a breakthrough, because I often see dark figures. I was so happy; maybe they are done tormenting me. I am also now more confident and happy with myself, so maybe that directly affects my OBEs. —CHRIS K., KILLINGTON, VERMONT

Our mental state has an immediate impact upon our experience. This is true because when we are having an OBE we are acting in a thought-responsive dimension of reality.

OBSERVATION OF THE SILVER CORD

The very fact that young children are observing the biblical silver cord is significant because they have not yet been led to believe in it. Children's observations provide additional evidence that the cord truly does exist.

Around the age of four I had an out-of-body experience while sleeping. I was floating in the upper corner of my bedroom and looking down at my body asleep in the bed. I was confused, and extremely frightened at what had happened. There was a "plasmalike" cord between my spirit and body, and I quickly went back into my body. —ANDREW W., MANASSAS, VIRGINIA

DUAL CONSCIOUSNESS

The experience of dual consciousness occurs when your awareness is divided between two energy bodies: During an out-of-body experience, a portion of our consciousness remains in our physical body to maintain the bodily functions while the majority of our consciousness is focused within our nonphysical form. Consciousness exists as a multidimensional continuum that allows us to shift between various energy bodies. This occurs because consciousness is fluidlike by its very nature. This fluidity is manifested in some out-of-body experiences as the feeling that you are in two places at once.

When I was a child, not even ten years old, I had a few out-of-body experiences while drifting off to sleep. While lying on my bed, I would feel a whirring sensation in my head. Next I would see my body and the bed from above. It felt as if I was in two places at once. I could feel the "me" up near the ceiling, but I could also still feel the "me" lying on the bed. By the way, the "me" near the ceiling never seemed to have a body—but it could see. After what seemed like a few seconds, the "me" near the ceiling could see the "me" on the bed spinning around—that is, the entire bed seemed to be spinning, with my physical body in it. The "me" near the ceiling then moved downward closer and closer to the spinning "me" until the two "me"s became one again.

I would usually feel a little bit dizzy after this took place. What I've just described happened very infrequently, and usually only when I was physically exhausted after a long day. I was never scared when it happened. It actually felt nice and natural. Since I was only a child at the time, I assumed it was some kind of weird dream. It wasn't until my early twenties that I realized that these incidents were probably OBEs. I now also realize that it wasn't the bed or the "me" in the bed that was spinning. It was the "me" in the air that was spinning above my physical body. —LAUREN O., ROCHESTER, NEW YORK

NIGHT TERRORS

Recently the phenomenon known as night terrors has gained public attention. This experience is essentially an intense wave of fear that both children and adults experience during sleep. For decades it was thought to be the result of nightmares or a possible chemical imbalance. The experience can be so intense and shocking for children that their lives can be disrupted. They are often too terrified to sleep and seek comfort in their parents' bed.

Night terrors are much more than a bad dream. They can be the direct result of vibrational-state phenomena, which may include paralysis, rushes of energy, loud sounds, voices, and other strange events. The energy effects of the vibrational state are often sudden, shocking, and unexplainable by modern science. These energy phenomena are the direct result of a rapid and extensive opening of one or more chakras during sleep. This massive inner-energy flow can create the strange and frightening sensations and sounds that initiate night terrors.

TEACHING CHILDREN TO OVERCOME FEAR

Parents and other caregivers struggling with the unwelcome results of spontaneous night terror experiences are wise to learn about OBE experiences. When we recognize and understand the vibrational state, we can actually teach our children to control it or even stop it. If you desire, you can teach your children to shut down the vibrational state when it occurs by instructing them to focus their complete attention on a single part of their body—say, their finger or toe. This will immediately end the vibrational state and bring the child back to physical reality.

Another option is to teach children to use the vibrations and sounds to explore beyond their physical limits. You can do this by instructing them to remain calm during such states and allow the vibrations to expand and spread throughout their entire being. They are then to surrender to the sensations and

sounds of the vibrational state as they focus an
complete attention away from their body. At
will begin to separate from the body and th
begins. Children are naturally gifted at spiritual
and proper instruction only enhances this gift.

Spiritual Protection for Children

THE GOLDEN BLANKET TECHNIQUE

Parents can use this technique with their younger children. Tell children that anytime they feel threatened or afraid, they can envision a blanket of protection surrounding them:

"Picture yourself lying quietly under a warm, protective blanket. This blanket covers you from head to toe and is made from special cloth. The blanket radiates a golden, protective light. This golden light covers you completely. Anything that is not welcome cannot come near your warm, golden blanket. This blanket protects you and keeps you safe from anything and anyone you don't wish near you. It is made of powerful, protective light, and no harm can come to you when you are surrounded by the glow of this blanket. It feels good to be safe. It feels good to be warm and cozy under your golden blanket. This is a happy place, where you are always safe. The warm golden glow of this blanket keeps guardian angels close to you at all times."

Any similar wording that you find appropriate will do. The key is to emphasize the protective quality of the blanket. You could also expand this technique by supplying a new physical blanket to the child.

A NATURAL EVENT

All of the evidence points to one fact: Out-of-body experiences are natural excursions into the spiritual dimensions of reality. The more open and receptive we are to the experience, the more prevalent they become.

In 1989, my husband and I were in a rented flat in Santa Barbara. It was about midnight. I was asleep, but I had gone

of body because my husband was snoring. My spirit was in the living-room area, on the couch. I was very aware that I was lying down and was perceiving the entire room. I then watched as a child came right through the wall. It was a boy about one and a half years old, and he came right to me. He was so excited to see me, he came running over and put his hands straight up in the air and then on my stomach. Only thing was, his hands went straight through me. We were both in our "light"- or ethereal-body form. I shot right back to my body in the next room and sat up in bed. What a rush! The next morning as we were leaving, so were the people who had rented the place next to us. Out came a woman, a man, and their year-and-a-half-old son. My mouth dropped open; his eyes lit up, and he squealed with delight. What an experience. The innocence of a child in another dimension. Children obviously go out of body far more than we adults are aware of!
—D. D., E-MAIL

As parents, our challenge is to become aware of the spiritual benefits and obstacles our children can experience during their spontaneous out-of-body adventures. The more knowledgeable we become, the more we will be able to assist our children in moving beyond fear and into enlightenment, and the more we will learn to accept and embrace the unlimited potential that out-of-body journeys offer both our children and us.

3

Combat- and Trauma-Induced Experiences

*A mortar round exploded near me, and the next thing
I knew I was floating above my body watching the
chaos around me.*

JIM M., VIETNAM VETERAN

Over the years I have heard numerous reports of out-of-body
experiences caused by the blast from explosives and the terrible trauma of war. We now know that the explosion of a shell
or bomb creates a shock wave powerful enough to literally
force the subtle spiritual or astral form out of the physical
body. Since we are but temporary inhabitants of our physical
body, it's only natural that this would occur.

COMBAT EXPERIENCES

I have received reports of combat-related out-of-body experiences from five nations and encompassing four wars. The
similarity and spontaneity of these reported experiences provide evidence that these are universal phenomena.

*I was a sergeant stationed at a fire base in the central high-
lands of Vietnam. During a recon mission, a force of North
Vietnamese regulars ambushed my platoon. All hell broke
loose, and a mortar exploded near me and I was knocked
unconscious. The next thing I knew I was watching the*

firefight from another perspective—I was above it! I could see everything happening as my platoon was overrun. I watched in horror as they stripped the boots and weapons from my dead friends. Then I saw a young Vietnamese soldier pulling the boots off a body and I recognized that the body was mine. In a rage I attacked the soldier with a kick to his head, but my foot went right through his body. I kicked and punched him again and again, and to my amazement he didn't even notice. At that point I watched in disbelief as he stripped my body and then joined his men. Moments later I was back in my body and I felt a searing pain. —TOM B., LONG BEACH, CALIFORNIA

What I find especially interesting is that the sheer intensity of emotion and stress created by life-and-death situations can initiate an out-of-body experience. It's as if a powerful survival instinct takes over our normal state of being in order to protect our consciousness from harm.

The following is a World War II out-of-body experience reported by Dr. Raymond Moody in his book *The Light Beyond.*

This happened to me in Sicily during the invasion of Italy. My platoon was passing through a field when we were pinned down from in front by a German machine-gun nest. Since I was a platoon sergeant, I considered it my job to get rid of the nest so we could continue to advance.

I went far around, using a grove of fruit trees for cover. In about thirty minutes I had looped around the field and ahead so that I came in behind them. I was ecstatic. There were three of them in this hole that was dug just on the other side of a bridge. They were so involved in keeping the platoon pinned down that none of them was looking behind.

I probably could have gone within six feet of them and not been seen. I thought about doing that, but instead I threw a hand grenade when I got to the top of the bridge.

I remember pulling the pin and preparing to throw it from twenty yards away. I cocked my arm, and just before throwing it, I yelled, "Here you go, suckers." Then I hit the dirt and waited . . . and waited, and waited. The grenade didn't go off. It was a dud, as worthless as a rock.

Before I could do anything, they had turned a machine gun on me and started firing. I curled up in a ball and waited for something to hit me, but nothing did. Maybe it was the rise in the bridge that gave me cover, or maybe it was just good fortune, but nothing that was fired hit me.

But a funny thing happened. As I lay there, I suddenly left my body—and Sicily, for that matter. I "traveled" to a munitions plant in New Jersey, where I floated over an assembly line of women who were putting hand grenades together. I tried to talk to them and tell them to pay attention to their work, but they wouldn't listen. Instead they kept chattering as they did their work.

I felt like I was there for fifteen or twenty minutes. Then I was suddenly back in Italy lying at the top of this bridge, still alive. By now the Germans thought I was dead and had turned their gun back around. I got up and pulled the pin on another hand grenade and pitched it into their hole. This time it exploded.

The platoon had seen everything and thought that I was dead. I was very calm about the whole experience, so calm that the company commander sent me to a psychiatrist. I told him what had happened, and he gave me a clean bill of health and sent me back into battle. He told me that he had heard of this happening to other men before and that I should keep the experience to myself so I wouldn't get sent to him again. That's exactly what I did.[1]

In addition to the blast from explosions, the trauma and physical intensity of gunshots and shrapnel can also initiate out-of-body experiences.

While advancing on a hedgerow in France I was hit in the right shoulder by a sniper's bullet. I fell backward, and when I stood up I saw that my body was still lying on the ground. As long as I live I'll never forget it. —TED S., RICHMOND, VIRGINIA

One of the more famous combat stories of an out-of-body experience is Ernest Hemingway's. It occurred when he was a young officer with the U.S. Ambulance Corps during World

War I. In the summer of 1918 a mortar shell exploded next to him and the shrapnel tore into his legs. In the agonizing moments following the blast he told a friend that he sensed his spirit leaving his body. Hemingway described his experience in his 1929 novel, *A Farewell to Arms*, in the episode in which the fictional Frederic Henry is wounded.

> I tried to breathe but my breath would not come, I felt myself rush bodily out of myself and out and out and out and all the time bodily in the wind. I went out swiftly, all of myself, and I knew I was dead and that it had all been a mistake to think you just died. Then I floated, and instead of going on I felt myself slide back. I breathed and I was back.[2]

A related event occurs to modern fighter pilots when they experience intense G forces during extreme combat maneuvers. It has been reported that pilots will lose consciousness during maximum G forces and undergo a brief out-of-body state of consciousness. The U.S. military has conducted extensive research into this potentially dangerous phenomenon and has officially named the experience "G-lock." The popular television show *Sightings* did an entire segment on G-lock-induced OBEs that was titled "Simulated Out-of-Body Experiences." Several U.S. military pilots participated in an experiment where G-lock was created in a NASA centrifuge. Each interviewed pilot reported that he had passed out and then described a detailed out-of-body state of consciousness.

Another reported war-related experience is the direct result of captivity. It's not uncommon for prisoners of war to spontaneously project their consciousness to their loved ones at home.

I was a German prisoner of war during World War II. I was very young and extremely homesick and would often think of the comforts of my mother's home. One night I drifted to sleep and awoke at my mother's house. I could clearly see her in the kitchen and waved my arms in an effort for her to see me. I knew she was desperately worried about me, so I tried to get

her attention and tell her I was okay: "I'm here, I'm alive!" I
was reunited with my mother in 1945 when I finally got back
to the States. During this reunion she excitedly told me, "I saw
you waving your arms in the kitchen." I was amazed that she
had seen me. —LEWIS S., MIAMI, FLORIDA

TRAUMATIC EXPERIENCES

Jack London, the celebrated American adventure writer,
documented one of the more famous examples of a trauma-
related out-of-body experience in his nonfiction book *The
Star Rover*. The book deals with the turn-of-the-century
California outlaw Ed Morrell. London describes how when
Morrell was a prisoner, his guards would torture him so
severely that he would spontaneously have multiple out-of-
body experiences.

It's not uncommon for trauma-related OBEs to be perceived
as near-death experiences when they are not. On closer examination of many trauma-induced events, it becomes apparent
that temporary physical death does not occur. Rather, it is
simply a "forced" out-of-body experience. The same kind of
trauma-induced out-of-body scenario is reported during violent accidents, such as car crashes and plane crashes.

Pain-Induced Experiences

Out-of-body experiences can be caused by numerous events,
such as illness, childbirth, or intense pain and emotional trauma. In situations of intense trauma we sometimes escape the
situation by spontaneously separating our consciousness from
our bodies.

In what follows, several people relate their trauma- or pain-
induced experiences. These are clear examples of consciousness escaping from physical abuse. I often speak about the
courage it takes to be a spiritual explorer; the same kind of
courage applies here.

My out-of-body experience was caused by the intense pain of an illegal abortion in Juarez, Mexico. I left my body with roaring in my ears and lights in my head, and I saw or was shown all of creation. It was incredible. I knew at the time that I would come back with only a tiny fraction of a memory of what I was shown or saw. The gist of it was that everything the human mind has conceived of is true. One never dies. The spirit goes on, able to travel faster than light. The stars of the universe had been left behind me as I sped through them. I think I may have even seen the Creator. —T. M., SANTA FE, NEW MEXICO

As a young girl of eleven, I was sexually molested. I got pregnant, and my mom and grandma gave me a coat-hanger abortion in my own bed. I remember reaching a point where the pain was so unbearable I "left my body" and floated up to the corner of the room, where I was met by three spirit entities and discussed whether I'd return to my body. Leaving my body released me from the pain of the physical. Years later when I first recalled this event, I realized as I replayed the experience that one of the spirit entities incarnated as my youngest daughter sixteen years later. —PAT E., HOUSTON, TEXAS

I was about twelve or thirteen when I had an OBE. I was in the process of being severely beaten to the point where my back, legs, and buttocks were bloody. The pain was horrific, and suddenly my spirit or essence drifted out of my body and I was "floating" just above, watching my body being beaten. There was no longer any pain—I could just clearly see what was going on. The beating stopped shortly afterward, and I was suddenly back in my body and the pain returned. I did not have any sensation of fear or anything like that. In fact, it was a peaceful experience. —SAM A., PARKTON, MARYLAND

Abuse-induced out-of-body experiences are more common than one would expect. The following is another example.

It began at the age of eight, during times of physical abuse from one of my parents. While I was being abused, an OBE would result after I wished for my escape. I would suddenly find myself, my awareness, on the ceiling in a lightbulb. For some unknown reason I felt safe there. After the abuse I would automatically exit the lightbulb and return back to my physical body. —STEPHEN H., DORAVILLE, GEORGIA

Childbirth

Out-of-body experiences are common during childbirth. They are generally brief and occur during the course of a difficult and painful labor.

I was about to deliver my second child after a difficult pregnancy. When taken to the delivery room, I was in such pain; then suddenly I was floating overhead. I could look down and see a woman in a bed being wheeled into a hospital room. She was in great pain and screaming. Suddenly I realized that the woman I was watching was me! Then, poof . . . it was gone. This "incident" has never left me over the past seventeen years. —LACEY D., SAN FRANCISCO, CALIFORNIA

Physical Attack

I have had only one OBE, and I didn't know that's what it was at the time. It was in October 1977, in Maryland. I was attacked by a rapist who had killed a lot of women by slashing their throats. I knew I was going to die. While in the midst of the rape, I suddenly came out of the top of my head and stood across the room and watched myself being attacked. I knew "I" was okay . . . that I was separate from my body and if it got killed, I would just go on to the next world. I spoke to "God" . . . trying to find a way to avoid this death and spare my parents having to go through this horrible experience. At some point, I knew all of a sudden that I had been given a task to do and would not be leaving this world now. Without trying or thinking of it, I was suddenly back in my body . . . through the top of my head. I started to panic and the rapist left and came back three times before leaving for good. After the experience I could remember what the man looked like even though I was blindfolded the whole time.

Later I reluctantly told the D.A. and the police investigators what had happened during the crime, and to my shock, the D.A. did not seem surprised at all. Several weeks later I was able to identify the attacker through photos brought around by the police. The man I identified was indeed the multiple rapist-murderer and was tried and convicted. —ANONYMOUS

Fear and Mental Stress

Intense fear or stress can act as a powerful trigger to initiate out-of-body experiences. Most of these events provide an escape from a negative situation.

I've had many OBEs, starting in my childhood and occurring infrequently throughout my life. I'm thirty-five now. I believe they started because of a traumatic experience I had while I was asleep as a child. I was molested during the night, and I think I first left my body out of fear. It then became a habit. Anytime I was under stress, if I slept on my back, I'd inevitably leave my body. Sometimes it was a great experience, flying over my neighborhood at night, feeling completely free. Sometimes it was the most unpleasant experience to leave my body, afraid of not going back, sensing evil spirits pulling me out, waking in a cold sweat.

While asleep, I would become aware of a loud sound inside my head. It sounded like a radio signal at full blast. I could feel electricity throughout my body, and I became fearful . . . a voice came to me and said, "Turn it down, tune it in." I "turned down the volume" inside my head, and the radio fre-

*quency tuned in to music. My logical mind thought that my
radio must have turned on by itself, so I tried to get out of bed
to turn it off. I realized, as I was moving across the room, that
I wasn't in my body. The fear came back, and the loud sound
came back. I returned to my body and awoke in a state of awe.
Since then I have heard that loud noise, followed by voices or
crystal-clear music. It seems to me that there are spirits on
another plane or frequency that can come through during an
OBE, or maybe they instigate the OBE, because, like I mentioned before, sometimes they pull at me while I'm sleeping.*
—J. B., BUTTE, MONTANA

*I have had maybe six spontaneous out-of-body experiences
like this. The first one was when I was in college. It was
induced by fatigue and terrible stress. I didn't know what it
was, and it terrified me because I found myself walking across
the room without my body. I could see my body sleeping on
the bed, and at first I thought I had died, and it scared me.
After many years I finally found out what it really was, and I
was extremely relieved.* —SHAWNA K., CANTON, MICHIGAN

Physical Stress

I received several letters that detail spontaneous OBEs during times of prolonged physical exertion. The most common
situations were long-distance running and treadmill exercising.

*It was while I was running in a marathon last year that I had a
very strange experience. I was at about the eighteen-mile
marker when I looked beside me and saw myself running. At
first I thought it was someone who was my build and wearing
the same shoes, but then I realized it was me! Even stranger
was that my running "partner" was drenched in sweat, breathing hard, and in obvious discomfort . . . while I felt amazingly
fresh and energized. The whole thing took only a few seconds.
When I shook my head—to clear the cobwebs—I was back in
my sweaty self again. I got to the finish line, still not sure what*

had happened. I am pretty much into my physical fitness—but this made me really think about the real me inside. —MARK J., BERLIN, GERMANY

Severe Depression

When I was seventeen and severely depressed, I was suicidal and just didn't care about anything anymore. One night I woke up suddenly from a dream and felt completely detached from my body—floating above it. There was also a very loud noise and a powerful energetic feeling like electricity or something. I was talking to myself, saying things like "Oh shit, oh shit, please stop, please stop," because I'd never experienced anything like it before. The weird thing is that I had wanted to die, but when this was happening I was suddenly scared and praying to survive. —LAUREN J., KINGSTON, JAMAICA

Sometimes the events that initiate an OBE are not a major trauma, but just an unexpected shock.

I had a spontaneous out-of-body experience as a child just after I had gone to bed. I had wet the bed and was jerked up and spanked by my father. I watched the whole thing from a corner of the ceiling. —NADINE G., BISMARK, NORTH DAKOTA

Illness

Illness and high fever are often reported as a cause of out-of-body experiences. Many believe the connection between the physical and spiritual bodies becomes more fragile during severe illness. The following are a few examples.

My first experience was at twelve years old. It was night. I was very ill with strep throat. It was dark, and my parents were asleep. I awoke to find myself floating at the top of my bedroom ceiling. I did not notice if my body was in my bed as I was so involved with the fact that I was at the top of my bed-

room ceiling. I felt light and transparent, and I moved from one corner of the ceiling to the next. This experience repeated itself several times until I found myself outside and above the treetops and flying while looking down at the landscape. It was wonderful. —BOBBI P., CORPUS CHRISTI, TEXAS

The very first memory I have of an OBE is when I was around five or six years old. I was extremely ill with smallpox and had a dangerously high fever. All I remember of the experience is calmly hovering up by the ceiling and looking down at myself being very sick in bed. My mother was very upset over my condition and was on the phone sitting near me on the bed talking to the doctor. He was telling her to give me an ice-cold bath to bring down the fever. I distinctly recall being very curious and concerned about myself in the bed . . . but other than that, I was extremely calm, peaceful, and silent. I enjoyed the sensation of floating and was glad to be separated from the obvious suffering my body was going through at the time. I wanted to tell my mother that I would be okay. The whole experience was very brief, really. The funny thing is, at the time, I never even questioned how odd it all was. I simply accepted it as if it happened all the time and was normal. It wasn't until I was much older, in my teens, that I realized how strange it was that my only memory of my illness was from the vantage point of the ceiling. I asked my mother about it then and was very surprised to learn that everything I remember seeing and hearing when out of body really did take place. —SALLY I., TORONTO, CANADA

I was home in bed suffering from a virus and had a very high fever. This had gone on for over two days when one night, almost reaching a convulsive state while in bed, I felt my ears begin to ring and it seemed as though I had no feeling in my body. There was also a sensation of falling. I had no fear, which was strange. Then I saw a light, getting larger and larger, almost warm in nature. I remember talking to someone—or *maybe it wasn't really conversing, but communicating. They said, "Don't worry, you will be all right." All the while I was thinking that it was my mother. I awoke the next morning feeling much better. It was very late in the morning, closer to noon, when my mother came in the room to ask how I was and if I was going to eat. I told her how much better I felt and that I did want to eat, that as she had said the night before, I would be all right soon. She looked confused and told me, "I didn't talk to you last night."* —PAT Y., MONTPELIER, VERMONT

Stress and Sleep Depravation: Charles Lindbergh's Unknown Flight

The most extraordinary moments of Lindbergh's 1927 transatlantic flight may have taken place during the trip's eighteenth hour. Enveloped in the dark of night, staring at the instrument panel, battling an overwhelming desire to sleep, Lindbergh clearly describes his thoughts of mind and body separation.

On a long flight, after periods of crisis and many hours of fatigue, mind and body may become disunited until at times they seem completely different elements, as though the body were only a home with which the mind has been associated but by no means bound. Consciousness grows independent of the ordinary senses. You see without assistance from the eyes, over distances beyond the visual horizon.

Lindbergh continues this premise with . . .

This essential consciousness needs no body for its travels. It needs no plane, no engine, no instruments, only the release from flesh which the circumstances I've gone through make it possible.[3]

Lindbergh realized that others would attribute his out-of-body experience to a hallucination; in his autobiography, the aviator responded to this conclusion.

My visions are easily explained away through reason, but the longer I live, the more limited I believe rationality to be.

These spontaneous experiences shed light on the wide variety of out-of-body journeys reported today. The separation of consciousness from the body can result from many different causes. Evidence suggests that each of us will experience the separation of consciousness from the body. These events can be spontaneous, induced by external circumstances, or self-initiated. The more knowledge we obtain, the more prepared we will be to use our experiences to explore our true nature and accelerate our spiritual development.

1. Raymond Moody, *The Light Beyond* (New York: Bantam Dell, 1989), 96–97.
2. Ernest Hemingway, *A Farewell to Arms* (New York: Simon and Schuster, 1929), 55.
3. Charles Lindbergh, *The Spirit of St. Louis* (New York: Scribner/Simon and Schuster, 1953), 352–53.

4

Transformational Experiences

This spiritual core is so awesome and overwhelming that the person is at once and forever thrust into an entirely new mode of being.

KENNETH RING, *HEADING TOWARD OMEGA*

Life-changing spiritual adventures are often part of an out-of-body experience. This is especially true of self-initiated out-of-body journeys, because the explorers are prepared for their adventures. They often report an instant and dramatic change in their awareness and their perception of the universe and themselves. Those who have had a profound out-of-body experience speak of an incredible acceleration in their personal evolution. This can be due to their expanded ability to obtain insights and knowledge, understand past-life issues, or overcome their fears. In addition, fully conscious spiritual meetings with loved ones, guides, or angelic beings can initiate a significant shift in consciousness and provide a powerful transformative experience.

SELF-REALIZATION

At the core of all transcendental and mystical states of consciousness is a shift of awareness away from the physical body and its senses to the formless spiritual essence within us. Many refer to such an experience as *self-realization* or *God realiza-*

tion. For thousands of years spiritual masters have taught that the act of withdrawing from the senses is essential in order to consciously experience our spiritual self. Spiritual texts around the world speak to the importance of transcending the body and embarking on the magnificent journey of soul into the pure realms of spirit. Authentic spiritual experiences have one thing in common: They all occur beyond the limits of the physical senses.

This process is important, because it brings us to the heart of our spiritual evolution. We begin to recognize that the direct path to self-empowerment lies in our ability to transcend the dense limits of our bodies and experience our true spiritual essence. There is simply no substitute for personal spiritual experience and our conscious connection to spirit. The following experiences provide examples of personal transformations that occurred as a direct result of out-of-body adventures.

In 1996, I experienced an emotional and spiritual explosion that led to two episodes of out-of-body experiences. Both occurred while I was lying in bed, doing deep breathing meditation and moving downward in consciousness toward my subconscious self. My body started to vibrate, and energy emanated from every pore of my body. At first I was filled with fear, but I let myself continue. As the experience continued I was in a place I can only describe as "the mind of God." I say place, *but there was no place or time. I was in the mind of Jesus on the cross, and Buddha, and all the prophets and holy persons throughout history. I was able to feel all of the births, lives, and deaths of humanity as if I were in an endless sea of souls. It was a place of endless, unconditional love pouring forth. No beginning, no end—just pure being. I was able to put my arms—not my physical arms, but I don't know how else to express this—around my parents, and love and forgive. I was able to forgive all and project nothing but love.*
—GRACE A., ST. PAUL, MINNESOTA

PROFOUND SPIRITUAL EXPERIENCES

One of the tremendous benefits of out-of-body exploration is the direct approach to spiritual development that it provides. Profound spiritual experiences are reported during both spontaneous and self-initiated adventures.

During my fourth self-induced out-of-body experience I screamed out that I had to see God. Words can't begin to describe it, but it felt like I suddenly shot upward through layers of colors. I completely surrendered to the intense motion. I experienced absolute oneness with all intelligence, all life. My awareness merged with the universe, with God, and for a few moments all knowledge flowed through me. It was the most incredible moment of my life. —KEITH G., HANOVER, PENNSYLVANIA

My out-of-body experience was in my search for God. I fell asleep but awakened again and felt a light and buzzing sensation. I then looked at my hand and felt it. My hand was real and solid yet without warmth. I left my body and went to a bright white room. I stood at the doorway and said, "Higher Self now!" At first nothing much happened, so I screamed out in my mind, "Higher Self now!" Suddenly I was like a rocket flying through lights and stars. My awareness was stretched across the universe. Words cannot describe any of this, for I was far beyond form and substance. I was suddenly in an incredible ocean of pure living light. Everything was there—all knowledge, all awareness, and all answers. I was part of it all. I didn't want to ever leave. —ROBERT J., YORK BEACH, MAINE

KNOWLEDGE EXPANSION

Many transformational experiences involve the acquisition of knowledge. During these experiences our ability to receive insights and knowledge is expanded far beyond our normal capacity.

When we are out of body, our minds will often manifest an

image of knowledge that is comfortable and understandable to us. Often this is represented as a book, a library, or a wise being.

I feel a vibrational energy and float from my body. I walk through the door and find myself in a new environment. I see a pillar of light that is about four feet high. I feel the intensity of the light and am drawn to it. As I move closer, I can see a large book at the top of the column of light. I move even closer and can feel a powerful energy radiating from the book. I instinctively know that it is the Book of Knowledge. I open the book and feel a surge of knowledge flowing into me. This is difficult to put into words, for I feel overwhelmed by a flood of pure knowledge entering me. I can't absorb it all; it seems to overflow. I try to hold it, but I cannot. It feels as if a massive electrical charge or jolt is surging through me, and I snap back to my body. Although I can't absorb all the knowledge, it is comforting to know that it is available to me. —BERT M., SHARPESBURG, VIRGINIA

I thought I was asleep, but I was awake and floating. I could see all around me, as if I had a dozen eyes circled around my head. I was in a brilliant blue sky, with a few white fluffy clouds. Ahead of me was a grand white staircase, like in those Hollywood dance movies from the fifties. It was wide and wound around to a white, shiny floor. The floor had a waisthigh railing surrounding it. There was a table and chair, all made of the white shiny material. I was thinking, "Is this what heaven looks like?" Sitting on the chair was a little man with a red bow tie. I'm sure he was wearing something else too, but that's all I could remember. He seemed a bit impatient with me and said, "Read the book." I said "What book?" "You know . . . Read the book!" As I pondered the question I was back in my body, and I felt paralyzed for several moments. I'm still not sure what book he was talking about, but since that experience I have increased my spiritual research and have become a regular practitioner of out-of-body travel. Whenever I do read a spiritual book, I think to myself, "Is this the one?" Maybe I'll never know. But I am more certain than ever of my continued existence beyond this body. —P. L., ROCHESTER, NEW YORK

When we return to our physical state of consciousness, we immediately become hampered by the limits of our biological brain, linear time, and the density of matter. I recommend focusing on the theme or message of the experience and writing down as many details as possible. As much as you can, capture the essence of the experience. Allow the information or imagery to flow without attempting to mentally edit the content. It's important to write our experiences because it's common for the insights we receive to make sense weeks or even months later.

THREE-HUNDRED-SIXTY-DEGREE PERCEPTION

One of the most commonly reported transformational experiences is the ability to perceive in all directions simultaneously. Based on many years of experience and research, I conclude that this is our natural mode of perception.

I felt intense vibrations and then a floating sensation. Several times in my mind I demanded awareness. I feel a surge of lightness and freedom flow through me. I was floating in what I can only describe as a sea of knowledge. For some reason I thought about the importance of my past lives—I was not a real believer in that—and I was instantly in a new environment. I was in what I can only describe as a 360-degree movie theater. An endless series of images appeared before me. All of these stories made perfect sense. Some were tragic, some were pleasant, but all of them were connected to me. They were me. I am in awe of the complexity and simplicity of it all. I know things about myself I can't explain. —ROBIN K., OLYMPIA, WASHINGTON

THE PRESENCE OF INTELLIGENCE

It is not uncommon for spiritual beings to exhibit no external shape or form. This is to be expected, because our natural state of consciousness dwells beyond three-dimensional concepts.

How we perceive and interpret these experiences is dependent upon our state of consciousness and beliefs.

While taking an afternoon nap, I awoke to find myself fully aware and in the presence of a huge ball of light. But it wasn't a sun; it was an intelligence. I was shocked by the reality of this experience. I immediately knew that this was God. I was so surprised, and before I had a moment to think of what I was saying, I shouted out, "You're real!" because at the time I did not believe that God was real. This brilliant sun or God had no face; it was just light. But I could feel that it was smiling at me. It seemed that it looked into me deeper than I had ever had anyone look into me before. I felt that I was totally transparent. Actually, I had no presence of a body at all; I was just an intelligence. I have never felt so naked in my life. It knew me, all of me, all at once. My reaction to this being was a very strong desire to hide myself. I was not accustomed to being seen so fully by anyone. Before I knew what I was doing, I moved away from this beautiful sun—even though I didn't have a body. I felt ashamed of myself for all of the things that I had done or had not done in my life . . . I had the impression as I moved away from this presence that I was getting no further from it at all; it was still with me as much as ever. —F. G., HONOLULU, HAWAII

MEETING LOVED ONES

One of the great benefits of out-of-body exploration is the ability to consciously meet our loved ones and verify our personal immortality. These experiences often create a dramatic shift in consciousness.

During an out-of-body experience I talked with a deceased relative and was offered a chance to stay. There was a loving being of light that said the choice was mine. Very quietly, I heard the voices of my children in another room, and I said I'd return to finish raising them. It was a profound experience that changed my life forever. I haven't been afraid of death since, and my priorities are far different from what they were before. —SANDI T., SEATTLE, WASHINGTON

LAYERS OF ENERGY AND COLOR

Out-of-body explorers often describe the perception of moving through layers of energy and color. Since the universe is a multidimensional continuum, all movement of consciousness is interdimensional in nature. I believe that the reported layers of color are our mind's interpretation of the various energy levels of the universe.

Several months ago I did an out-of-body technique every night as I fell asleep. I was very focused on finding answers and having a spiritual experience. One night I fell asleep normally and was shaken awake by what I thought was a train running through my bedroom. I tried to move but couldn't. I then thought about knowing God. I instantly shot through an incredible series or layers of colors and was suddenly floating in a endless ocean of white light. I was connected to everything and everyone. —ERIC L., DETROIT, MICHIGAN

When I am having my most profound out-of-body experiences, I move through a rainbow and my entire being is completely surrounded by an endless sea of liquid color filled with loving light. I feel as if I am the light, but yet somehow I am still an individual. An incredible feeling of peace and love surrounds me. I'm part of the universe. All knowledge is present. —ALAN D., PALM BEACH, FLORIDA

SHIFTS IN CONSCIOUSNESS

Out-of-body experiences by their very nature can provide dramatic shifts in consciousness and perception. This can create rapid changes in behavior.

I was lying in my bed, thinking deeply about death and wanting to kill myself. As I was doing this I began to fall deeper and deeper into the back of my mind. Then I was stricken with an overwhelming amount of pressure on my chest, and I thought I was really going to die. The next thing I knew there was a flash and I was floating above my body, watching myself. It was the most intense thing I have ever felt, and it made me realize how truly beautiful and worth living life is.
—CARLA G., LOS ANGELES, CALIFORNIA

The profound act of projecting your consciousness beyond the body can have an immediate life-changing impact. You dramatically confirm your immortality and experience yourself in a shocking new light. You fully recognize, often for the first time, that you are a spiritual being and that you are completely responsible for all of your actions. This is a powerful, transformational shift of consciousness that initiates immediate and lasting benefits.

It's been a month since my out-of-body experience, and I can't believe how real it was. Everything suddenly changed that night. I saw and experienced things I can't begin to describe. It's tough to explain, but I realize I am so much more then I ever believed possible. —LARRY H., CALIFORNIA CORRECTIONAL FACILITY

An out-of-body experience is a powerful wake-up call capable of shaking up even the most hardened criminal. An inmate currently imprisoned in a New York correctional facility reports the following experience.

I am not a believer in this kind of stuff but decided to try one of the techniques from your book [Adventures Beyond the Body] for about a month. After about three weeks weird things started to happen. A loud engine sound woke me up several times during the night. The next day I was scared awake by sounds and I couldn't move my body for several minutes. I hate to admit it, but this was really scary to me. I know you say to expect this stuff and give in to it, but nothing

*in this world can really prepare you for the real thing.
Anyway, I continued the techniques every night for two more
weeks and then "it" really started to happen. I woke up completely paralyzed, but this time I stayed calm and thought
about the door. Bang, I was suddenly standing by the steel
door and I could see through it. The door and the walls were
like layers of fog. I touched the fog and then stepped through
it. I was suddenly in a new place, a green field. I was so
shocked by the change that I seemed to be sucked back into
my body. I opened my eyes and felt paralyzed for a few seconds. Then it all hit me like a bolt of lightning: It was completely real. I lay there in total amazement: "This is bigger
then anything I can imagine; how can I tell people without
sounding like a nutcase? This changes everything I ever
thought I knew or thought was true. I need to know more,
see more.* —T. R., NEW YORK CORRECTIONAL FACILITY

Crimes are committed because people have lost contact with
the truth of themselves and their spiritual existence. In a sense,
they are suffering from a form of amnesia. They have forgotten
that they are immortal spiritual beings with absolutely unlimited creative abilities. They are disconnected from the greatest
single truth of the universe—that they are powerful spiritual
beings that create their reality and their life, both the positive
and the negative.

TRANSFORMATIVE QUALITIES RESULTING FROM OBEs

- Increased respect for life
- Expansive self-concept extending beyond the physical
- Increased spiritual connection
- Reduced hostility and violence
- Greater awareness of reality
- Increased interest in a personal search for knowledge
  and wisdom
- Increased self-respect and sense of responsibility
- Personal verification of immortality

- Expanded awareness of our interconnection with others
- Dramatic psychological changes due to potential encounters with spiritual beings, loved ones, or guides

*A relative got me your book [Adventures Beyond the Body], and I studied it for a month. I did the techniques every night as I fell asleep. I experienced the sounds and vibrations you described several different times for weeks. Then one night I heard a tremendous rush of sound and I experienced paralysis. I was scared but didn't freak out; I did what you said and "let go." I felt a sense of movement and found myself in a field surrounded by dead and wounded soldiers. It was a green valley between three mountains, and the air was very cool. The fighting men I assumed to be Scottish because they wore plaid, but not any kind of military uniform I was familiar with. I was drawn to one man who had a sword raised over his head, about to attack a wounded man on the ground. He hesitated, and I read his thought: "I can't do this anymore. People have got to stop killing." At that moment, an opposing soldier ran up behind him and took his life. I felt helpless and vulnerable—not a feeling that I am familiar with. It occurred to me that this man was caught up in a situation where he did not want to fight but he had no choice because of the lifestyle he had chosen. And then the whole picture became clear: This man was me. As I came out of the experience I felt numb, unable to move. My waking thoughts took me back to the field of dead men, and I realized that I would continue to find myself in some kind of battlefield where it was kill or be killed until I made a major change in my life. That was several months ago, and I have been focused on changing my direction since that experience. I now know that there is a cycle I must consciously break before I can move ahead. —*JEROME J., MARYLAND CORRECTIONAL FACILITY

Jerome's daily out-of-body techniques opened the door for an important shift in consciousness. This created the opportunity for his soul to orchestrate the experience necessary for his personal development. Often personal change requires a dramatic wake-up call for us to truly "get it." We must remember that a profound out-of-body experience can awaken even the sleeping soul.

PAST-LIFE REVELATIONS

When we explore beyond our physical body, time and space do not exist as we otherwise perceive them. As a result, it is common for us when out of body to spontaneously experience various time lines: past, present, and future. Based on my experiences and the substantial feedback I have received, I believe that all experiences and events possess an inherent energy signature and that we are naturally attracted to the energy that is important for our spiritual development. During an out-of-body experience we are often drawn to the strong energy signature of an unresolved past event that is exerting an influence on our current state of consciousness. All energy seeks balance, so each experience provides the potential for balance and resolution within the person.

Spontaneous past-life imagery and revelations during OBEs are often reported. This is especially true of experienced travelers who self-initiate and direct their adventures. It's important to know that we can use our out-of-body experience to obtain clarification or additional information about an immediate situation or encounter by asking focused questions—for example, "What year [or What country] is it?" or "Why is this important to me?" Often the answer will manifest itself in the form of inner knowledge or a clear unseen voice or message. The following are two examples.

I had a rushing sensation and found myself in a new environment. As I headed downstairs to the kitchen, I suddenly realized that the house in which I am currently living does not have a kitchen downstairs. But I "knew" every detail of the house, and it was my house. I noticed the refrigerator and looked inside and it was full of ice blocks, like those old-fashioned refrigerators. Then I noticed a calendar on the wall and saw that it was September 1936! I went with my husband—not from this life—on a fishing job, and a foreman came up to me and suggested that I give up my job as there were men out of work who needed jobs. I have been reading about the illusion of time, and I feel like this could have been a previous existence. This experience has given me a new perspective on spirituality in my current life. —T. L., JOPLIN, MISSOURI

I occasionally will have a spontaneous out-of-body experience when I'm asleep. This is often shocking to me because the reality is absolute, not dreamlike at all. The most memorable was an OBE that put me in a World War II battle in France. Me and my men were pinned down by German machine-gun fire, and two of my closest buddies were killed right next to me. I was so scared that I wet myself. I lost it completely and fought like a madman until I was jolted by an explosion. Instantly everything became real quiet and I was floating above what was left of my body. This was as real as anything I've ever experienced in my life and made me realize that reincarnation is absolutely real. —TOM G., DAYTON, OHIO

VISITING A FUTURE SPIRITUAL HOME

Several people have expressed to me that they have visited their future spiritual home. They state that there is a knowledge about the location that is unmistakably familiar.

When I go out of body, I feel very good, exceedingly free and happy. I usually walk through a wall, because I almost always end up someplace that I don't expect. This time I say to myself, "I want to see where I'll go when I die." I am instantly in a gray place and say again, "I demand to go to the place where I'll go when I die." This time I am moving inward through grayish blue clouds, and I experience a sucking feeling, like my head is being sucked in. Suddenly I am floating above a place that is totally beautiful. I recognize the place and say, "The lake!" I know that a part of me has been here

before. It is large—maybe ten miles to the other side, where there is a low mountain range. The sun is coming up so the mountains are reflected in the water. There is a mist above part of the lake, and I am overwhelmed with emotion and joy. I feel at home here. I do not fear death. I've returned home.
—CATHY L., FARMINGTON, MICHIGAN

ENERGY MEMBRANES

Energy membranes are the energy fields that appear to separate two dimensions. They are dense layers of energy that are often reported as a dense mist, layers of color, channels of liquid, or various kinds of walls or borders. Our movement through the membranes is one way to determine our location and progress from one energy level to another. It's common for the environment to change when we move through a perceived wall or membrane.

As I moved away from my body I immediately found myself plunging through some kind of layer or membrane into darkness. I was instantly in a darkness filled with stars or points of light as if I were traveling through space. Then I moved through another layer filled with darkness and stars, and then another and another. The farther I went, the faster it seemed I traveled. I ended up in a new reality of vibrant energy.
—HENRY N., SEDONA, ARIZONA

WAKING OUT-OF-BODY EXPERIENCES

Even though OBEs that occur during waking states of consciousness are rare, they are occasionally reported. The following is one such experience.

I have had thirteen out-of-body experiences since the age of seven. I am now forty-seven. The last OBE was a God-awareness experience. I was working late on November 13, 1992. I leaned back in my chair and stretched, and bang! *I was* out of body and seeing in a 360-degree viewpoint. I could see everywhere at the same time! I was looking to the front and was viewing a black shimmering curtain that stretched off into infinity. I became aware of a pinpoint of light directly behind me. I thought, "How cool, a lone star." I was feeling childlike wonderment at what I was seeing. The star seemed to hit me in the back of my head, and my soul-body was shattered and flung into the shimmering reality in front of me. I instantly remembered my soul's life—all my past lives, everything my soul has been responsible for since its creation in the vast universe of God. I was reminded of my soul's eternal duty, or what my soul was created for. I also learned that my soul was created before the creation of the physical universes. That my soul, along with billions of other souls, was responsible for the creation of the physical universes. It also reminded me why I was brought back to earth in this life, and that I had a mission or duty to put into action that only my soul has the power to do. —Drew B., St. Augustine, Florida

EXPERIENCES WITH ANGELS

Encounters with angels can be interpreted many different ways. Some believe that these ethereal beings are spiritual guides and helpers, while others insist that they are indeed biblical angels. However we interpret such experiences, the important fact is that they are very real to the experiencer. The underlying reason for the "vision" is an internal shift in consciousness, attested to by the reported increase in spontaneous out-of-body experiences that occurs as people approach death. (The latter phenomenon is covered more extensively in chapter 8, "A New Vision of Death and Dying.")

Lying on my back, I silently repeated two affirmations: "I remain aware as I drift to sleep" and "Now I am out of my body." It took about fifteen minutes before my body became sleepy and tired, so I repeated the affirmations in my mind. When my body transitioned to sleep, instantly I was out of my body. *I became aware that I was just outside of my body, close to the door. I noticed that a person was walking into the room wearing dark clothes. My vision was blurry and lazy even though I was quite conscious and aware. Then my thoughts became focused on that person. The room was still dark, because the person had not turned on the light yet. Then the scenery changed and I was in a cloudlike environment. There I was next to an angel who was sitting on what appeared to be a cloud, a book in his lap. The reason I knew it was an angel was that, for one, I felt it, and it was dressed in white. The whole time, I was quite calm and knew what was going on. The environment was somewhat dim. On the other side of the angel was a white path leading up to the higher heavens. Focused on the book, I asked the angel, "What is in the book?" The response was like images entering my mind: "Let's see what you have done with your life." I was shown things about myself that are important, and I was amazed at the simplicity of it all. Now I really watch my thoughts and deeds, and I thank God for the reassurance that I am progressing.* —L. B., New Brunswick, Canada

Often these ethereal encounters are spontaneous events initiated by emotional intensity or the overwhelming need for reassurance or information.

When my son was very sick in the hospital, I spent every available moment by his side. One late night, sitting in a chair next to his bed, I heard a loud noise and felt like I was being pulled out of my body. I was drifting through the room and noticed that somehow my surroundings had changed. I saw the hazy outline of the playroom in the hospital. It wasn't very clear, but I was certain that my son was playing with another child. They were building with Legos on a table. You know how you can pick out your child, even if just from an outline. He noticed me and sent me a telepathic message: "Don't worry, I'll be okay real soon." He pointed to the other child and said, "He told me." I tried to walk toward them, but the scene vanished just as quickly as it had appeared. I woke up with a startled feeling, as I could not move my legs right away.

Several days later my son had gotten well enough to leave the hospital, and he couldn't stop talking about the friend he'd made while playing with Legos. I've always felt privileged to see what my son experienced. —GLORIA H., LAS VEGAS, NEVADA

HIGHER-SELF EXPERIENCES

Out-of-body exploration offers us a highly effective method for experiencing our spiritual essence. However, we must have the courage to transcend not only the physical body but also the limits of our culture and our beliefs. We must exercise the self-reliance, self-discipline, and courage of a true spiritual explorer in order to experience our higher selves.

For a few years I have had out-of-body experiences but wanted to take it further. I was reading about the higher-self experience and decided to focus on it as a personal goal. Every night as I go to sleep I repeat affirmations like "Now I'm out of body and I remain aware." Sometimes nothing happens, and sometimes powerful sounds and energy sensations awaken me. I never know what to expect. One time I felt the vibrations and surrendered to the energy flowing through me. I focused my attention on the window and began to feel myself floating upward. What happened next was incredible: Faster than I could imagine, I found myself being pulled through level after level of living color and light. When the motion slowed, I asked for clarity and was overwhelmed by the absolute energy I felt within and around me. I could see 360 degrees of an infinite light, and yet it wasn't the physical me that was experiencing this. It was as though I suddenly knew everything about everything and was totally in a peaceful, loving place. When I came back to my physical body, I knew that my life would never be the same. —SEAN W., DOVER, DELAWARE

We possess the inherent ability to direct and control our experiences. The key is to remain calm and exercise our control. The following is an example.

This OBE started with the paralysis and a rushing out of my body. I found myself on at the time what I figured was a lower astral plane. I felt heavy, like I was floating in molasses, and my vision was blurry, as if I was looking through olive oil. I had heard that you can use an OBE to connect with your higher self. After willing this, I immediately felt myself rush upward at an incredible speed. When I stopped, I was in the most beautiful place I had ever been. The first thing I noticed was that I had a glowing, translucent, sparkling body. Then I noticed I was floating over this flat expanse that seemed to go on forever in all directions. The colors were bright and pure, almost like fluid light. After drinking in the beauty of the scene—which seemed like an eternity—I came back to my body. It was incredible. —LESLIE D., VIA E-MAIL

Higher-Self Technique

Immediately after complete separation from the physical body, center yourself by firmly declaring "Clarity now!" or "Awareness now!" When you are fully aware within your non-physical body, clearly declare, "Now I experience my higher self!"—your soul or spiritual essence. Make this request a focused demand for immediate action. Be prepared to be propelled inward or upward at tremendous speed. The sensation is one of extreme inner motion, like being drawn into a powerful vacuum. Layers of light and color will flash by your awareness as you move deeper and deeper within the universe that is your self. Some people report the sensation of shooting into space or a void. The key is to let go of all preconceptions and completely surrender to the inner motion. Be aware that this rapid motion can be startling and powerful. Trust yourself, for this perceived motion is intense. After several moments, the motion will cease. Your limitations and fears will melt away as you experience your true essence existing within an incredible dimension of pure light and knowledge far beyond all concepts of form. This experience can be viewed as the expansion or extension of your awareness from the relatively dense astral body to the higher-frequency existence of pure consciousness or soul.

This is a life-changing spiritual adventure that must be experienced to be understood. For many, this is the primary purpose and goal of their out-of-body training and practice.

For about two months I did the techniques as I went to sleep. First I noticed that my dreams started to make sense, and then one night I was awakened by a weird buzzing sound and I realized that I could not move. I stayed calm and immediately began to think about my higher self and the idea of floating up. I felt myself slowly move up. It was all very peaceful for a moment; then I thought about my higher self and all hell broke loose. Suddenly I was sucked upward at an incredible speed and I moved through a blur of colors and stars. I felt like I was stretched across the universe. When the motion finally stopped, I was in a vast pool of pure energy, love, consciousness. I can't begin to describe it, because it was everything and nothing at the same time. It was far beyond words, but it felt like my home. It is, without comparison, the most profound experience of my life. —Lori W., Lansing, Michigan

SPIRITUAL HEALING

For thousand of years, shamans in many different cultures have performed healing practices during sacred ceremonies. Shamans induce altered states of consciousness and out-of-body states of consciousness. During these ceremonies they often strive to make energy adjustments to the subtle nonphysical body of the patient. By doing so they essentially manipulate and adjust or expel the negative or restrictive energies from the energy field or aura of their patient. Healing is achieved when the patient's essential energy flow is returned to its normal state.

Healing oneself and others is one of the significant benefits reported during of out-of-body exploration. The unseen causes of physical illness and disease are the energy blocks or disturbances that occur within the nonphysical body. This is only natural, since the subtle body is the direct substructure to our physical body. When we adjust and balance this subtle energy substructure, physical healing can rapidly occur. Many believe that this unseen energy process is the true source of all reported "miracles." With focus, training, and control, out-of-body exploration gives us the ability to consciously interact with and readjust the underlining energy cause of any physical disease.

During my OBE I felt myself begin to shrink, and I was in a place that was completely foreign to me. Everything was dark. I heard many sounds that were unrecognizable. All of a sudden for some unknown reason I realized where I was . . . I was actually in my father's body. My purpose there was to scan his body to see where all of his "trouble spots" were and to try to heal them. I could see that his blood was a very dark red, almost black looking. I tried as best as I could to heal that. I noticed that my form now took the form of white light energy. I sent light all throughout his body and I knew that was my purpose for being there. After I was done scanning his body, I began to feel a very strong vibrational feeling, stronger than I had ever felt before. —CARL M., PHOENIX, ARIZONA

Spiritual Healing Technique

The following healing technique focuses directly upon the underlying energy cause of a physical illness. By using this technique it is possible to influence and balance the unseen energies flowing within yourself or another person.

1. Begin by doing your favorite out-of-body technique. Immediately after separation, request complete clarity of awareness by saying, "Clarity now!" Repeat the clarity request until your consciousness is crystal clear.

2. When your full awareness is centered within your nonphysical body, begin to mentally or verbally request the healing light and energy of God—the universe—to enter you. Ask for and clearly feel the positive healing energies of the universe flowing within you. Request that the healing light permeate every level of your mind. Allow yourself to be completely immersed within the intense healing light.

3. Verbally request that the healing energy be directed to a specific person or to a specific part of your own physical body: "I request the healing energy of the universe to assist and heal [name of person]. The healing power of the universe flows throughout my mind and body."

4. When you direct your thoughts toward your physical body, you will often return to it. After returning to the physical, remain still and feel the healing energy and light flowing through every cell and system in your body.

5. Take your time, and welcome the energy flow throughout your entire body. Allow any vibrational adjustments necessary for you to obtain your optimal health. Be open to receiving a complete energy adjustment and healing of your body and mind.

Do not underestimate the power of this healing technique. Be thankful for your healing experience. You have received a special gift of energy awareness, adjustment, and healing. Use your gift to assist others in recognizing the inner healing energy that flows through all of us.

Transformational experiences are our destiny. We possess the God-given ability to obtain answers, explore our past lives, resolve conflicts, direct healing energies, and—most important—experience our true spiritual essence. However, we must have the courage to let go of our physical limits and embrace the unlimited spiritual potential that dwells within us.

5

The Thought-Responsive Universe

All matter is frozen light.

DAVID BOHM, PHYSICIST

Just for a moment, imagine that you live in a magnificent ethereal world of indescribable beauty—a world consisting of subtle energies, where every thought you create instantly molds and shapes the immediate environment around you. Imagine a perfect world where your thoughts instantly create any reality you choose. Whatever your heart desires is suddenly made manifest before you. It is a glorious land overflowing with living light, a land where death, disease, and limitations are nonexistent. Imagine yourself in an ideal world where everyone is free to explore and develop their creative pursuits and experience their unlimited potential. Does this sound like heaven?

Just think what an immature or undisciplined being could and would do in this ideal thought-responsive world. Picture the chaos and destruction that a single primitive mind could create. One undisciplined mind would wreak complete havoc, destroying the perfection of the subtle environments and the privacy of all the inhabitants.

Now for a moment imagine what kind of educational environment would be the perfect training ground for this undisciplined mind. What kind of school would you create to educate this primitive state of consciousness? What kind of lessons would effectively train this disruptive mind to coexist in the thought-responsive heavenly dimensions?

Welcome to the slowed-down molecular training ground of consciousness. Welcome to the dense training ground of matter, where focused thoughts are required in order to create and prosper. Welcome to the ideal environment where the young and undisciplined mind can learn by trial and error without contaminating the pure realm of spirit. Welcome to your life.

This is one of the primary spiritual lessons we are here to learn. The unaware remain in the dense outer dimensions of the universe until they learn to exercise complete responsibility for their thoughts and actions. They then must learn to escape from the dense gravity field consisting of matter, form, and emotion. Eventually they recognize and break free from the illusions of form and to consciously pursue and experience their spiritual essence. One highly effective method of achieving this goal is self-initiated out-of-body exploration.

THE BENEFITS OF OUT-OF-BODY EXPLORATION

I have received many letters from people who have experienced the life-changing benefits of out-of-body exploration. During self-initiated out-of-body experiences, new insights and miracles are frequently reported. For example, it is common for the blind to see and the disabled to walk or even fly. This occurs because the spiritual body that we experience during an OBE is the subtle energy duplicate of our physical body. This spiritual body is the direct energy substructure of our physical body. It can be viewed as an energy vehicle that is molded by our state of consciousness. Our expectations and beliefs have an immediate impact upon our nonphysical body. This subtle energy form automatically adapts and adjusts to our self-concept and our thoughts both conscious and subconscious.

It is critically important for us to recognize that our thoughts shape and mold our personal reality. Out-of-body exploration has confirmed that our nonphysical body and its surroundings are extremely thought-responsive. Over the years I have experimented with changing my spiritual form and density during numerous out-of-body experiences. On several occasions I directed my nonphysical body to change into a sphere, and in seconds my humanoid form was transformed into a globe of consciousness that could perceive in 360 degrees. During other out-of-body experiences I focused my undivided attention on flying like a bird, and my spiritual body became an eagle soaring high above the ethereal landscapes below. In addition, over the last three decades I've noticed that during my OBEs my nonphysical body is consistently that of a relatively young man no matter how much my biological body continues to age. It became apparent that my subconscious self-conception was automatically shaping my nonphysical form. This creative-energy process explains why departed loved ones encountered during OBEs and near-death experiences are often reported to appear younger, often in the prime of life. It is common during these experiences for a departed elderly person to appear as a twenty- or thirty-year-old. This occurs because our thoughts and personal expectations mold our subtle nonphysical body according to the image we hold of ourselves.

During an out-of-body adventure, the abilities and limitations we experience are created by our mind. Our focused thoughts will manifest any energy shape and form that we concentrate upon. This realization opens the door to incredible opportunities for accelerated personal growth.

Unfortunately, some people are unaware of this energy process and continue to manifest their limitations even when out-of-body. The solution is to jettison all personal limitations and demand immediate positive results. One technique is to repeat a powerful affirmation during your out-of-body experience: "Now I can see!" or "Now I can walk!" Focus your thoughts, and expect immediate results. If necessary, shout your affirmation aloud. As I have said many times in workshops, a wimpy request creates a wimpy result. We must demand and expect immediate action; nothing less will do. Our focused intention is extremely powerful. Keep in mind that our spiritual essence possesses no physical attributes such as arms, legs, eyes, or ears. Our thoughts and expectations create the subtle energy forms and capabilities that we experience.

Because of this, we can manifest any outer form or ability that we focus upon. The following lists of energy principles and energy mechanics are presented to assist you on your journey.

BASIC ENERGY PRINCIPLES

Everything is a form of energy.

Focused thought possesses the innate ability to influence, restructure, and ultimately mold energy.

The less dense the energy structure or environment, the faster the pace at which the restructuring may occur.

The effectiveness and speed by which thought energy restructures an energy environment is determined by the intensity of the thought and the density of the energy it is acting upon.

BASIC ENERGY MECHANICS

The nonphysical universe is progressively less dense in substance and increasingly thought-responsive as we explore inwardly toward the spiritual source of energy.

Our thoughts are a form of creative energy and have a natural tendency to interact and affect the nonphysical environments encountered. The farther within the multidimensional universe we explore, the more rapid and pronounced this thought reaction is upon the energy environment.

Our thoughts, both conscious and subconscious, will influence the nonphysical energy that we observe. The degree of influence we experience is in direct proportion to the intensity of our thoughts and the density of our surroundings.

The reality perceived in a thought-responsive environment is determined by the personal energy frequency—density—of the observer and their prevailing thoughts.

These energy principles are extremely important to all of us, because we absolutely possess the natural ability to shape and mold our individual reality. However, we must first recognize and embrace our creative abilities in order to manifest our desired reality. This process of energy restructuring occurs much faster when we are out of body because the experienced energy environment is extremely thought-responsive. The now popular use of creative visualization is based on these energy principles. When we hold an image in our mind, we are actually creating an energy mold within the unseen dimensions of the universe.

All matter, form, and substance are first born in the unseen dimensions of the universe. The creative power of pure consciousness acts upon the thought-responsive subtle energies that constitute the dimension of the subconscious mind. Here is where the first elements of form are created. At first it may be just the mental archetype of form, but as we maintain focus, a specific energy shape and form solidifies. With continued focus this subtle energy mold eventually manifests itself as form in the physical world.

From now on, put aside your doubts and simply demand to experience your ideal body of consciousness, and it will be so. Repeat the following energy technique until you receive the desired result. Don't underestimate your personal creative abilities; a focused mind-set is an extremely powerful tool. An awakened mind has no limitations, so enjoy your new capabilities and freedom.

Manifesting the Ideal Body of Consciousness

1. After separation, move away from your body and center yourself by requesting "Awareness now!" or "Clarity Now!"

2. Focus your complete awareness on your desired improvement or capability: "Now I can see!"; "Now I can walk!"; "Now I can hear!"; "Now I can fly!" There are no limits. Keep your demand short and powerful, and always in the present tense because our subconscious mind does not operate in linear time.

3. Absolutely expect to experience the desired result immediately. Completely know it, feel it, and expect it.

4. Be completely open to immediately experiencing and receiving your request. Have no doubts, fears, or indecision.

Repeat this process until you experience the desired result. Accept no compromises. The ideal mind-set is to expect your request for change to manifest itself instantly and at the same time be completely open to receiving your request.

This simple and direct demand for action will effectively mold your spiritual body into your ideal self-concept. It is important to understand that the reverse is also true. If you harbor self-doubt or fears, you can restrict or even hinder this natural energy process. In other words, when you psychologically accept a limitation or disability of any kind in your life, you will then create and shape the reality of it. Your thoughts and expectations have breathed life into an energy mold that must take form.

The creative power of this energy-molding process is demonstrated in many ways. Here are some examples:

I have been blind since I was nine years old. My mother bought me your book and would read it to me every night before bed. I was especially intrigued with the part about crippled people being able to walk during their out-of-body experience. She read that part to me many times, and I decided that if it would work with walking, why not with seeing? Every night as I went to sleep I would walk around the house and feel my way through several rooms. After a while I became very good at it. During the second week I started to get a buzzing sound in my head, and I got excited and woke up. It was in the fourth week that it happened. I fell asleep and felt paralyzed and heard weird sounds; then it felt like I was being lifted up and out of my body. I rolled sideways and seemed to fall to the floor and crawled around for a moment. To my surprise I couldn't see at all and began to actually get mad. Then I remembered about control and demanding results, so I spontaneously shouted out, "I can see now!" Slowly I began to make out shadowy forms around me. I shouted again, "I see now!" Everything around me became a little brighter, and I was thrilled. I stood up and actually looked around. I could see, even though I knew it had to be dark! I was so excited I wanted to fly, and suddenly I shot up through the ceiling like a rocket. Everything was happening so fast it scared me, and I felt like I was jerked back to my body with a jolt. —TOM T., DALLAS, TEXAS

Dr. Kenneth Ring, the well-known researcher and author of *Life at Death,* has studied the results of near-death and out-of-body experiences for over two decades. In a recent book, *Mindsight,* he concludes that the blind can see after leaving their body. He sums up his research in the following statement:

> In summary, as a whole, our interviews with both NDErs and OBErs offer abundant testimony that reports of visual perception among the blind are common, that their impressions concern both things of this world and other worldly domains, and that they are often clear and detailed, even in narratives furnished by those who have been blind from birth.[1]

The same creative-energy principles apply to any limitation, whether it is physical or psychological. A woman who has not walked in ten years reports the following experience.

I have been paralyzed from the waist down and dependent upon a wheelchair for over ten years. It sounded too good to be true, but I did the techniques you recommended. For the first month nothing much happened. During the second month I started to get the vibrations and buzzing you spoke of. In the third month I woke to a loud sound and vibration. I stayed calm and focused on going to the door, as you said. I slowly floated up and then seemed to float to the door. I was so excited, it was incredible; and I thought about standing, and suddenly I was standing at the door. Yes, standing! Then I thought about walking, and I began to walk from my room and down the hallway. It was incredible. —JUDY C., CHICAGO, ILLINOIS

It is not unusual for spiritual guides or loved ones to offer their assistance by reminding us of our personal creative abilities. The following is a self-initiated out-of-body experience reported by a woman who is deaf.

I successfully went out of body and noticed that outside it was light when it was supposed to be dark, and that people could see me. All of a sudden I became lucid while I was sleeping. I couldn't move, and my mind was quiet. So I said in my mind, "Vibration!" and suddenly I got the vibration—so powerful that it almost woke me up. I tried to remain calm and remain asleep. "Okay, let's go out of body!" I said in my mind. It was successful. I got out and I opened my eyes. I looked at my body. I was in a state of awe. I turned around and flew through the window. It was night, and the stars were shining beautifully. Suddenly I heard a voice—I am deaf, and I cannot hear anything—for the first time: "Did you know that you don't have to fly, you just have to think and then you will immediately be there?" When I heard the voice, I panicked, which caused me to return to my body. Darn! And I woke up and looked at the time. Only one minute had passed.
—SANDY P., TUCSON, ARIZONA

SELF-EMPOWERMENT

Keep in mind that everything is a form of energy, and be aware that your thoughts and intention will affect any form or structure it is focused upon. The same creative process that applies to our nonphysical body will just as effectively work in our immediate environment. The following experience demonstrates this process in action.

I have about six out-of-body experiences a year. During my last one, which occurred two nights ago, I found myself in a strange rustic cabin that I didn't like. I immediately demanded to move from there and I did. Then I was in a beautiful parklike setting. I moved to a small tree and decided to try one of the experiments you talk about. I concentrated on the tree and thought about it being much bigger, like a giant redwood. In seconds it began to grow and change into the biggest, most beautiful tree I have ever seen. I was in awe and felt a wonderful surge of energy flowing through me. It sounds weird, but I felt somehow empowered. —JOHN F., ROCHESTER, NEW YORK

This creative process impacts all of us in every energy dimension of the universe. When we embrace our creative abilities, we are often amazed at the miracles that occur in our life. This energy process is also the key to manifesting our desires while in the physical world. The only difference between the physical and nonphysical is the time it takes for the formation of the new reality to become manifest. The density of matter simply slows the energy-restructuring process.

One of the great lessons that many of us are now learning is that we mold our personal reality with our thoughts. We are powerful creative sparks of God, and we shape our lives by the way we focus and direct our thoughts. Our awareness of our creative abilities is an important step forward in our evolution. When we fully embrace our personal creative abilities, we become spiritually empowered to create any reality we focus upon; we recognize that we are the architects of our lives and that our every thought and deed are our creative action. Once you are empowered by this knowledge, it matters little what dimension of the universe you are experiencing; you will never again be a victim of your surroundings or circumstances.

1. Kenneth Ring and Sharon Cooper, *Mindsight* (Palo Alto, CA: William James Center for Consciousness Studies at the Institute for Transpersonal Psychology, 1999), 60.

6

Extraterrestrial Contact and Abduction

*It is certainly the case that many abductees report
floating to the alien [craft] . . . In near-death
experiences, people feel themselves floating along or
up a tunnel towards a light. Abductees sometimes
experience being drawn up a light beam towards the
"craft." The imagery and sense of motion are very
similar. There are many facets shared by abduction,
out-of-body, and near-death experiences. It is a
similarity that should not go unnoticed.*

PAUL DEVEREAUX, EARTH LIGHTS REVELATION

While I was conducting the out-of-body experience survey
described in the introduction to this book, I began receiving letters related to alien contact and abduction. After reading
more than two hundred such letters, I noticed a startling similarity: The letters describing extraterrestrial contacts and abductions were almost identical to the thousands of letters I have
received describing OBEs. In fact, I often could not distinguish
between letters. If you replace the words *alien abduction* with the
words *out-of-body experience,* the two types of letter become
very nearly identical. The same kind of phenomena and descriptions—such as paralysis, electrical sensations, strong vibrations,
and strange, unearthly sounds and contact—are reported.

The following is presented as an overview of the similarities
and differences that exist. I do not profess to be an expert in

alien contact or abduction; I am simply sharing the information that I feel is important to all of us. I am often asked if I personally believe in the existence of extraterrestrials, and my response is in the affirmative. However, evidence suggests that a large percentage of alien-contact experiences are actually multidimensional experiences. Out-of-body and near-death experiences have confirmed that life does exist just beyond our physical vision.

I have personally seen and experienced a wide variety of nonphysical intelligent beings. Many of these beings exhibit no solid external shape or form as we understand such things. In fact, it is feasible that truly advanced beings may have evolved beyond the need for dense biological form. (It appears that the current human dependence on and obsession with form and shape is one of the primary earmarks of a more primitive species.) In addition, some nonphysical beings are reported to possess the ability to manipulate and manifest form, substance, and matter when required. This may sound strange at first, but keep in mind that science has confirmed that the human mind can alter the motion of primary particles of energy and matter. Just imagine what a highly evolved and focused mind could accomplish.

Out-of-body explorers have consistently reported the universe to be a multidimensional continuum of subtle nonphysical energies inhabited by immeasurable variations of conscious and intelligent life. It appears likely that the more-evolved beings that inhabit the universe travel, explore, and interact on a multidimensional basis. Many believe that a truly advanced civilization would have little need for a primitive material starship to initiate contact. The exploration of the universe both physical and nonphysical could be achieved by the direct use of focused consciousness and inner-dimensional motion. Three-dimensional form could be manifested as needed for the denser contact situations but would be unnecessary for physical observation or exploration.

MULTIDIMENSIONAL TRAVEL

Multidimensional travel by nonphysical explorers provides a logical explanation for the many biblical references to beings such as angels that are reported to appear from thin air, interact and communicate with the primitive local inhabitants, and then abruptly disappear when their mission is completed. This also explains the ethereal glow that is so commonly associated with these spiritual visitors. For centuries the astral body was commonly called "the body of light," and is well known for its inherent radiance. Today many people perceive this spiritual body to be a stable energy matrix of light that consciousness uses for expression within the unseen dimensions of the universe. It is possible that the modern reports of alien contact and the numerous sightings of angels and deities throughout history may very well be instances of the same phenomenon interpreted from different cultural viewpoints.

The real frontier for humanity is the exploration of consciousness and the nonphysical dimensions that exist just beyond our vision. As we evolve, we will move beyond our current obsession with matter and join the multidimensional community of consciousness. Until we do, we will continue as primitive outsiders who stare into the sky and wonder about our place in the universe.

SIMILARITIES BETWEEN
ALIEN ABDUCTION AND OBES

The following information is based on the results of my survey and on feedback I have received from around the world. As *Adventures Beyond the Body* was published in six languages, the survey reached an international audience.

The primary reference used for the comparison that follows is Dr. John E. Mack's book *Abduction*.[1] I chose Mack's work because his documentation is excellent and I respect his dedication to detail. Mack is a professor of psychiatry at the Cambridge Hospital, Harvard Medical School, and won a

Pulitzer Prize in 1977. He is also the founder of the Center for Psychology and Social Change, a research organization.

The observations presented here are the result of information received from my OBE survey, personal interviews, and workshops. Even though the survey was not designed to be a valid scientific study, I strongly feel that the sheer number of participants makes the survey results an important database of information and insight. The real jewels of the survey, though, are to be found in the thousands of personal stories I received. This information broadens our understanding of the elusive topics of alien abduction, contact, and out-of-body experiences, because at their very core these topics are primarily rooted in consciousness. Each of the following topics is described by Mack as a phenomenon associated with alien abduction. The comments and experiences that follow each discussion are taken from various out-of-body descriptions. The similarities speak for themselves.

Odd Humming Sound

An overwhelming 85 percent of respondents to the out-of-body survey reported sounds such as buzzing, humming, or roaring as an immediate prelude to their experience. Many described the sounds as electrical, unearthly, and extremely powerful. The sounds were often combined with other phenomena, including high-energy sensations and temporary paralysis. Such sounds make up one of the most universally reported preludes to an out-of-body experience. They can be very strange and even frightening. I have heard many descriptions of loud enginelike sounds, thumping, and voices. I reported in my previous book that the sound I often hear immediately before an out-of-body experience is similar to a "roaring jet engine in my head." It should be noted that the reported sounds immediately dissipate after separation from the body is completed. Alien abductees also report hearing strange noises, especially during the early stages of these experiences.

*One experience I remember clearly was awakening to a pow-
erful buzzing sound, and I both audibly and physically felt as
if I were being paralyzed by electricity. I had the distinct sensation there was someone at the foot of the bed I was in, but I
panicked and it soon ended.* —FRED D., CLEVELAND, OHIO

Strong Vibratory or Energy Sensation in the Body

The OBE survey results indicate that 56 percent of the participants report experiencing vibrations or high-energy sensations.
This generally occurs at the initial phase of the out-of-body
experience commonly referred to as the vibrational state. The
vibrations are often combined with other phenomena such as
strange sounds and paralysis.

*For the past year or two, I wake up in the middle of the night
feeling like I've merged with an electrical transformer. I hon-
estly thought the energy was invoked by extraterrestrials . . . I
couldn't talk about this to anyone. Doctors don't know what
to make of it. It wasn't until I read your book [Adventures
Beyond the Body] that things began to make sense. On page
157 you describe signals associated with the initial experience
of out-of-body travel . . . I have experienced every one of those
signals as recently as last week.* —BILL V., PENSACOLA, FLORIDA

Temporary Paralysis

Paralysis is reported by 72 percent of the OBE survey participants and is commonly described during abductions. This
is often portrayed as the most frightening aspect of both experiences. Paralysis is generally experienced with unusual sounds
such as electrical humming or buzzing and high-energy sensations.

*I heard noises that sounded like a high level of energy was
above me. It gave me the impression that a UFO was overhead. I was paralyzed, unable to move or make any sounds.*

The experience lasted about two minutes, and each time I could feel a magnetic force going through my body. —LISA K., NASHVILLE, TENNESSEE

Shift in Consciousness

One of the essential elements of an out-of-body experience is a dramatic shift of consciousness from the physical body to the nonphysical. This shift of consciousness is essential in order to have an out-of-body experience.

I found myself floating above my body and looking down upon the room below. I felt free. —KIM N., LONDON, ENGLAND

Appearance of an Unexplained Light

During a nighttime out-of-body experience, the surrounding environment is often reported to be significantly brighter than the physical environment itself. It is common to hear phrases such as "The room was illuminated by a silvery glow" and "I experienced bright moonlit surroundings even though it was pitch black in my bedroom." An OBE survey by researchers Stuart Twemlow, Glen Gabbard, and Fowler Jones found that 30 percent of their OBE participants reported a brilliant white light, and of this group 46 percent found the light to be strongly attractive while 33 percent felt it was a being.[2] In addition, it should be noted that the astral body is known to naturally radiate light. The term *astral* comes from a Greek word meaning "related to a star" and originally described the abodes of the Greek gods.

During my out-of-body experience everything around me was illuminated by a strange glow, like a silvery full moon. When I returned to my body it was 2 A.M. and the bedroom was dark. —KELLY M., LISBON, PORTUGAL

Sense of Presence of a Being or Beings

Twenty-two percent of the respondents to my survey report that they have seen or felt the presence of an unknown non-physical being, and 24 percent report that they have seen, heard, or spoken to a deceased loved one. Many people believe that there is a nonphysical being close to us during every out-of-body experience. Some refer to this presence as a spiritual guide, watcher, or helper, or as an astral being. How we interpret this presence is of course based on our individual beliefs and perceptions of reality. I have heard descriptions that span the limits of imagination: angels, devils, aliens of all sorts—even animals. The most commonly reported sightings are humanoid forms that appear to be watching as the out-of-body experience unfolds. We frame our nonphysical adventures and contact based on our individual mind-set.

It is important to understand that we do not possess eyes when out of body; we perceive our surroundings with our minds. And it is our minds that create a comfortable facsimile similar to our normal physical vision. This is why vision is often described as 360-degree vision by experienced explorers. They have simply expanded their individual concept of visual perception beyond the human physical norm. This is important, because it describes how we perceive and interpret our nonphysical surroundings. Vision and perception are not static three-dimensional observations but interactive communications in which our mind determines the meaning of the energy forms or consciousness that we encounter. In effect, our mind not only interprets the perceived reality but also influences and molds it. For example, if you believe that spiritual guides will appear as monklike beings wearing long robes, you will likely perceive your nonphysical contacts in that light. If you believe in alien grays with large eyes and heads, you are predisposed to "see" such an image. This knowledge does not nullify the reality of the experience; it simply increases our understanding of it.

Expanding this thought a little further, I would like to point out that we eventually must take responsibility for our thoughts and experiences, for we are the cocreators of our perceptions and our experiences in every dimension of the universe.

I awakened to the shock of a strange being touching me. I was so scared and paralyzed and tried to scream, and then the thing disappeared. —KRIS C., TROY, MICHIGAN

Telepathic Communications

The universal form of nonphysical communication is telepathy. This is experienced as a flow of pictures entering your mind. Projected mental imagery is a far more precise method of communication than primitive word symbols; it is like a movie that also includes thoughts and emotions.

I don't know for sure if this was an out-of-body experience. I was asleep for the night, and I woke up to find two beings at the foot of the bed. I don't think they were human, more like creatures or aliens. One was tall and thin; the other was shorter and rounder. But they had similar heads and faces. The taller one said, "Let's go," and waved for me to follow him. I was not afraid, but I didn't want to go, so I tried to shake my head no. I got the feeling they were reading my mind more than anything, because I couldn't feel my head shake. But they seemed to get the message and left. My husband was sleeping beside me. He didn't see or hear anything and says I must have been dreaming. It just didn't feel like a dream to me. —ARLENE G., BRISBANE, AUSTRALIA

Moving Through Physical Objects

Moving through walls, doors, or windows is a common element of many out-of-body experiences. In fact, this is one of the first things I recommend that explorers accomplish after they gain full conscious control. When out of body, we are experiencing an extremely subtle energy body that can easily pass through any dense physical barrier or object.

I heard a loud electrical sound and floated up . . . I moved and floated right through the wall. —EILEEN B., LAS VEGAS, NEVADA

Abductees often report that they have been transported into another reality. They describe this as a waking reality, but one different from the normal physical world. Those who experience OBEs often report the same thing. In fact, the statement above is a good general description of an out-of-body experience.

Missing and Distorted Time

The phenomenon of missing or distorted time is commonly reported during both OBEs and abductions. This is to be expected, because linear time does not exist as we understand it when we leave our physical body. Evidence suggests that out-of-body and most abduction experiences are actually multi-dimensional experiences that occur beyond the external reference points of time.

I was traveling out of my body for some time and was surprised when I returned and looked at the clock and only a few minutes had passed. —TOBY V., TRENTON, NEW JERSEY

Sense That One Is Not Dreaming or Imagining Things

Out-of-body experiencers frequently make the same statement. They often describe their OBE as a stark reality. According to the OBE survey conducted by Twemlow, Gabbard, and Jones, 94 percent of respondents stated that their OBE was "more real than a dream."[3]

Nobody could ever convince me that my out-of-body experience was a dream. It was as real as anything I've ever done. —ROBERT F., BIRMINGHAM, ALABAMA

Seeing Home and the Earth Itself Recede

It's not unusual to hear reports of out-of-body explorers flying high above their city or town. For many, one of the most memorable joys of OBEs is the ability to fly free from the dense limitations of matter. Even though reports of spacecraft are rare, the perception of flight before and during an OBE is universal. Eighty-one percent of the respondents to my survey reported flying in a dream as an immediate prelude to their out-of-body experience. Many believe that flying in a dream is actually our mind's interpretation of an out-of-body experience.

I felt the vibrations and surrendered to them. The next instant I shot up through the ceiling like a rocket. A sense of incredible speed filled me, and I was floating in space or some kind of void. —VICKIE W., TACOMA, WASHINGTON

Based on my experience and research, I believe that the majority of alien-abduction experiences involve multidimensional contact with nonphysical life forms.

In *Abduction*, Mack makes an interesting statement in reference to the connection between abduction and OBEs: "The individual may have an out-of-body experience while others see that he or she has not left the house."[4]

OTHER PHENOMENA

There are specific elements of some abduction experiences that are not normally reported during an OBE. One example is the report of various intrusive medical procedures administered under the control of an extraterrestrial. Even though medical procedures are rarely reported during OBEs, it is interesting that 33 percent do speak of being touched and even moved by nonphysical beings. In addition, 46 percent report seeing, feeling, and even speaking to some sort of being near them.

There are also stories of abductees who are taken by some degree of force. Often this is perceived to be a beam of light or some other form of energy used by the alien beings. Paralysis, floating, and strange humming or buzzing noises frequently accompany the experience. I would like to point out that the majority of OBEs also include these kind of phenomena. In addition, a large percentage of the survey respondents considered their OBE to be a startling or even frightening event, with 46 percent reporting a panic attack during their OBE. Often this was an initial fear response to the paralysis and strange sounds that are common elements of the vibrational state. Both out-of-body experiences and abductions are spontaneous events that completely shock the participant. I have had many people tell me that, were they not aware of the vibrational phenomena associated with OBEs, they would swear that some external force was creating their experiences.

It felt like a powerful beam or surge of raw energy spread through my body, and I was completely paralyzed. I was absolutely terrified and just wanted it to end. I tried to scream but couldn't. —JUDY Y., BOSTON, MASSACHUSETTS

Various vibrational-state phenomena are clearly evident in the following experience.

It began as a dream. In the dream, I was in the backseat of a car and we were driving along the highway chasing a UFO that was high and to the right of us. Suddenly I awoke and couldn't move. I heard the buzzing you talk about, but it was more of an ear-piercing type of high-pitched scream. It was very mechanical sounding, and the first thing I thought was that I was being abducted by aliens. I freaked out. I tried to scream but couldn't. I tried to thrash about in bed but couldn't, and after a minute or so of fighting, it was over. I was always spooked by it and never told anyone about it. —ANDY W., ARLINGTON, VIRGINIA

CONTACT WITH NONPHYSICAL BEINGS

I was sleeping on my back in a small camp trailer and gradually awakened to a low humming sound. When I was able to open my eyes, there was a spherical "object" floating about two feet over my chest. The "object" seemed to be hundreds or thousands of tiny points of pale blue light of about the same color as an electric arc. They were not bright, though— just the same color. The points of light seemed to be randomly moving about in a well-defined spherical space about the size of a basketball. There did not appear to be any "skin" to the object, but the points of light seemed contained within a very well defined boundary. I realized, when I tried to slide or creep from underneath this object, that all my voluntary muscular activity was paralyzed except for being able to open and close my eyelids and move my eyes. After a couple of minutes the object lifted up and suddenly shot out through the trailer's small side window. I inspected the window after finding I was once again able to move. The object went unimpeded through the screen and window frame, which was smaller than the object, leaving no trace. —BLAIR S., OKLAHOMA CITY, OKLAHOMA*

Was this experience an alien contact, or a visitation from a nonphysical being? Your answer depends upon your personal beliefs and viewpoint. It should be pointed out that nonphysical beings are often described as various shapes and forms of light. These ethereal beings are commonly described as consisting of thousands of tiny points of light and exhibiting a stable outer form. During my out-of-body experiences I have observed that my nonphysical body will often appear to consist of a mass of tiny blue stars with a stable outer shape and form. I detailed this observation in the first chapter of my previous book. In fact, self-examination is one of the things I feel is important for all of us to do, especially during our first few fully conscious out-of-body experiences. I believe that this personal examination helps to validate our experience on a conscious and subconscious level. This personal verification process opens us psychologically to more and better-controlled out-of-body experiences.

I found several books with steps and exercises for having an OBE. After attempting it several times, I woke up at night and I couldn't move or talk. All I could do was look around my room. I saw a shadowed figure at the end of my bed. As soon as it realized I could see it, it drifted off to the left and vanished. For a moment I was scared to death and thought I was going to be abducted by aliens or something. Then I came to realize what was going on, and all my fears dwindled.
—TED M., DAYTON, OHIO

The following experience is an interesting combination of imagery that combines a classic abduction description with a common OBE theme.

I woke up on something like an operating table. I was surrounded by a circle of intense white light. I recall being loosely tethered to something—including a pulling feeling in my abdominal area. Looking to the left, I saw someone seated with their back to me. I reached out and put my hand on their shoulder, and they turned around. It was my mother.
—LOUISE I., VIRGINIA BEACH, VIRGINIA

PURPOSE OF THE INCREASING CONTACT PHENOMENA

I believe that the true significance of alien sightings, contact, and abduction rests in the impact these phenomena have upon the individual and group consciousness of our species. These interactions in any of their forms have an immediate impact on the experiencer, whose state of consciousness is often dramatically altered by the encounter. Experiencers inevitably view their world and themselves with a new and broader perspective. Often a new mind-set emerges that questions the status quo and is driven to acquire additional knowledge and answers. On many unseen levels contact experiences may initiate important shifts of consciousness and perception that impact the individual in ways we do not currently understand. These encounters thrust the experiencer into a dramatically new way of thinking in much the same way that encounters with angels have influenced humanity for centuries.

I have witnessed evidence of this shift of consciousness during my speaking engagements at various UFO conventions around the country. In their search for UFO and alien abduction information, those who are interested in such phenomena are often introduced to the subjects of out-of-body experiences, multiple dimensions, past-life exploration, and the spiritual nature of reality.

Of one thing I am certain: The underlying purpose of the worldwide increase in reported alien phenomena is to be found in consciousness itself. All observed phenomena are the direct result and manifestation of consciousness. As a species, we are being methodically prepared for and guided toward a significant shift in our group consciousness.

As we evolve, the time for subtlety is rapidly drawing to an end. As the evolution of consciousness accelerates, so will reports of extraterrestrial sightings and contact experiences. The universe is a continuum of consciousness that uses every available opportunity to awaken the masses of people still wandering within the physical labyrinth. If the outer image of an angel or an alien is effective in awaking our potential, such images will continue to appear.

Out-of-body exploration provides substantial evidence that we are evolving beyond the dense limits of matter. Is it not possible that some other species may have already achieved this evolutionary leap? I contend that all life-forms are slowly evolving beyond the need for biological form. Eventually we will recognize and consciously explore our multidimensional nature and take our place in the magnificent thought-responsive realities of the universe.

If you are seriously interested in experiencing and comprehending the phenomena of extraterrestrial contact, I strongly suggest that you become skilled at out-of-body exploration.

Learn and practice the principles and techniques of nonphysical exploration. The key to effective contact will always be found in the exploration of consciousness, for this is the true home of the evolved.

1. John E. Mack, *Abduction* (New York: Ballantine Books, 1995).
2. Stuart W. Twemlow, Glen O. Gabbard, and Fowler C. Jones, "The Out-of-Body Experience Phenomenology" (paper presented at the annual meeting of the American Psychiatric Association, San Francisco, 5–9 May 1980).
3. Ibid.
4. Mack, *Abduction*, 392.

PART 2

THE
TECHNIQUES

7

A Brief History of
Out-of-Body Experiences

You must be born again to
enter the kingdom of heaven.

JOHN 3:3

The very beginning, the intrinsic core, the essence,
the universal nucleus of every known high religion . . .
has been the private, lonely, personal illumination,
revelation, or ecstasy of some acutely sensitive
prophet or seer.

ABRAHAM MASLOW, *RELIGIONS, VALUES, AND PEAK EXPERIENCES*

Throughout history, adventurous individuals who have had out-of-body experiences have molded our religious and spiritual beliefs. The early prophets of every religion recorded and interpreted their spiritual experiences according to the cultural and religious viewpoints of their day. Thus for thousands of years out-of-body experiences have been revered as holy and transcendental, and often viewed as a profound communion with God. In every corner of the world sacred texts describe incredible spiritual journeys to dimensions that exist beyond our vision. Out-of-body experiences are described in many of mankind's oldest written documents, including the twenty-five-hundred-year-old Egyptian Book of the Dead. In this ancient text the Egyptians detail the separation of the subtle body, which they referred to as the "Ba," from the denser body, called the "Ka" (fig. 2). In Egypt, some of mankind's most ancient pictographs clearly display the separation of the soul from the body.

EARLY CULTURES

The separation of consciousness from the body was of great importance to many early cultures. The earliest civilizations of Greece, Rome, India, and China all speak of individuals who traveled into the heavenly dimensions. On his deathbed the renowned philosopher Socrates was reported to have said, "And what is the purification but the separation of the soul from the body?" During the third century B.C. Plato wrote about adventures into the unseen dimensions in book 10 of the *Republic*. He gives a detailed account of a Greek soldier named Er, who moments before he is about to be cremated awakens

Fig. 2. The Egyptian Ka

and describes how he left his body and entered the "land of the dead."

In the fifth century B.C. the great Persian mystic Zoroaster was known for his explorations of the unseen areas of the universe. He was the founder of Zoroastrianism, the ancient Persian religion of the magi. This religion evolved into the current Parsi faith. Zoroastrianism was founded and is based on Zoroaster's many out-of-body journeys into what he called the "spiritual worlds." He is credited with the reform of the old pantheistic religious systems and the downfall of idolatry.

TIBETAN BUDDHIST EXPLORATION

The culture and religion of Tibet offer multiple references to adventures beyond the body. In Tibetan literature, it is reported that the mother of Buddha experienced an out-of-body state prior to his birth. There are also reports of Buddha and his disciples transcending time and space during their journeys beyond matter. In areas of Tibet, it is common for people who leave their bodies to be called *delogs*, meaning "those who return from the beyond." In 1972 the *International Journal of Parapsychology* published an article by D. Scott Rogo, titled "Astral Projection in Tibetan Buddhist Literature," that presents fascinating accounts of Tibetan out-of-body explorations.[1]

BIBLE AND KORAN

The Bible and the Koran are overflowing with vivid references to out-of-body travel. For example, in Ezekiel 3:12, it is stated: "Then the spirit lifted me up and I heard behind me the noise of the Lord rumbling as the glory of the Lord rose from its place." Ezekiel goes on to describe dozens of out-of-body experiences throughout his writings.

The New Testament is filled with references to out-of-body travel. In 2 Corinthians 12:2, Paul speaks of experiences in the nonphysical regions of the universe: "I knew a man in Christ who, fourteen years ago, (whether in the body, I cannot tell; or whether out of the body, I cannot tell: God knoweth) was caught up to the third heaven." Paul's use of the phrase "third heaven" displays his personal knowledge of the multiple spiritual dimensions and out-of-body exploration. In Revelation 1:10, John describes one of his out-of-body experiences when he says, "I was caught up in the spirit on the Lord's Day and heard behind me a voice as loud as of a trumpet." He then goes on to detail his incredible adventure in the thought-responsive areas of the inner dimensions.

It should be noted that such early biblical phrases as "noise of the Lord rumbling" and "voice as loud as of a trumpet" reported by Ezekiel, John, Paul, and many other prophets could easily be descriptions of the vibrational sounds commonly described today during separation from the body. This coincides with the descriptions of modern out-of-body experiences. The results of my OBE survey indicate that 85 percent of the sixteen thousand participants reported sounds such as buzzing, roaring, or humming as an immediate prelude to their experience. Often these sounds are described as extremely loud and emanating from the head. Another national survey by Twemlow, Gabbard, and Fowler indicated that the reported sounds are distributed as follows: buzzing (the most common), 29 percent; roaring, 19 percent; and music or singing, 16 percent.[2] The multiple survey results provide additional evidence that many of the early spiritual leaders were indeed experiencing out-of-body journeys.

One of the most famous quotations from the New Testament is Jesus' statement in John 3:3: "You must be born again to enter the kingdom of heaven." For hundreds of years there has been an ongoing dialogue regarding the meaning of this powerful statement. Religious sects and scholars have interpreted these words to mean a total mental and emotional commitment to Jesus. Unfortunately, they are interpreting a mystical observation using an intellectual mind-set. What is often overlooked is that Jesus, Muhammad, and others were spiritual explorers and mystics of the highest order. They were spiritual explorers who refused to blindly follow the established religious beliefs. Each of these great spiritual leaders was not just a believer in God, but experienced God. It is very likely that traveling out of body was a common practice for each of them.

EARLY SPIRITUAL EXPLORERS

Five centuries after the birth of Jesus, Muhammad, the founder of Islam, described himself as riding a magnificent stallion through what he called "the seven heavens." Each dimension that Muhammad encountered is described in detail. He speaks of seven incredible dimensions, each radiating different brilliant colors. He describes wondrous areas made of pure flowing light as well as hell-like, frightening environments. An examination of these accounts makes it clear that the personal beliefs and perceptions of reality of these early spiritual explorers influenced what they perceived when out of body. In other words, it may be that our modern religious beliefs were influenced by the way the early prophets interpreted the nonphysical environments they experienced.

Today Muhammad would likely see himself riding in a magnificent white vehicle instead of a horselike animal throughout the spiritual dimensions of the universe. Instead of John saying in Revelation, "I was in the spirit," he would likely say, "I was out of body." This knowledge does not diminish the inspired writings of our early spiritual explorers; it only provides additional insight into the unseen meaning of these explorations. Many of the early spiritual leaders who influenced and molded our major religions were out-of-body explorers. They documented their nonphysical journeys in accordance with the cultural and religious perceptions of their day. There are many parallels between the lives of Ezekial, John, Zoroaster, and Muhammad. All of these men describe similar out-of-body explorations into unseen dimensions of the universe.

PERSIAN SUFIS

The twelfth-century Persian Sufis were well known for inducing deep trance states and exploring "the land where spirits dwell." In their writings they speak of the *"alan almithal,"* dimensions created by thought. Numerous spiritual teachers or guides, called the *imam,* inhabit these invisible realms. What is especially interesting is that in the Sufi teachings the nonphysical environments and cities are described as very real and are created by the group consciousness or imagination of the inhabitants. In addition, the residents of these unseen lands possess subtle energy or thought bodies. The magnificent realities that the Sufis so eloquently describe coincide with descriptions provided by modern out-of-body explorers.

One of the great Sufi poets, Hafiz, began to have profound out-of-body experiences at an early age. At the age of nine he had his first such experience: "I refused to tell the family that the spirit [consciousness] left my body and visited God to receive instructions in this life." In his writing he details numerous spiritual journeys: "God rewarded my devotion hundreds of times. Many times I was in deep meditation, my body in my room, my soul in the great heavens with God." The writings of Hafiz and Rumi, another Sufi poet, as well as those of Zoroaster and Muhammad contain powerful examples of the benefits received from out-of-body exploration.

SWEDENBORG

The Swedish scientist and mystic Emanuel Swedenborg was born in 1688. He became well known throughout Europe as the Leonardo da Vinci of his time. He spoke nine languages and was an inventor, mathematician, and astronomer. Swedenborg wrote some twenty texts on various topics including chemistry, metallurgy, and physics. Later in his life he became famous for his ability to leave his body and visit the heavenly realms. During his countless out-of-body journeys he documented encounters with the "spirit world" and detailed communication with angels and various nonphysical beings. He vividly describes his explorations of multiple levels of heaven and how he would move between the energy levels by way of steps. His writings describe beautiful environments in which time and space were no longer relevant. Swedenborg illustrated different nonphysical environments and magnificent areas that he called realms of "streaming light."

> It has pleased the Lord to . . . open the interiors of my mind or spirit, whereby I have been permitted to be in the spiritual world with angels, and at the same time in the natural world with people, and this now [has happened for] twenty-seven years.[3]

YOGI MASTERS

In more modern times, many of the Yogi masters speak of transcending the flesh and exploring unseen spiritual dimensions. One of the most influential Yogis was Sri Yukteswar, a well-respected Hindu holy man who died in 1936. Yukteswar would speak eloquently of visiting invisible dimensions composed of "various subtle vibrations of light and color" that are "hundreds of times larger than the physical cosmos." He described in detail how nonphysical inhabitants communicate by a form of telepathy he called "light pictures." Reports from many of today's out-of-body explorers confirm these observations.

Another example is the Yogi Paramahansa Yogananda. He is well known throughout the West as the founder of the Self-Realization Fellowship and author of the best-selling book *Autobiography of a Yogi,* published in 1946. In his writings he describes how he separated from his body and actually met his deceased guru Sri Yukteswar.

VARIOUS CULTURAL DESCRIPTIONS

The anthropologist Erika Bourguignon, conducting a cross-cultural survey in the early 1970s, obtained data from 488 societies around the world. She found that some form of out-of-body state of consciousness or disassociation existed in 89 percent of all the cultures sampled.[4] The fact that this experience is so widespread is reflected in the number of societies that have had a name for the subtle body that separates during an out-of-body experience. The early Romans used the term *larva* to describe the nonphysical existence. The Norwegians called the out-of-body phantom the *fylgje* and the *vardøgr*. The ancient Britons had many names for the astral body, including *fye, task, fetch,* and *waft*. Pre-Germanic tribes used the term *litr* to describe the fine ethereal substance that connected the physical body to the senses. The German term *Doppelgänger,* meaning "double," has been borrowed by English. Doppelgängers were reported to be apparitions of a physical person. In the Highlands of Scotland, apparitions called *tamhasg* were thought to be specters of the living. These entities were believed to be living beings having an existence of their own. These descriptions and concepts, found throughout a myriad of cultural traditions, all seem to point to the idea of an ethereal body that traveled beyond the physical body.

CATHOLIC SAINTS

Numerous Western mystics, including several Roman Catholic saints, have reported the ability to leave their bodies. Saint Teresa of Ávila's autobiography contains detailed descriptions of her out-of-body travels. She reports: "One feels one has been transported into another and different region. The soul is suspended in such a way that it seems to be completely outside itself." Other Catholic saints and monks known for out-of-body experiences and bilocation include Saint Francis Xavier, Father Padra Pio, and Saint Anthony of Assisi.

ABORIGINES AND NATIVE AMERICANS

From the Amazon rain forests to the mountains of Peru, the stories of transcendent journeys beyond the body are well documented. For centuries in Australia, Aborigines claimed that their "clever men" could project beyond their bodies at will. The Arand tribe of central Australia calls the astral double the *ngancha*. Many Native American tribes believe in the projection of the spirit body. During the seventeenth century the Huron, the Seneca, and other Iroquoian peoples described the capacity of the spirit body to journey beyond the physical during dreams and vision quests. An example of this is the tribal leader Black Elk, well known for his ecstatic out-of-body travels.

SHAMANISM

Based on my travels and contact with several South American shamans, there is a clear connection between out-of-body experiences and the ancient practice of shamanism. In a sense shamanism may be the oldest known spiritual practice still existing today. In brief, the shaman's role is to interact with and influence the subtle unseen world. Shamans are often called upon to provide healing and communication with the beyond. The quintessential skill of the shaman is the ability to separate from the dense body and venture into the spirit world. It is here that they interact with and influence the finer vibratory levels of reality in order to make adjustments to the energy field of the person they are working with to help or heal. During sacred ceremonies shaman will self-induce an altered state of consciousness though various methods such as drumming, chanting, and in some cases the imbibing of medicinal or psychotropic plants and herbs. They then separate their consciousness from their physical body and proceed to make energy shifts to the subtle etheric substructure or energy field of their patient. This interaction and the resulting energy adjustment can result in a dramatic physical healing.

According to the anthropologist Michael Harner, the shamans' descriptions of journeys into the afterworld are virtually identical to certain passages in the Book of Revelation.[5] It should be noted that this is also true of the descriptions of modern out-of-body explorers. During several of my journeys I have encountered strange beings such as a giant sloth with the face of a dog and a large winged lion that communicated with me though a stream of vivid "thought pictures." In many ways modern out-of-body experiences parallel reports from the early spiritual explorers, the Book of Revelation, the Koran, and other revered texts.

MODERN SPIRITUALITY

Today there are many modern spiritual movements that acknowledge the importance of out-of-body experiences. Eckankar, the religion of the light and sound of God, is essentially based on the premise that spiritual growth is accelerated through the use of self-initiated out-of-body exploration. This concept of accelerated spiritual evolution through out-of-body experiences has an ancient history. Today many people pursue self-initiated out-of-body exploration by themselves and in small groups.

Most of the religions around the world are essentially based on the profound out-of-body experiences of a small group of individuals who consciously explored the spiritual dimensions of reality. Practically every religious movement known today refers to out-of-body states of consciousness. Unfortunately, many people remain unaware of this critical connection that heavily influenced all religions.

Even the newer religious traditions, such as the Mormon faith, mention out-of-body states of consciousness. In the *Journal of Discourses,* Mormon leader Heber Kimball describes an experience that occurred to Jedediah Grant when he met his deceased family in the "spirit world."

> He said to me, Brother Heber, I have been into the spirit world two nights in succession, and of all the dreads that ever came across me, the worst was to have to return to my body, though I had to do it. He saw his wife, she was the first person that came to him. He saw many that he knew, but did not have conversation with any but his wife, Caroline. She came to him and he said that she looked beautiful and had their little child, that died on the plains, in her arms, and said "Mr. Grant, here is little Margaret; you know that the wolves ate her up; but it did not hurt her, here she is all right."

TWENTIETH-CENTURY WRITERS

Several modern writers have contributed to a resurgence of interest in out-of-body exploration with their writings. Sylvan

Muldoon, Yram, Robert Crookall, Oliver Fox, Robert Monroe, and others have written fascinating accounts of their out-of-body adventures. Other well-known writers who have reported having OBEs include D. H. Lawrence, Jack London, Goethe, Aldous Huxley, Fred Alan Wolf, Michael Talbot, Michael Crichton, and Richard Bach, to name a few.

Muhammad, Swedenborg, the Sufis, Yogi masters, shamans, the biblical saints, and modern out-of-body travelers have all explored the subtle realms of the universe. They have all experienced the multidimensional universe and have described what they encountered there based on their individual cultural viewpoint. These cutting-edge explorers traveled far beyond the established norms of science and religion. They blazed a trail that all of humanity must eventually follow. Their exploration is critically important to us, because there is no escaping the fact that each of us will eventually return to the inner dimensions of reality as we experience the ultimate out-of-body adventure—that is, death.

When you examine the lives of the great spiritual leaders you find that they all had one thing in common: All experienced profound personal spiritual adventures beyond the limits of their bodies. Their lives were not directed by the prevailing religious and social beliefs but based upon their individual experiences and the insights they gained from those explorations. Many of these great spiritual explorers were considered radicals because they didn't follow the established religious norms of their day. Most important, the great spiritual explorers were not just believers; they were courageous explorers of consciousness, explorers of the unseen dimensions of God.

SPIRITUAL DIRECTION

The doctrine-immersed theologians who dominate today's religious traditions may never truly comprehend or experience the mystical experiences of Jesus, Muhammad, and others. The simple act of memorizing religious texts or just believing in words does not bring wisdom, understanding, or an authentic spiritual awakening. It requires true courage to explore beyond the dense limits of the body and the prevailing beliefs of man. It takes daring and determination to transcend the flesh and enter the ethereal realms of spirit. It takes personal experience beyond the body to even begin to comprehend the thought-responsive realities that are encountered during a profound out-of-body adventure. True spiritual leaders have little need for the beliefs of others, for they are self-directed by spirit.

History teaches us that personal spiritual experience is the key to our existence and our evolution. A good example of this is found in the Book of Revelation. For two thousand years biblical scholars have studied and attempted to interpret this magnificent text. The end result is a futile attempt to find logical religious symbolism where it does not exist. Simply put, Revelation, the Koran, and many other spiritual texts are primarily personal journals of the exploration and observations of the thought-responsive inner dimensions of reality. The only way to truly understand these mystical observations is to experience the subtle spiritual dimensions for yourself.

When we separate from our bodies we are following in the footsteps of the great spiritual leaders. Anyone who has ever had an out-of-body experience can relate to John's spiritual concept of being "born again." This is without a doubt the finest biblical description of what it feels like to separate from your physical body and enter a new environment of spirit. During the first moments of an out-of-body experience we are truly born again, as we awaken within a new subtle energy body and enter a new world. The New Testament analogy is incredibly accurate because, like a newborn baby, we must learn to adapt to an entirely new environment. We must learn to function, control, and communicate within our subtle spiritual body.

HUMANITY'S GREATEST DISCOVERY

I contend that the discoveries of out-of-body explorers are far more important than we can even begin to imagine. In fact, they represent a true quantum leap in the evolution of our species. These explorers may be so advanced that our current physically immersed states of consciousness cannot acknowledge, much less comprehend, the sheer magnitude of their discoveries. As modern science continues to concentrate on particles of matter, a few brave souls are exploring and mapping the unseen universe. These explorers have discovered incredible dimensions of reality that exist just beyond our vision. Their discoveries are far more important than a few rocks from the moon. In fact, all existing human discoveries pale in light of this new knowledge. I find it amusing that every day we swim in a magnificent ocean of multidimensional energy while our sciences are still examining the grains of sand on the beach. How long will it take us to recognize that the greatest discoveries of humanity are those of the existence of the multidimensional universe, of our multidimensional nature, and of our place within this incredible ocean of consciousness?

PERSONAL SPIRITUAL EXPERIENCE

As we evolve, the need for firsthand spiritual knowledge and experience is growing. Millions of people are searching for the answers to their existence and are exploring beyond established assumptions and beliefs. As we enter the new millennium, increasing numbers are no longer satisfied to just read and study the ideas and beliefs of others. As we awaken to our spiritual potential, spontaneous and self-initiated out-of-body explorations will become an established path to self and God realization. Millions more will recognize that out-of-body adventures are a powerful tool for experiencing the spiritual realms referred to by the early mystics who founded many of the religious traditions practiced today.

My fondest hope is that one day we as a species will "wake up" and see that each of us possesses the God-given ability to become a spiritual explorer. Eventually, we all will awaken to the fact that it is our destiny to transcend the crude confines of the flesh and break free from the binding chains of matter and belief. Eventually, we will come to experience the blazing truth of our multidimensional existence. The great history of out-of-body exploration is just beginning to be written, and at its core this history is truly about the evolution of consciousness beyond the facade of matter.

1. D. Scott Rogo, "Astral Projection in Tibetan Buddhist Literature," *International Journal of Parapsychology* 10 (1968): 277–84.
2. Twemlow, Gabbard, and Jones, "Out-of-Body Experience Phenomenology," 21.
3. Emanuel Swedenborg, *True Christian Religion*, section 851.
4. Erika Bourguignon, "Dreams and Altered States of Consciousness in Anthropological Research," in *Psychological Anthropology*, ed. F. L. K. Hsu (Cambridge, MA: Schenkman, 1972), 418.
5. Harner, Michael. *The Way of the Shaman* (San Francisco: HarperSanFrancisco: 1990), 6–7.

8

A New Vision of Death and Dying

*To civilize death, to bring it home and make it no
longer a source of dread, is one of the great challenges
of the age. Gradually, dying may come to hold again
the place it used to occupy in the midst of life: not a
terror, but a mystery so deep that man would no more
wish to cheat himself of it than to cheat himself of life.*

THE NATURAL DEATH HANDBOOK

I s it possible that the most transformational single event of
your life may occur at the moment of your death?

SPIRITUAL AWAKENING AT DEATH

Today many people are beginning to understand that they
create their own reality by the way they focus their thoughts
and actions. They are often surprised to discover that they can
use this same ability to influence the most important transition
of consciousness—their death.

Few of us think about the process of death. In fact, many
people in our youth-dominated culture intentionally avoid the
subject of death as much as possible. In the world of medicine,
the death of a patient is often looked upon as a failure of modern
science. Of course, those of us who have had out-of-body and
near-death experiences know better. We know from firsthand
experience that after we die, we continue to exist and flourish in

a higher vibratory dimension of reality. We know with certainty that death is an essential transition of consciousness.

Most people live their entire lives in total ignorance of their "final destination." They worry about and try to plan every detail of every day but leave the most important event in their existence to fate. It's as if they are on an eighty-year cross-country journey but possess no knowledge of their final destination. Of course, some people believe that if they accept the proper faith, obeying the established rules of their religious tradition, they will magically end up in heaven or paradise. This rather simplistic view has become the accepted norm in most modern cultures.

One of the oldest and most universally accepted beliefs is that there are a variety of afterlife environments that we may enter at death, based on our actions during our lives. The commonly held assumption is that we automatically go to the afterworld that is in sync with our personal spiritual evolution or vibratory rate. In addition, many feel that we have no control over our ultimate destination, so it is not worthy of much thought.

Surprisingly, many of the established religions of the world do not adequately address this important subject. They simply provide a few prayers for the dead and comforting words for the living; the transition of death is largely left in the loving arms of God. As you will see, this was not always the case.

ANCIENT SPIRITUAL PERSPECTIVES

Revered texts like the Egyptian Book of the Dead and the Tibetan Book of the Dead were written to provide extensive instruction and guidance for the "journey of soul at death." Spiritual leaders from divergent cultures have gone to great lengths to document detailed and elaborate methods for influencing and assisting the soul's journey to its final destination.

Many ancient tombs and burial places are inscribed with specific directions, maps, and advice for making the journey. One of the oldest written texts, the five-thousand-year-old Egyptian Papyrus of Ani contains information about the transition of death and the separation of the Ba-soul from the body. Numerous cultures throughout history have given this subject considerable thought and determined that external guidance can influence the transition of consciousness that occurs at death.

THE TIBETAN BOOK OF THE DEAD

The Tibetan Book of the Dead is one of the best-known texts detailing the transition of consciousness at death. The title of this eighth-century reference, in the native tongue of its writers, is *Bardo Thodal*, meaning "Liberation by Hearing on the After-Death Plane." In a sense this is a training manual to provide preparation and guidance for the separation of consciousness from the body at the point of death. This book is to be read aloud to people who are going through the process of dying to provide detailed assistance for navigating the various transitional stages of consciousness. The basic objective is to help direct the consciousness of those dying to the highest possible state of awareness, so that the higher spiritual realms of the universe are experienced and achieved.

The Tibetan Book of the Dead thus instructs us to assist the dying by providing detailed spiritual guidance. The following extract from this book offers a brief example of what a Tibetan Buddhist would read to a loved one nearing death. This and other phrases are repeated to the dying person in order to impress it on the mind as much as possible.

> O nobly born [insert name], the time hath now come for thee to seek the Path. Thy breathing is about to cease. Thy guru hath set thee face to face before with the Clear Light; and now thou art about to experience it in its Reality in the Bardo state, wherein all things are like the void and cloudless sky, and the naked, spotless intellect is like unto a transparent vacuum without circumference or centre. At this moment, know thou thyself; and abide in that state.[1]

Throughout the Tibetan Book of the Dead, the basic premise of the instruction is to direct our awareness to the "Clear Light" beyond all three-dimensional concepts of shape and form. This point is emphasized again with the phrase "transparent vacuum without circumference or centre." The Tibetan masters clearly understood that most people experience the Bardo state (i.e., the astral state and body) immediately following death. They are essentially instructing the dying to focus their undivided attention upon their formless spiritual essence that exists far beyond the astral, or Bardo, body. They are directing the soul to bypass the astral plane and embrace the formless essence of pure spirit.

THE BARDO BODY

The spiritual observations of the early Tibetan monks are remarkably similar to observations from other cultures. For example, modern out-of-body and psychic explorers confirm the description, function, and energy systems of the Bardo body. Today, the Bardo body is commonly called the astral or etheric body or sometimes the densest energy body. This non-physical body is an energy duplicate of the physical one and contains various energy centers. The early Tibetans' description of the "psychic nerve system" in their Book of the Dead clearly displays their advanced knowledge of the chakras, or energy centers, so essential to all life.

> The Bardo body, formed of matter is an invisible or ethereal-like state, is an exact duplicate of the human body, from which it is separated in the process of death. Retained in the Bardo body are the consciousness-principle and the psychic nerve system (the counterpart . . . of the physical nerve system of the human body).[2]

This knowledge is important in our spiritual development because the Bardo body is the energy body that is experienced during most out-of-body adventures.

One of the keys to initiating a profound experience beyond the body is our ability to stimulate and open the psychic nerve system, or chakras. Additional information about this is presented in chapter 9, "The Direct Path to the Soul."

A NEW VISION OF SPIRITUAL EMPOWERMENT

In addition to ancient spiritual teachings, dramatic evidence obtained from out-of-body explorations provides a new perception of death and dying. The ultimate journey and destination of soul is not a simple predestined event that we must endure, but a highly creative process. At death we are not powerless victims, but rather interactive participants in a wondrous and natural transition of consciousness. Let us awaken to a new vision of death and dying.

THE TYPICAL TRANSITION

The average person approaches their death with no conscious knowledge or understanding of their final destination. As death approaches, they may experience some degree of fear and uncertainty, followed by a brief state of confusion and disorientation. After final separation from the body, they are often met by loved ones who have already made the transition. This is a wonderful and joyous reunion. The newly deceased are reunited with past friends and loved ones, and are immediately reassured that everything will be all right. In time, they reorient themselves to their new reality. Many people are simply relieved and overjoyed to discover that they really do continue to exist after death and, as a result, gladly accept the first nonphysical reality they experience as their "new spiritual home." After a short time, new arrivals adapt to their environment. They are, of course, happy and content within their new spiritual home. And why not? These nonphysical dimensions are extremely pleasant when compared with the physical world. There is no disease, starvation, or physical death as we know it. Many of earth's most beautiful environments and vistas both present and past are available to be explored and enjoyed. "Life" is good. One experiences a much-needed respite from the heavy trials and tribulations so common in the physical world.

However, there is one very serious problem with this comforting scenario that few are aware of and no one addresses. You

ted and adapted to a thought-consensus environ-
tral plane. You have just accepted a reflection of
f the true essence of it. You have done what bil-
e before you. You have merged your conscious-
nonphysical reality far from your true spiritual
home. By doing so you essentially guarantee the continuation of
your form-based existence and your reincarnation. The end
result is that most people accept the denser spiritual realities of
the astral plane as their new home. They settle for and adapt to
the physical-like areas of the astral plane because these environments are familiar and comfortable. Thus they chain themselves
to the astral realms of form and substance, and the ancient cycle
of rebirth is maintained and assured.

THE IMPORTANCE OF BEING SPIRITUALLY PROACTIVE

Today, many people travel through life without clear spiritual direction. They cling to the popular religious beliefs of
their culture. They settle for tradition and faith instead of
seeking personal spiritual experience. The same holds true for
the journey of death. We possess the inherent ability to influence and direct our spiritual progress and our transition.
When we become spiritually proactive, we also have the ability to assist others.

I propose that we go beyond just providing comfort to the
dying. We possess the God-given ability to assist and guide our
loved ones to a higher state of consciousness before, during,
and after the process of death. At present, those near death are
often pumped with drugs and left alone to die "in peace." The
primary emphasis of the family, the church, and the medical
profession is on patient comfort and pain control, while the
critically important issues concerning the transition of consciousness are seldom addressed.

By focusing upon spiritual empowerment, we can embrace a
more evolved approach to death and dying. We have the ability
to do so much more; we can assist our loved ones in making
the ideal transition to a higher state of awareness. However, to
do so we must become more aware of our own abilities.

ASSISTING THE TRANSITION OF CONSCIOUSNESS

During my workshops, I teach a simple method that can assist us during the transition of death. As you sit by someone who is dying, you can help them to go to their higher spiritual self, even if they are in a coma or incoherent. Focus upon your spiritual intention. Use terms that mean pure spiritual essence to the individual and absolutely know that your uplifting guidance and assistance will be effective.

I am not suggesting an elaborate ceremony or ritual, but simple direct advice and guidance. Offer suggestions that will encourage the individual to be open to and experience the spiritual core of their consciousness. As much as possible use terms that will be understood, but keep in mind that your clear spiritual intention is far more important than the words that are used.

The following example shows that you do not have to be physically present to assist a transition. Simply direct your thoughts and guidance to the person, wherever they may be.

Last January I got a call from my mother to come to Las Vegas. My father was dying. I literally jumped on the first plane out. Needless to say, I was most upset. All I knew was that I had to get a message to my father to let him know that I was on my way to see him. I closed my eyes and projected myself to my parents' house and saw my sister and mother on either side of my father. My father looked very weak . . . colorless. It was becoming very hard for him to breathe. At the foot of his bed I saw pink and white lights. I kept telling my dad to go to the lights . . . not to be afraid; that it was okay to go anytime he wanted to. I also told my dad that I loved him and that my brother—who lives in South Carolina—and I were on our way to be with him. I tried to help make the transition easy for him. I left my parents' house after I felt my dad become more relaxed within himself. I opened my eyes and noticed I was still on the plane. About fifteen minutes went by and I felt an immediate pulling of my body. I saw that I was above the plane, and I felt an energy inside my body. But this energy I felt was a loving, peaceful feeling . . . I felt like it was a good-bye feeling. I must have been gone for all of forty seconds. When I plunked down into my body, at first I felt very dizzy and nauseous, but I no longer had an anxious feeling. I felt at peace . . . very restful. I immediately looked at my watch. I noticed the time. It was 1:30 P.M. I finally got to Las Vegas at 8 P.M. Pacific time. I got off the plane, and at the gate were my mother and sister. The first thing I asked was, "Is Dad already gone?" They said yes. I asked them if he had died around 1:30 Eastern time. They said, "Yes. How did you know?" I told them that Dad had come to me to say good-bye and to tell me he loved me. We all just embraced and cried. That evening my sister told me she had felt my presence that morning. She thought she heard my voice telling my dad to go to the light. We just looked at one another in awe. —JANET M., CLEVELAND, OHIO

PREPARING YOURSELF TO PROVIDE ASSISTANCE

To begin, I suggest doing a brief meditation to center and open your self. Ask and allow your self to be a clear and open channel for the unlimited power of God. It is critically important to guide and assist our loved ones beyond all aspects of form. Be aware that any form-based concept or image creates limitations that can direct the individual to the lower manifestations of spiritual reality. As much as possible, guide your loved ones beyond all form-based concepts and beliefs. Encourage them to seek and experience the pure essence of their being. It is important to recognize that we are conditioned during our physical life to accept various dense forms as our reality. Even many of our concepts of heaven and God are form based.

Our form-based preconceptions of reality create defined limits within the conscious and subconscious mind. The result is that our awareness is conditioned to accept form-based reflections of heaven as the real thing. These astral-plane heavens are beautiful environments that incorporate the most magnificent scenery and vistas found on earth. Compared with the physical world, they are indeed heavenly. However, they are but a reflection. Unfortunately, what most people don't realize is that they "end up" dwelling on the middle to upper astral realms. They have accepted physical-like forms as reality. Their identification and obsession with three-dimensional substance have limited them to the form-based manifestations and reflections of heaven instead of the pure essence of it. As shocking as it may sound, this is a common experience for many people after death. This is why I stress the importance of self-initiated out-of-body exploration, and why I strongly emphasize the importance of consciously experiencing our higher selves and exploring beyond all form-based realities while we are still living. Until we do so, we will continue to settle for less than our spiritual potential and severely limit our personal evolution.

SPIRITUAL GUIDANCE AT DEATH

1. Center and open yourself to the unlimited power of God—the universe—flowing through you. Sincerely ask to be an open, receptive channel for the power of God: "Now I am a clear, open channel for the power of God flowing through me!" Take your time and allow the inspiration, thoughts, and words to flow through you.

2. As much as possible, talk about, direct, and guide the person to dwell upon their spiritual essence beyond all concepts of form and substance. Focus on spiritual potential, freedom, beauty, and all the positive aspects of the approaching adventure.

3. Instruct and guide the person to release and reject all forms of fear and guilt and to embrace the unlimited freedom of their spiritual essence.

4. Instruct and guide the person to forgive and release any person or group that may have harmed them in any way. For example, they could say: "I sincerely forgive and release [name] completely and forever. I am free and I set all free that may have harmed me." The purpose here is to break the unseen emotional and intellectual

energy chains that bind us to the density of form and
matter.

5. Repeat an affirmation or mantra that focuses the person
   on their ultimate spiritual goal. Keep this extremely
   clear, brief, and in the present tense: "Now I experience
   my pure spiritual self!" Use whatever terms will most
   mean "pure spiritual essence beyond the manifestations
   of form" to the individual.

6. Maintain this process before, during, and for some time
   after the transition is complete.

As you feel yourself or a loved one approaching the transition point, focus and maintain your undivided attention upon
an affirmation that focuses your awareness upon your spiritual essence. Use language that for you denotes pure spiritual
awareness beyond all form and substance. Make this statement
a powerful mantra in your mind, and remember to keep it in
the present tense. When assisting a loved one, you can adapt
the approach to fit the situation. Your assistance can be given
silently, or verbally if it is acceptable. When assisting a loved
one, add their name as appropriate. The following are a few
examples of effective affirmations.

- Now I experience my higher self.
- Now I experience the highest spiritual aspect of my soul
  (consciousness).
- Now I experience my true self beyond all thought and
  form.
- Now I cut all attachments to form.
- Now I am reunited with my higher self.
- Now I experience my spiritual essence.
- Now I release all anchors of thought and emotion.
- Now I experience the essence of God.
- Now I go beyond all form and experience my true spiri-
  tual essence.
- Now I am one with the pure essence of God.

- Now I experience my spiritual essence beyond all concepts of form.
- Now I sincerely forgive all others and myself and experience my higher self.
- Now I release all of my attachments to form and experience my spiritual essence.
- Now I forgive all who may have harmed me in any way and I release them forever.
- Now I demand to experience my higher self now.
- Now I forgive and release myself from all attachments of the mind and body.

The ideal scenario is for several of the dying person's friends and loved ones to unite and provide spiritual guidance in shifts or teams. During a lengthy transition, consider recording your spiritual advice, guidance, and affirmations. When you are not able to be present, play the recording by the person's bedside. If you are not comfortable with recording your own affirmations, you can find professionally created recordings in bookstores and online.

The Self-Empowerment of Soul

The same principles apply to our individual journey of consciousness. We can influence our state of consciousness at the transitional moment by directing our awareness to experience our higher spiritual self. As you approach your last breath, repeat a focused affirmation such as "Now I experience my higher self!" As much as possible, hold this affirmation as your last conscious thought. Don't underestimate the potential of this simple technique. The proactive approach to death is far more effective than the current cultural dominance of fear, loss, and despair. The perfect mind-set would be to be prepared both mentally and spiritually and embrace the great adventure to come. As much as possible, release all attachments and fear and embrace the absolute joy and freedom of the ultimate out-of-body experience.

Using the Higher-Self Technique

I highly recommend using the "Higher-Self Technique" described in chapter 4, "Transformational Experiences." Remember, the ultimate journey of soul is not death but the self-realization of our spiritual essence. Eventually we must make the important transition from religious believer to spiritual explorer. This is the path we all must travel sooner or later.

The following are two examples to help you better understand what you may see or feel during a higher-self or spiritual experience.

*I heard and felt vibrations and then floated out of my body. I was surprisingly calm, and after a few seconds I decided to do the higher-self method. I shouted out in my mind, "I experience my higher self now!" The results were immediate. It's difficult to describe, but I felt myself, my awareness, pulled upward at an incredible speed. It felt like I was pulled through the entire universe and shot through layers of colors. The intensity was beyond belief, but I didn't back down. The next thing I knew the motion stopped. I was floating in an endless sea of stars. It's beyond words to describe, but I felt connected to everything in the universe. Everything was instantly clear; everything was here and now. It was pure ecstasy and knowing. I didn't want to leave. —*TAMMY R., COLUMBUS, OHIO

I have been having spontaneous out-of-body experiences for many years. However, I never attempted to go beyond the boundaries of my house. After attending your workshop I decided to take your advice and really explore what is out there—or should I say in here. During my last OBE I moved away from my body and demanded "awareness now"; then I waited for a moment and with all my heart I demanded, "Now I experience my higher self!" I was launched like a rocket, moving so fast it scared me. My mind and spirit were stretched to infinity. Then all of a sudden I was floating in what I can only describe as an ocean of pure living light. It was incredible,

a magnificent state of complete bliss. Everything was so peace-
ful. I know this must be heaven. I felt like I was floating in the
mind of God and I was absorbing all the love and knowledge
in the universe. It was beyond my wildest expectations.
—TIM G., SOUTHFIELD, MICHIGAN

THE IDEAL PREPARATION FOR SPIRITUAL TRANSITION

Evidence strongly suggests that the very act of having OBEs
is a natural and necessary preparation of consciousness in
order to make the transition of death a smoother process. I
firmly believe that spontaneous deathbed OBEs are a universal
method for consciousness to adapt to its new spiritual body
and environment. It is nature's way of providing assistance for
the transition of consciousness that will soon be experienced.
What better preparation for death can there be?

The ideal spiritual preparation is to become an experienced
out-of-body explorer. Each adventure beyond the body provides
valuable insights into our multidimensional nature and our spiritual capabilities. We are truly "born again."

Out-of-body explorers simply do not fear death. They fully
understand that death is a natural and exciting transition of
consciousness. They have a tremendous advantage over the
fearful masses that cling to the density of flesh. This is important for many reasons. Out-of-body explorers are prepared for
the thought-responsive dimensions that await us. They are not
paralyzed by fear and negativity or imprisoned by the limits of
the body. As they grow spiritually from their experiences, they
recognize and use their multidimensional abilities on a regular
basis. This is evident when Paul states in the New Testament,
"I die daily." Maybe today he would say, "I leave my body
daily."

As we evolve, we grow beyond our dependence upon the five
physical senses and become more conscious of our spiritual
abilities. The more we embrace and experience our multidimensional nature, the greater is our spiritual freedom both now and
after death. It is up to us to learn how to navigate the unseen

worlds of spirit and to travel the path to our spiritual essence. Out-of-body explorers know from personal experience that the path is within. They also know that spiritual experience is absolutely essential in preparing us for the incredible thought-responsive dimensions that await us.

ADVANTAGES OF OUT-OF-BODY EXPLORERS

- They know from experience that they are multidimensional spiritual beings.
- They are not attached or addicted to temporary realities based on form and substance.
- They experience a far greater range of spiritual freedom and choices in any dimension that they explore.
- They can consciously experience their true spiritual home beyond all concepts of form.
- They are far more likely to experience the higher vibrational heavens because they are more spiritually prepared, empowered, and experienced.
- They navigate the thought-responsive nonphysical realms with more ability and confidence.
- They understand the importance of raising and adjusting their personal vibrational state.
- They comprehend the absolute spiritual necessity and purpose of inner-dimensional travel.
- They know from experience that their consciousness is the inner-dimensional path to God.
- They know from experience that thoughts are a powerful and creative force. Thoughts have a tremendous impact upon our various nonphysical bodies, our perceptions, and our surroundings.
- They are accustomed to and at ease with the vibrational-state experience.
- They know how to confront and dissolve internal energy blocks and fears.

The Power of Forgiveness

In life and at death we are often our own harshest critic and judge. There is much talk about forgiveness, but many are unaware that it is critically important to forgive ourselves for our perceived sins. Evidence received from near-death and out-of-body experiences suggests a radically different final-judgment scenario than is widely accepted today: At death we are not judged by God or angels on a heavenly throne; instead, we must face the most demanding judge imaginable, our own spiritual self. The pure spiritual essence of our consciousness appraises our development. Our every thought, word, and deed are known. Our life is an open book where every secret, every desire is clear and present. The art of forgiveness is often the practice of self-forgiveness. Don't underestimate the liberating spiritual power of its use.

OBEs: The Natural Process of Soul

To emphasize how natural out-of-body experiences truly are, I would like to point out that we separate from our bodies during sleep. Every night our nonphysical body moves out of phase with the physical. This natural process allows us to recharge energetically and spiritually. In addition, those who are approaching death often begin to have spontaneous OBEs as a natural prelude to their transition. This phenomenon has been well documented by Dr. Raymond Moody and other near-death researchers. I have received numerous reports from hospice workers and nurses, as well as from friends and loved ones who have assisted with dying persons. They describe a substantial increase in out-of-body states of consciousness and communication with unseen guests as death approaches. The following are some examples from hospice nurses.

As death approaches, the incidence of deathbed visions and out-of-body experiences increases substantially. —SALLY J., NEW YORK, NEW YORK

I can tell when the time of death is near, because the patient is slipping in and out of consciousness. Such people often describe detailed conversations and meetings with friends or relatives who have passed on. —RUTH, WASHINGTON, D.C.

Many refer to this process as the thinning of the "veil" between the physical and spiritual dimensions.

DEATHBED VISIONS

It is common for out-of-body states of consciousness to become manifest in the form of communication with a non-physical loved one. The hundreds of letters I have received have led me to believe that the phenomena of deathbed visions are often out-of-body experiences. Here are some typical comments.

I was just speaking with my (deceased) mother; she looks wonderful. She told me everything will be fine. —JANICE W., BEL AIR, MARYLAND

I talked to my (departed) grandmother standing over there in the corner of the room. —CATHY B., LOS ANGELES, CALIFORNIA

Angelic visitations are also often associated with deathbed visions and near-death experiences. The underlying reason for the "vision" is an internal shift of consciousness from the physical body to the spiritual. Additional evidence supporting this conclusion is the reported increase in spontaneous out-of-body experiences that occurs as people near death.

When my sister was dying from cancer, she would awaken from unconsciousness to tell me of her meetings with our grandmother and other family members that had passed on. She would speak of detailed conversations where she was offered reassurance that she was going to be in a wonderful place when she decided to "let go." These daily visits occurred for about two weeks, and then one night she quietly died. —AMY S., TORONTO, CANADA

In the past many have assumed that these visitations were some form of vision or dreamlike encounter, but my research has led me to believe that many of these reports are actually out-of-body experiences that occur naturally as we draw closer to death. Their occurrence is caused by the loosening and deterioration of the ethereal connection between the physical body and the subtle spiritual form (first energy body). As we move closer to death, the incidence of spontaneous out-of-body experiences and deathbed visions increases dramatically. This is soul's way of preparing its earthbound consciousness for the approaching transition of death.

COCREATING OUR NEW SPIRITUAL REALITY

Heaven is not a single place or city but many different nonphysical dimensions and realities. Most people who have died find themselves in realities that are in many ways similar to their past physical surroundings. They live in communities and homes, social and soul groups where they feel welcome and at ease. Many nonphysical residents carry on a surprisingly busy but a rather physical-like existence. This occurs because we have a strong tendency to gravitate toward what is comfortable and familiar to us. We are essentially creatures of habit. We not only accept what we perceive to be the norm but also help to manifest it with the creative energies of our thoughts.

One of the surprising observations during out-of-body experiences is the wide diversity of realities. There are reports of everything from poverty-stricken ghettos to magnificent castles, from inspiring and magnificent temples of learning to dark and dingy rooms filled with every imaginable form of addiction. It's amazing how many people report an existence that seems almost "everyday" and "mundane." For example, if you were born and lived your entire life in a crowded city apartment, it is likely that this is the reality you may find comfortable after death. It appears that many people's concept of heaven is often limited to their physical conceptions of reality. Some people are content in a home in the country overlooking some sort of panoramic view, while others live in a busy city. Of course this is to be expected, since our mind-set will determine and mold our experience.

Be aware that if we have accepted mediocrity or lack in any form as our norm in this life, we will likely continue to experience the same sort of reality when we make the transition of death. We shape and mold our concept of reality; it matters little whether it is a beautiful home on a hill or a small city tenement. We "make" it so. When we accept any limitation as a reality, that limiting mind-set continues after death. Even though death may mark the exit from the body and the end of physical life, there is no escaping the creations and limitations of our minds.

ASSISTING SOULS DURING
AN OUT-OF-BODY EXPERIENCE

As mentioned in the previous chapter, one of the greatest spiritual explorers of all time was Emanuel Swedenborg. He became famous in seventeenth-century Europe for his ability to leave his body in full awareness and venture into the unseen dimensions. In his extensive writings he describes numerous trips into various different heavens where he assisted lost and disoriented souls. He speaks in detail of guiding souls from the lower heavens (the lower astral plane) to the higher vibrational dimensions. The following is from a letter I recently received that describes an experience with lost souls.

During an astral projection I went to my uncle's farm. When I was outside in the field, I was approached by several people who seemed to know me. I could see their forms, but not the details of their faces. Somehow I could tell they had all passed over. I wasn't afraid, because they seemed to need something from me. They were all talking at once and moving toward me. I wasn't sure what to do; there were too many to listen to. They seemed confused or lost. I wasn't sure how to help them, so I just told them to go to the light. —GINNY M., BANGOR, MAINE

During an out-of-body experience, the interconnection between different dimensions and environments is often represented by stairs, elevators, or some form of energy portals. We have the ability to assist others to a higher vibrational reality by escorting or directing them to these energy areas. Be aware that energy portals can also be created by focused thought.

During one of my recent out-of-body experiences I found myself in a foggy area filled with people. They seemed to be confused and lost, and I sensed that a few were angry. One of these people approached me and asked for directions. This was odd, since I didn't even know where I was at the time. I spontaneously told them that they had to concentrate and think their way out of this place. I mentally told the group to create an elevator with their thoughts and ride it up to the top floor. I somehow knew that this would work. They thanked me, and then I slammed back into my body. I felt paralyzed for several moments. —KEVIN F., DALLAS, TEXAS

THE RAPID TRANSITION

One of the most tragic results of a sudden or violent death is what can immediately occur to the spiritually unprepared. Sometimes the rapid transition of consciousness that results from murders, heart attacks, automobile accidents, or other violent, sudden deaths can propel the dead into a startlingly new reality so quickly that the individual becomes extremely disoriented and refuses to accept the dramatic change. Just imagine: One moment you are driving home after a normal day of work, and the next you are forcefully ejected into a parallel reality where you are unable to communicate with the people you know and are unable to touch the surroundings that you are accustomed to. You feel fine, your body looks the same, but you are somehow separated from everything and everyone that you believe is real. In this scenario it is not uncommon for the accident or war victim to refuse spiritual assistance and to attempt to remain as close to the physical world as possible, clinging to their last perception of reality. Throughout history, this individual is sometimes identified as a ghost. Our expanded knowledge of the process of death can eliminate the confusion resulting from sudden transitions.

I've had a few out-of-body experiences since I was a teenager, but by far the most memorable happened a few days after my cousin died in a car wreck. I felt the vibrations like I was lying down next to a moving freight train; then it was like whoosh and I was sitting with my cousin in his car. He seemed confused, and although he didn't say anything, I had the feeling he didn't know what had happened to him. I'm not very religious, but I asked him whether he knew how to get to heaven. Right after I said that, the car sort of melted or faded away. Then there was a wide beam of light with little stars and sparks in front of us. I told him, "Follow the light, and don't stop until you get there." —DONNIE B., PHILADELPHIA, PENNSYLVANIA

One of the great benefits of being a conscious spiritual explorer is that you are far more prepared for the transition of death and the thought-response energies that mold our future home.

TAKING RESPONSIBILITY
FOR OUR SPIRITUAL EVOLUTION

As we grow, we must take responsibility for our personal life and our spiritual evolution. It's not enough to simply believe, hope, and pray. We must act by taking focused spiritual action, for we possess the God-given ability to experience and enjoy the ultimate spiritual realities. However, it is up to us to recognize and experience our full creative and spiritual potential. Nothing stands in our way but our own self-induced limitations. The sooner we embrace our spiritual responsibility, the faster we will reclaim our place in the pure realms of spirit.

There is an old saying that you will continue to get what you always got if you continue to think as you always thought. I believe that the same principle applies to our spiritual evolution. Continuing on the popular path of belief instead of opening our minds to our unlimited spiritual potential will only ensure the status quo.

TAKING SPIRITUAL ACTION

This is why it is so important that we consciously recognize and exercise our personal creative and spiritual abilities. Our thoughts build our reality in every dimension of the universe. Many people never recognize this universal truth because the density of matter slows the creative manifestation of thought and obscures this fact. The dense molecular surroundings make the creation process more challenging because it takes longer for thoughts to influence matter than it does for them to influence the subtle energies that make up the inner dimensions of reality. To be creative in the physical world it is necessary for us to focus and maintain our thoughts for an extended period of time. This process provides the ideal training ground for consciousness to learn and develop its creative abilities. The entire physical universe is essentially a slowed-down molecular training ground designed for the evolution of developing consciousness.

It is essential that we take spiritual action in order to propel our consciousness away from the dense gravity field of matter. The great spiritual masters throughout history were well aware of this fact. Buddha instructed us to detach from the physical world and release the attachments and desires that bind us to matter. Jesus taught us to seek first the kingdom of God with all our heart and our entire mind. If you examine the teachings of any spiritual master you will hear a resounding call for spiritual action. Belief and faith are only the first steps of spirituality. Granted, belief is an important first step, but belief alone was never intended to be the sole core of religion and spirituality. Jesus, Buddha, Muhammad, and other enlightened spiritual leaders never taught us to become dependent upon man-made beliefs. Their lives were vibrant examples of personal spiritual action and spiritual exploration. Ask yourself this critical question: Are you content to settle for man-made traditions and beliefs, or are you ready to take the next step in your spiritual evolution?

For many, the important next step in our personal development is direct spiritual action. This action can manifest itself in many different ways such as meditation or breath work.

However, one of the most effective methods of spiritually empowering ourselves is to practice the methods and techniques of self-initiated out-of-body exploration.

A NEW PHILOSOPHY

Let us embrace a new philosophy of death and dying. Instead of fear, let us feel joy, for we know that we continue to live and grow beyond the dense illusion of flesh. Our exit from this temporary stage is a glorious return to our true spiritual home. Let us open our hearts and minds to the formless void of pure spiritual consciousness. Let us accept and embrace the journey of death as another self-empowering out-of-body experience to the very spiritual core of our consciousness. This is a magnificent opportunity for us to go beyond the astral plane and all form-based realities. As the Tibetan Buddhists would say, let us enter the "clear light of the void."

I believe that the elimination of our fears concerning death and dying is a major step forward for all humankind. Slowly, a new vision of life, death, and our multidimensional nature is emerging. We are awakened to the fact that death is a natural transition of consciousness, a continuation of life.

Just imagine the potential benefits that are attainable through conscious out-of-body travel. You approach death with a clear knowledge that you are immortal. You are empowered to focus upon your spiritual goals and actions instead of your fears. As you approach your final physical breath, you concentrate on your clear spiritual intentions and goals. As the moment draws near, you mentally focus on and demand to experience your highest spiritual essence: "Now I experience my spiritual essence!" Your spiritual goals are firmly set in place as you separate from your body and move rapidly inward through layers of energy and color to the very core of your spiritual self. The possibilities are limitless, but we must be empowered to take positive action.

The Tibetans understood that the Bardo, or astral body, is an energy duplicate of the physical body. They were also well aware that a large percentage of humanity clings to this energy body at death. The great challenge is to break free from our attachments to form and substance. We must empower our self to go beyond the astral and embrace the formless essence of soul.

Those who doubt the potential or speed of this spiritual awakening process should keep in mind that time and space are fleeting perceptions based only in matter. Soul or pure awareness simply is. Soul exists beyond the concepts of time, space, and form. No external force is keeping us from the spiritual realms. We have separated ourselves from self-realization and God realization. We possess the God-given ability, through our focused spiritual actions, to experience our spiritual essence right now. For many the unseen gravity field they must escape is their personal attachment to all form and substance. Their state of consciousness and their obsession with the temporary forms around them impede their progress toward their true spiritual home.

When you examine the sacred texts throughout history you discover that the central theme of all religious traditions is an awareness of the unseen dimensions that are commonly called heavens and the recognition that our consciousness or soul continues beyond the physical body. What is so often forgotten is the fact that these critically important observations were obtained by spiritual explorers who possessed the courage to explore beyond the limits of the physical body. To arrive at these important conclusions, they had to consciously transcend the physical body. The answers to the truly important questions of our existence—Where do we go at death? Where do we come from? What is our purpose? What are we?—are not found in the physical world. Nor are they found in books. We find these answers only through spiritual experience beyond the physical body.

In the midst of transition, many people actually make a statement describing their "vision" of the afterlife. The following are examples of what some well-known people have reported seeing as they exited their physical body.

I still live . . . pretty. —DANIEL WEBSTER

It's very beautiful over there. —THOMAS A. EDISON, MOMENTARILY EMERGING FROM A COMA

More light! —JOHANN WOLFGANG VON GOETHE

I suffer much less. The music is so beautiful . . . Listen, listen. In the midst of all those voices I recognize my mother's! —LOUIS XVII

It is all light. —GEORGE AUGUSTUS SELWYN (BISHOP OF LICHFIELD)

Now I am at the source of blessedness. —FRÉDÉRIC CHOPIN

I never felt better. —DOUGLAS FAIRBANKS

Beautiful. —ELIZABETH BARRETT BROWNING

THE POWER OF SPIRITUAL ACTION

I am often asked what I will do when I take my final breath. This is a critically important question that too few people ask themselves today. My answer is this: "I will demand to experience my higher self, my spiritual essence!" I am not content to simply "go to the light." I am not content to accept past acquaintances and comfortable surroundings as my new reality. In fact, I am not content to settle for any form-based reality as my spiritual home. I absolutely know that there is so much more available beyond the realms of form. There exist magnificent dimensions of living light simply waiting for us; all we need do is awaken and accept their reality. Two powerful truths are apparent. First, all form is but a reflection of pure spirit. Second, we are not helpless victims of an external force that dictates or directs our reality and our lives; we are bestowed with the power of free will and the ability to take spiritual action. Why would you settle for a pale reflection of reality when the pure realms of spirit are always present?

Let us begin to take responsibility not only for our physical life but for our afterlife as well. We determine the realities that we accept and cocreate. So, from this moment on, let us be aware and choose well.

1. Evans-Wentz, W. Y., The Tibetan Book of the Dead (London: Oxford University Press, 1936), 91.
2. Ibid., 92.

9

The Direct Path to the Soul
Demystifying the Process
of an Out-of-Body Experience

*Unless you find paradise at your own center, there is
not the smallest chance that you may enter.*

ANGELUS SILESIUS

The key to our evolution is our ability to consciously experience our spiritual essence. Unfortunately, knowledge about the nature of authentic spiritual experiences is sadly lacking in our society and culture. To comprehend the nature of such experiences, we must gain a deeper insight into ourselves and become aware of the energy mechanics of the spiritual process. This knowledge will help us weather the storm of the vibrational state while assisting us in expanding an out-of-body experience into a profound spiritual adventure.

It is important to recognize that spiritual experiences are magnificent natural processes. We are spiritual beings temporarily clothed in matter. We can and will instinctively experience our spiritual nature when the proper conditions are present.

Today we have a growing desire to consciously reconnect with our spiritual essence. This inner yearning for spirit is one of the major reasons for the worldwide increase in and acceptance of spiritual practices such as meditation and yoga. We possess a primal drive to experience and know our true essence beyond the facade of matter.

The soul exists at a much higher frequency than matter. It dwells beyond emotions, thought, form, and substance as we know them. The soul can be viewed as pure awareness, completely independent of linear time and space. Because of the soul's extremely subtle nature, it requires a method or mechanism in order to interact within the denser areas of the universe. The soul accomplishes this interaction by effectively using different energy vehicles as tools of expression. These energy vehicles include our biological bodies, our emotions, and our thoughts both conscious and subconscious. Essentially, these energy forms allow us to project, interact with, and express our awareness in the denser dimensions of the universe. In a very real sense the soul is extending its awareness throughout the multidimensional universe by the use of these energy vehicles or bodies of consciousness. The soul uses them to effectively interact within the outer dimensions of the universe.

The following list presents an overview of the reported phenomena associated with authentic spiritual experiences. I use the word *authentic* because the physical world is filled with those who pretend to have spiritual experiences and claim to be consciously connected to spirit. We have all witnessed their antics on television. Today many people have no idea what it is like to have an authentic spiritual experience.

COMMON ELEMENTS OF
AUTHENTIC SPIRITUAL EXPERIENCES

- Consciousness shifts inward and away from the physical body and its senses. This shift often manifests itself as an altered or trance state followed by out-of-body and expanded states of consciousness.
- The physical body often appears to be in a deep state of trance or sleep.
- They are preceded by the withdrawal of consciousness from the physical senses. Vibrational and Kundalini

phenomena such as sounds, energy surges, and paralysis are often experienced.

- There is an awareness of expanded modes of inner perception. These may include 360-degree vision, vivid imagery, and direct knowledge that expands beyond form. Images and thoughts may be experienced simultaneously.
- There is an overwhelming sense of pure love—a pure state of being that surpasses all form and thought.
- There is a conscious connection to all existence.
- There is an awareness of a completely nonphysical, non-form-based reality. This reality may manifest itself as an ocean of light, a loving void, or a magnificent transcendent presence.
- There is recognition of an enhanced form of communication by direct knowing or pure awareness.
- There is a complete disassociation or release from the physical body and the ego. The concepts and limits of time, space, and form are transcended.

THE UNSEEN NATURE OF MANKIND

We are far more complex than the established concepts of body, mind, and soul. Each of us is an incredibly expansive multidimensional being. We possess many different energy bodies consisting of different vibrational frequencies. The physical body is of course the outermost and densest of our bodies. The energy form that many people experience during an out-of-body adventure is essentially the first inner energy body or subtle energy mold of our physical form. The nonphysical body that many experience during an OBE can be viewed as an energy duplicate. Many refer to it as the etheric or astral body, the vital sheath, or the Bardo body. In a sense this subtle body acts as a transformer to step down the higher frequencies of soul into the density of flesh. There are specific energy adjustments and changes that are necessary in order for our awareness to transfer from the dense physical body to the subtle nonphysical and spiritual bodies within us.

CHAKRAS AND THE SPIRITUAL EXPERIENCE

The first subtle spiritual body contains seven primary energy centers, commonly called *chakras*. You can think of these energy centers as a transference system for nonphysical energies. Chakras and the various energy bodies make it possible for the extremely subtle, higher-frequency energies of soul to flow into the denser areas of the universe. This system is essentially nature's way of providing an effective method for the subtle spiritual energies to enter and sustain the denser vehicles of soul. Chakras function similarly to organic valves that control and distribute the flow of life-giving energy into our body. When one or more of our chakras are stimulated, they begin to open, resulting in the flow of nonphysical energy. This unseen energy process marks the beginning of the well-known phenomenon known as the vibrational state (fig. 3). The commonly reported sounds, sensations, and vibrations so often experienced during the initial stages of an out-of-body adventure are the direct result of this massive energy flow. Nonphysical energy floods our etheric body, causing it to expand, and initiates the conditions required for the occurrence of an out-of-body experience.

Generally this entire process occurs rather quickly, with many people reporting that it takes only ten to sixty seconds to move from the beginning of the vibrational state to separation from the body. The more comfortable we are with the process, the more open we are to it, the faster it seems to occur. The key to enjoying the full benefits of this magnificent energy flow is to surrender to the process. Simply allow the energy to expand throughout your body without analyzing the process. In a sense, go with the flow. Many people, shocked by the intensity of the energy flow, focus their attention on their physical body. Unfortunately, this immediately shuts down the entire process. As you will see, our response to this inner energy flow will often determine the results we achieve.

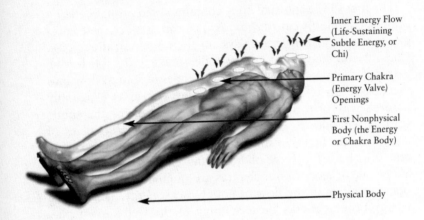

Inner Energy Flow
(Life-Sustaining
Subtle Energy, or
Chi)

Primary Chakra
(Energy Valve)
Openings

First Nonphysical
Body (the Energy
or Chakra Body)

Physical Body

Fig. 3. The Unseen Energy Process
That Initiates Out-of-Body Experiences

The vibrational state and out-of-body experiences are initiated by the substantial opening of one or more of the primary chakras, or energy centers, that exist within the first subtle energy body. This opening creates a massive flow of nonphysical energy that activates and expands our first energy body. The starting point and intensity of the vibrational state and the resulting out-of-body experience are determined by the location and aperture of one or more primary chakras.

THE DAILY ENERGY CHARGING PROCESS

Every night as we sleep our energy body moves out of phase with our biological body. A subtle trickle of nonphysical energy flows through our chakras and into our dense bodies. Our biological and astral bodies are recharging during this process.
WILLIAM BUHLMAN

This powerful energy process also provides an explanation of the well-documented phenomenon known as the *Kundalini experience*. During this experience the base chakra opens dramatically, creating a massive energy flow up the spine. This potent energy flow systematically activates the various energy centers as it moves up the spine toward the crown chakra. This explains why profound and spontaneous out-of-body and spiritual experiences are so often reported during a full-fledged Kundalini experience.

I would like to emphasize that this energy process, though it may seem amazing to us, is a completely natural event. During sleep we normally recharge ourselves by the same basic process. The only real difference is that in the latter case the energy flow is a slow trickle, similar to what a battery receives on a slow charge, instead of the massive surge that initiates an OBE. The more knowledge we have about this energy process, the better prepared we will be to master the art and practice of spiritual exploration.

THE MULTIDIMENSIONAL NATURE OF SPIRITUAL EXPERIENCES

Each energy body that we process is a vehicle and expression of our consciousness. To interact with matter, we must use a physical form for expression. The same applies to all energy levels of the universe. In other words, we are a microcosm of the multidimensional universe (figs. 4, 5). For example, for us to consciously experience the third heaven that Paul speaks of in 2 Corinthians, we must shift our conscious awareness from the physical body to the corresponding third inner-energy or spiritual body. This process of inner-dimensional movement of consciouness is the essential core of all spiritual exploration and experience.

When Muhammad, Zoroaster, Buddha, Paul, and other spiritual explorers undertook their explorations of the various heavens, they were actually extending their conscious awareness from their physical body and into the various higher-dimensional bodies within themselves. The great spiritual

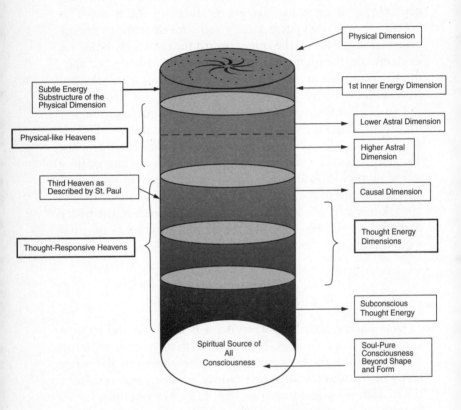

Fig. 4. The Multidimensional Universe

All dimensions occupy the same time and space. They are separated by their individual vibrational frequency and resulting density. As we move in toward the energy source, each heaven becomes progressively more thought responsive. Multiple heavens exist within each dimension created by the group consciousness of the inhabitants.

WILLIAM BUHLMAN

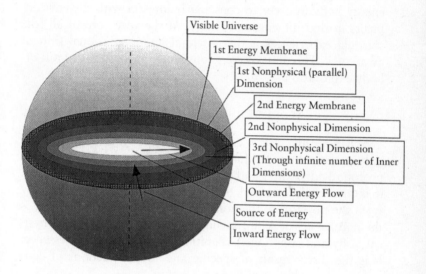

Fig. 5. The Multidimensional Universe

The universe is a continuum of energy frequencies emanating from a nonphysical source. The physical universe we observe is the molecular epidermis layer of the complete multidimensional universe.

WILLIAM BUHLMAN

explorers became proficient at transcending the flesh and shifting their awareness throughout the various energy dimensions of the universe. For example, John's vividly described experiences as recounted in the Book of Revelation, be they perceived as positive or negative, were firsthand accounts of his out-of-body explorations of the inner dimensions of the universe. John shifted his awareness from his physical body to his inner subtle energy body in order to consciously interact with the environments in that dimensional reality. At the very core of all true spiritual experiences is this essential interdimensional shift of awareness. This shift of consciousness is at the heart of out-of-body exploration!

FOCUSED SPIRITUAL ACTION

Spiritual adventures are not random mystical events that only a few lucky individuals experience. In order for us to have profound adventures and become authentic spiritual explorers, it is absolutely essential that our awareness move internally from the physical to the nonphysical. A spiritual experience is the natural act of withdrawing our awareness from the physical body and consciously reuniting with our spiritual essence. It is the direct result of specific and focused actions of consciousness, and it is available to all of us.

First, we must recognize and accept our ability to have a profound spiritual experience now. It's important to embrace this very moment and not some vague time in the future. Second, we must learn how to expand our awareness beyond the confines of the physical body and its senses. Third, we must consciously transcend the dense limits of flesh. And finally, we must continue this inner exploration of our consciousness until we experience union with the very core of our spiritual essence.

One essential truth is evident: We must either consciously transcend the dense body or remain a prisoner of it. The ultimate spiritual goal for billions of people is to transcend the outer remnants of soul and experience union with their true spiritual essence. The word *yoga* means "union" in ancient Sanskrit. Of course, this conscious union with God is the ultimate purpose of all true spiritual paths and practices. This ultimate union is achieved by the inner-dimensional movement of consciousness from the physical to the spiritual source within us.

FOCUSING UPON INNER EXPLORATION

The ever-changing beliefs of our society have little bearing on an authentic spiritual experience. This ultimate spiritual awakening can occur in any culture or in any belief system if the individual has the courage and drive to explore beyond the limits of the body. In fact, mastery is earned by those unique individuals who have expanded their consciousness beyond the dense outer covering of soul and maneuvered their awareness throughout the multidimensional universe until they have fully experienced their true spiritual self.

A profound spiritual experience is the direct result of effective spiritual training and action. Spiritual mastery is often acquired after many lifetimes of interdimensional exploration and experience. No matter which path or religion we have chosen to follow, we must transcend the limits of the body to experience our spiritual essence. This is why mystics and prophets throughout history have emphasized the necessity of transcending the senses and all attachments to the body. This is also why many of the great spiritual explorers were often viewed as rebels in their time. They did not blindly follow the prevailing religious beliefs and traditions of their day. Instead, they pursued personal spiritual experience.

THE INNER-DIMENSIONAL PATH OF SOUL: THE JOURNEY OF CONSCIOUSNESS

During an authentic spiritual experience we undergo the transition of consciousness as we move beyond the outer physical body and inward toward our true spiritual source. The first essential step of this magnificent process is to transcend the dense physical body. Then we must systematically transcend each of the subtle vehicles of our awareness until we consciously experience the blazing reality of our pure awareness—our soul. This process is the inner-dimensional path of soul (fig. 6).

When you have an out-of-body experience, your awareness moves or shifts from the physical vehicle to one of your subtle inner-energy vehicles. For example, when our conscious awareness shifts to our astral body, we experience astral projection. As we move further inward, we experience the realms of pure thought and then spirit.

This process of the soul extending its awareness throughout the various energy dimensions is at the core of all life throughout the universe. At this moment you are experiencing this process as you utilize the perception vehicles of your body and mind to hold, see, and absorb the information in this book. Your every thought and deed is an expression and extension of your soul within the inner-dimensional universe. The recognition and conscious exploration of our various multidimen-

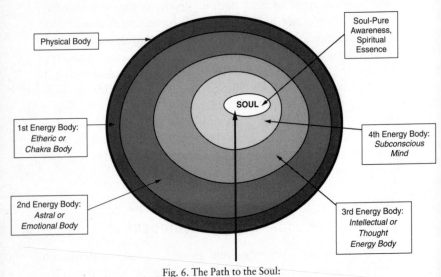

Fig. 6. The Path to the Soul:
The Multidimensional Nature of Man

Self-realization is achieved when we transcend the dense outer bodies of the soul and consciously experience our spiritual essence. This movement of consciousness is the inner-dimensional passage within us. This is spiritually directed out-of-body travel.
WILLIAM BUHLMAN

sional bodies is a major leap forward in our spiritual evolution. When we awaken to and experience our multidimensional nature, we take the great leap from being physical creatures tied to the animal senses to becoming conscious spiritual beings with unrestricted abilities (fig. 7).

I contend that learning the art and practice of out-of-body exploration is of tremendous value for any seeker of the truth,

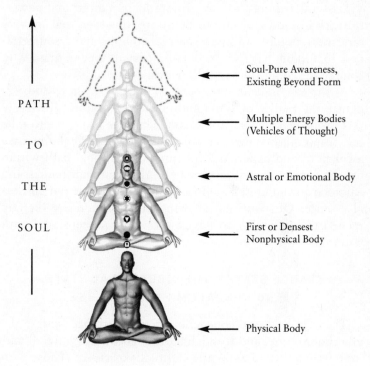

PATH

TO

THE

SOUL

Soul-Pure Awareness,
Existing Beyond Form

Multiple Energy Bodies
(Vehicles of Thought)

Astral or Emotional Body

First or Densest
Nonphysical Body

Physical Body

Fig. 7. The Inner-Dimensional Path to the Soul

The universal path to self-realization is the multidimensional path within each of us. This inner path consists of a series of subtle energy vehicles or bodies. All bodies of soul function as the necessary expressions and vehicles of consciousness within the various dimensions of the universe. Each out-of-body adventure is a powerful opportunity to explore inward and consciously experience our true spiritual essence. This is the direct path to God within us.

WILLIAM BUHLMAN

for anyone seeking self- and God realization. No matter what path you follow, this knowledge and skill will eventually be required. There is an old saying that there are many paths to God. This may be true, but all direct paths involve the ability to transcend the physical limits and consciously connect with spirit. All true spiritual paths teach the necessity and benefits of a profound spiritual experience.

Self-initiated out-of-body exploration is a direct and powerful path to God realization. Be aware, however, that its very directness requires an inner spiritual courage and resourcefulness that many have yet to obtain. It is not for the timid who cling to the comfort of established beliefs.

As the new millennium opens, so must we open to and recognize the reality of our multidimensional nature, for truly this is our personal spiritual path. The time has come to take full responsibility for our spiritual growth. The sooner we awaken to and experience the inner-dimensional path within us, the sooner we will evolve beyond our animal bodies and embrace our unlimited abilities to fully experience our spiritual essence. Our spiritual growth and evolution are directly related to our ability to navigate the multidimensional path within us.

TRANCE STATES, THE VIBRATIONAL STATE, AND KUNDALINI EXPERIENCES

There is a direct connection between trance states, the vibrational state, and Kundalini experiences. They are all natural preludes to an authentic spiritual experience. Those who are prepared for the intensity of these states of consciousness will often experience a rich spiritual connection. Those who are uninformed about trance and vibrational states of consciousness and inexperienced with them are often startled by the energy of the experience; many report being frozen with fear and prematurely ending their pending out-of-body adventure. The key to moving beyond this fear is the accumulation of accurate information and knowledge. Simply put: The more prepared you are for the phenomena that occur immediately before a spiritual experience, the greater the potential results.

THE FIRST STEPS IN SPIRITUAL EXPLORATION

The first steps in spiritual exploration involve recognition of and response to trance-state phenomena. When we explore inward, we shift our state of consciousness from the physical body and its senses to the subtle inner world of spirit. During this process we experience specific changes in our body and our mind. Our breathing and heart rate slow as our brain-wave patterns change from the active beta state to the slower alpha state. As we progress in our inner exploration, our body and brain waves slow even further into the theta state. At this point we often experience a feeling of dissociation from the physical body and its senses and a distortion of time. These changes in consciousness are often referred to as a trance state (fig. 8). It is important to recognize that trance states are natural manifestations of the process of relaxing and focusing our attention inward.

We live our entire lives perceiving the world through our outer biological senses. Our physical body is our dense vehicle of perception, our window to the world around us. What is so

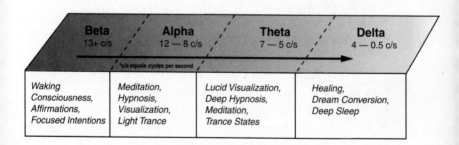

Fig. 8. The Progression of Trance States of Consciousness

WILLIAM BUHLMAN

often forgotten is that our biological body is but a temporary vehicle of soul, a rather crude and limited tool of consciousness. We essentially use our five physical senses to observe and interact with the world around us. When we begin to explore our spiritual essence, we naturally disengage from our physical senses. Essentially, this process of disengaging from the outer vehicle of soul creates the trance state.

Each person experiences the trance state differently. A slowing of breathing and a sense of heaviness or lightness often indicate the beginning of this state. Various phenomena— including internal energy sensations, sounds, and vibrations— are associated with this state.

A positive reaction to the energy changes within you will assist you in taking advantage of every opportunity to explore beyond your physical body and experience the ultimate adventure. Recognition of and response to the various trance phenomena are important steps in preparation. The following list will help you recognize the internal sensations and sounds associated with trance states.

COMMON TRANCE PHENOMENA

- Heaviness or a sinking feeling
- Slowing of breathing
- Distortion of time
- Disassociation from the body
- Unusual tingling or energy sensations
- Kundalini energy experiences
- Voices, laughter, or your name being called out
- Buzzing, humming, or roaring sounds
- Numbness or paralysis in any part of your body
- Weightlessness or spreading lightness
- Any internal vibrations out of the norm
- An electrical-like sense of energy
- Coolness or heat
- Arms or legs floating

- A surge of energy flowing through your body
- Strange noises: wind, engine, music, bells, etc.

The way we respond to trance, vibrational, and Kundalini phenomena will often determine how effectively we are able to explore inward and open ourselves to a spiritual experience. The following provides the basic guidelines for responding to these phenomena.

HOW TO RESPOND TO THE TRANCE STATE

1. Remain calm. Energy phenomena in any form or manifestation—heaviness, floating, vibrations, sounds, numbness, catalepsy, etc.—are a normal and positive experience.
2. Allow and encourage any unusual feelings such as numbness or vibration to spread throughout your entire body. Remember not to move or think about your physical body. Physical movement will often shut down the trance process.
3. Completely surrender to the heaviness, vibrations, and/or sounds. Allow the energy phenomena to expand and envelop you. Don't analyze or judge the experience; simply allow it to spread through every level of your being.
4. When you feel a sense of separation from the body— such as floating, sinking, or spinning—visualize yourself, your awareness, moving away from your physical body. This visualization can be enhanced by a repeated affirmation: "Now I float upward!"; "Now I move to the door!"; and so on—any location away from your body. After weightlessness or separation is obtained, the vibrations will immediately diminish. At this point it's important to focus and maintain your complete attention *away* from your physical body.

5. Mentally focus and demand to experience your spiritual essence: "Now I experience my spiritual self!" Use terms that clearly denote your true spiritual or higher self. Be completely open to experiencing the result of your request.

During this process it is common to experience a sense of rapid inner or upward motion, often accompanied by a feeling of intense movement through layers of light and energy. Remain calm and enjoy the sensations and motion. The path to the soul is the inner-dimensional path within each of us. In reality, an authentic spiritual experience is an amazing journey of consciousness. The motion that we perceive is often our conscious awareness moving inward toward the core of our multidimensional existence.

Our knowledge of and positive response to trance states provide one of the primary keys to initiating an out-of-body adventure. During the early years of my OBEs, I was often startled and sometimes even scared by the intensity of the trance and vibrational phenomena. As I look back I realize that I learned the hard way. During the early '70s there was little information available on this subject, and what written material there was scarcely mentioned the topic.

After repeatedly experiencing heaviness, vibrations, and buzzing sounds during meditation, sleep, and dreams and when practicing out-of-body techniques, I began to realize that these events are a natural prelude to a spiritual experience. The unusual vibrations and sounds were some of the best early indicators that I was ready to explore beyond my physical limits. After several experiences I started to enjoy the vibrations and even began to look forward to them. In retrospect I realize that my positive attitude and my positive response toward the trance phenomena had a major impact on my ability to have an out-of-body experience. They effectively opened the door to the ethereal realms within myself. As my anxiety concerning the energies and sounds slowly turned to anticipation, my personal ability to explore increased substantially. Eventually I got to the point where the various trance phenomena were welcome friends that heralded the beginning of an exciting adventure.

I began to recognize different energies and sounds during deep relaxation, meditation, sleep, and dreams. The intensity of the phenomena varied. Sometimes they were subtle; at other times, overpowering. I also found that when I experienced a mild trancelike state, I could surrender to the experience and allow it to expand throughout my entire being. For example, on one occasion I woke in the middle of the night with a slight vibration at the back of my head. I closed my eyes, completely relaxed, and enjoyed the sensation. I surrendered to the trance state and allowed it to spread from the back of my head throughout my entire body. Slowly a feeling of numbness and paralysis seemed to spread down my spine and then outward, enveloping my trunk and limbs. After what seemed like several minutes, the paralysis enveloped my entire physical body and I directed myself away from my body. Within seconds I was standing outside of my body and ready to explore.

This process is completely natural and extremely enjoyable once we get accustomed to it. In addition, our new understanding and reaction to the various trance states give us an expanded ability. We can now take advantage of every possible opportunity to explore beyond our physical limits. Always keep in mind that the sensations and sounds of the trance state are an important reference point that can go a long way toward enhancing our abilities to have a profound out-of-body experience.

The key to responding to trance-state phenomena is to stay calm and focused on your spiritual intention. Then mentally direct yourself to move beyond your physical limits and demand to have an authentic spiritual experience.

VIBRATIONAL-STATE PHENOMENA

The vibrational state is generally identified with any phenomena that occur immediately before an out-of-body experience. These include vibrations, strange energy sensations and surges, sounds, and paralysis. This state is commonly reported to begin at the head, neck, and stomach areas and then spread to envelop the entire body. The vibrations are often accompanied by numbness, paralysis, and noises such as a buzzing, humming, voices, or a roaring sound. The intensity and duration of these phenomena varies tremendously. It should be noted that the vibrational state energies are often reported during Kundalini experiences and trance states of consciousness. In fact, the lines between the three often blur beyond recognition.

*I was teetering on the edge of sleep, very relaxed, and very awake. Then it hit me: I was enveloped by the vibration that precedes full paralysis. This time I paid really close attention to what it felt like. This is something that distinctly emanated from deep within my body, especially from inside my head or neck, and spread everywhere, and not just along the surface. For lack of a better term, it feels more vibratory than tingly. The vibration starts at an even, constant level, and then seems to distinctly flow from one part of the body to the other. Both feelings, while different, are euphoric in nature. While I had the experience, I could hear everything that was happening around me. —*Lazlo V., Tecumseh, Michigan

Some 82 percent of the survey participants reported floating, sinking, or spinning as an immediate prelude to their out-of-body experience. In addition, 54 percent stated that they felt vibrations or high-energy sensations in their body during the early stages of their experience. And 85 percent also reported strange sounds such as buzzing, humming, or roaring.

As you enter into deep states of relaxation, meditation, sleep, dreaming, or trance, it's helpful to notice any internal changes you may experience. Pay close attention to any unusual vibratory feelings or sounds, even if they are subtle. Many people routinely experience vibratory sensations and sounds but disregard them as dream related or as unexplained physical phenomena.

Your recognition of and response to these sensations and sounds will, many times, determine how successful your exploration becomes. Be aware that it is common for people to be so startled by the sensations and sounds that they focus their attention to their physical body. This creates an instant return to the beta state.

THE KUNDALINI EXPERIENCE

There are numerous reports of full Kundalini experiences culminating with a transcendental out-of-body state of consciousness. In fact, many people consider this experience to be the ultimate path to enlightenment. The basic premise is to encourage the flow of Kundalini energy up the spine and toward the top of the head—the crown chakra—thus projecting your awareness into the higher heavenly dimensions of the universe. It should be noted that this process is almost identical to that of the "Higher-Self Technique" I describe in chapter 4, "Transformational Experiences," and which I often speak of. The result is an indescribable expansion of consciousness into spiritual realms beyond form and thought.

The author Hiroshi Motoyama is considered one of the leading experts on self-initiated Kundalini experiences. He began practicing yoga at a young age and reports in his fascinating book *Theories of the Chakras* that his first Kundalini experience occurred at the age of twenty-five. His experiences began as energy movement: "An incredible power rushed through my spine to the top of my head . . . I felt as if my head would explode with energy."[1]

As Motoyama's Kundalini experiences continued to blossom, he wrote a detailed description of his adventures.

As the Kundalini rose from my heart to the top of my head, it became shining white. It left my body through the top of my head and I rose with it to a much higher dimension . . . Since then I have been able to do psychic healing . . . my psychological state also underwent some profound changes with this awakening. Notably, I developed an attitude of non-attachment to worldly things.[2]

Motoyama also reports the following Kundalini experience. The connection between Kundalini and out-of-body experiences is clear.

A shining light began to enter and leave my body through the top of my head and I felt as if the top of my head protruded ten to twenty centimeters. In the astral, but not the physical dimension, I saw what looked like the head of Buddha, shimmering purple and blue. Gradually, I lost the sensation of my body, but I held a clear awareness of consciousness, of super consciousness, . . . I could see my spiritual self gradually rise higher and leave my body through the top of my head to be restored in heaven. I descended through the same path, and returned to my body through the gate at the top of my head. I consciously had to permeate my whole body with spiritual energy, because it was rigid and my extremities were paralyzed. Finally, I was able to move my hands and feet a little, and the normal sensation gradually returned.[3]

On the basis of my own experiences and the reports of hundreds of people, I have concluded that there exists an inseparable connection between the vibrational-state phenomena and the Kundalini experience. It is apparent that the central elements in both experiences are chakra related. When our chakras are activated, a massive surge of nonphysical energy flows into our subtle body, creating the ideal conditions for dramatic shifts of consciousness. As the worldwide evolution of consciousness continues to accelerate, this kind of powerful spiritual experience will become increasingly prevalent.

THE ADDICTION TO MATTER

To experience our spiritual essence, it is essential that we break free from the chains of matter that hinder our progress. Many people have become addicted to three-dimensional form, substance, and the intensity and drama of physical life. They have identified themselves with their body to such an extent that they are psychologically attached to its form. The addiction to form and emotion is one of humanity's greatest obstacles to spiritual development and one of the primary energies fueling the reincarnation process.

When my aunt passed away, we drove back home to attend the funeral services. We had lived two doors away from my aunt and uncle while I was growing up, and our two families were very close. Being a heavy smoker most of her seventy-three years, my aunt died from a lengthy bout of emphysema. My uncle had been taking care of her for several years and took her passing very hard.

Later, while on vacation, I was in bed early in the morning halfway between sleep and wakefulness when I had an out-of-body experience. I was suddenly in my uncle's living room with him, spending some time helping him through his grief. My aunt appeared in the room. She was dark haired and thinner than I remembered. A healthy color was in her cheeks, and she seemed to be content. Testing my vision, I asked my uncle if he noticed anything different in the room. (I didn't want to alarm him with what I saw.) He had no clue that she was there. Although my aunt did not speak, I knew she was there to stay by my uncle's side. She wore a pastel housecoat over a white nightgown, and the housecoat changed colors from pink to lavender to blue. I noticed a box in her pocket, and I asked her what it was. She pulled out a pack of cigarettes—as I had suspected it was—and gave me a devilish grin. It was a red pack of Pall Malls. I asked her if she really intended to smoke them, and her one verbal reply was yes. I was amazed that after such a distressing illness she would still crave cigarettes. —LINDA L., WOODLAND, MARYLAND

Linda's experience illustrates her aunt's attachment to her previous life, and her addiction to cigarettes. All of these circumstances bind her aunt to the physical-like realities of the astral plane. The lower or denser vibratory regions of the astral plane are similar to an energy duplicate of the physical. If you are physically addicted to any substance such as food, alcohol, or drugs, this addiction will continue to manifest itself even after you have died. This is especially true for addictions that are psychologically based, for they are created and maintained by our mind. Such addictions include attachments to people, places, money, lifestyle, social status, and power.

BREAKING OUR ADDICTION TO FORM

Everything seen and unseen is a form of energy, and there is no escaping the subtle energy creations of our own mind. We must conquer our personal addictions and attachments, for these are the anchors that hold us to the density of form and matter. One of the great benefits of self-initiated spiritual exploration is our expanded ability to resolve blocks and attachments by experiencing and confronting their subtle unseen source.

In order to break our addiction to form, the following may be helpful.

- The soul possesses no form or substance of any kind. In fact, we are not even humanoid; we are pure consciousness—spiritual beings without form or substance.
- All form is temporary. The human form that we identify with is only a temporary vehicle and expression of consciousness. All energy forms and bodies—both physical and nonphysical—are tools of consciousness.
- Many humans have become addicted to their body and all the sensations and emotions associated with it.
- The human attraction and obsession with form and emotion is one the primary causes for reincarnation.

OUR SPIRITUAL GOAL

Our great spiritual task is to awaken to and consiously experience our spiritual essence beyond the dense limits of the body. Self-initiated out-of-body exploration provides a direct and powerful method for doing this. From this moment on, empower yourself to be open to personal spiritual experiences. Create a new mind-set that focuses on your spiritual intention and experience. Become a full-time spiritual explorer. This attitude is the essential step toward a profound experience. Let us begin.

1. Hiroshi Motoyama, *Theories of the Chakras* (Pasadena, CA: Theosophical Publishing House, 1989), 241.
2. Ibid., 253–54.
3. Ibid., 254.

10

The Art and Practice
of Out-of-Body Exploration

*Self-initiated out-of-body experience is the cutting
edge of human exploration.*

WILLIAM BUHLMAN

This chapter will introduce you to the wide variety of current-ly practiced methods for initiating out-of-body exploration. Many of the techniques described here are self-explanatory, while others may require some additional study.

Spiritual exploration is a highly creative process where we select and customize our approach to fit our abilities and lifestyle. For example, some people can visualize well while others cannot. If your visualization abilities are poor, focus on other approaches such as the motion or tactile methods. Many people who currently pursue the path of out-of-body explo-ration do so as the direct result of a spontaneous out-of-body experience they had while meditating. They realized the impor-tance of the event and decided to learn more about this elusive subject. Today many are wisely incorporating their knowledge of out-of-body exploration into their other spiritual practices.

PREPARATION

The ideal way to prepare for having an out-of-body experience is to create a designated exploration area similar to a meditaton area. (Actually, any room other than the bedroom will do; we are conditioned from birth to sleep in our beds, and here we desire a different experience.) I am often asked about my personal preparation. For over twenty-eight years I have followed the same basic pattern. Generally between eleven in the morning and one in the afternoon I lie down on my living-room sofa. I turn the phones off, relax completely, and read about out-of-body experiences or a related subject until I feel sleepy. Then I begin a technique of some kind. Often I use silent affirmations combined with specially designed brain-synchronization music.

While doing a technique, focus on your intention. Really get into it: Feel or sense it, see it, absolutely enjoy it. It's extremely important to hold this image or feeling as your last consciousness thought as your body drifts to sleep. Don't make the common mistake of mentally exhausting yourself by starting your technique too soon. Five minutes of focused imagery and intention as you drift to sleep are far more effective than an hour of vague visualization.

EXPERIMENTATION AND PRACTICE

I would recommend experimenting with several techniques until you find one that fits you. Then proceed with your chosen method for at least thirty days. Daily repetition is extremely important, because it helps to condition the mind to open and accept the reality of fully conscious out-of-body exploration.

During one of my workshops in California a young man who is an avid surfer told me that he initiates out-of-body experiences as he drifts off to sleep by imagining himself surfing a perfect wave at his favorite location. He told me that he enjoyed his personal OBE technique so much that it was easy for him to hold his surfing image as his last conscious thought and thereby initiate regular out-of-body adventures.

Today there are an extensive variety of out-of-body exploration techniques available. I believe that a focused mind-set, our intention, and perseverance are more important than the technical correctness of the method we select. The very act of inner exploration is a highly creative process that transcends all attempts to establish rules and procedures. For example, there are many different variations of what I call the inner-motion method (see the "Inner-Motion Techniques" section starting on the next page). The most effective method for you will likely be the one you feel most comfortable with. We do not have to be experts in subtle energy movement and metaphysical principles in order to have an out-of-body experience. I know people who have had profound out-of-body adventures without ever having studied the mechanics of the process.

ENJOYING THE PROCESS

Ideally, take your time and select a technique that you will really enjoy. Out-of-body exploration is as fun and exciting as you make it. The mind-set of total immersion applies to all the methods presented here. Out-of-body experiences arise from the natural process of consciousness exploring our multidimensional nature. Conscious out-of-body adventures represent a universal journey of awakening. Open your mind to your unlimited ability to experience your true spiritual self and allow your consciousness to fly.

Inner spiritual exploration is a natural process; we are simply experiencing our inherent abilities to explore beyond our physical limits. Enjoy the techniques; each method is an adventure in and of itself. Don't allow yourself to get hung up on results, because this can create a psychological block. In many ways the best mind-set is to view out-of-body exploration as a daily meditation session. The very act offers its own rewards: You are more relaxed, rested, and at peace with yourself. As much as possible, be open to the unlimited spiritual potential that out-of-body exploration offers. Many of the following methods are simple, so the descriptions are brief.

INNER-MOTION TECHNIQUES

When we use out-of-body techniques we are stimulating our subtle spiritual body and energy centers into action. Each thought and image has an impact on our inner energy form. However, a deliberately focused image of inner motion initiates our energy body to move or expand from its normal stable position. This inner motion initiates the onset of the vibrational state, which often leads to separation from the body. The successful use of motion techniques lies in our ability to visualize and feel the motion as we drift to sleep.

We can loosen and then free our subtle energy body by creating a form of imaginary motion as we drift to sleep. Basically, any form of continuous inner motion can begin to activate and loosen our subtle energy or etheric body—the more intense and realistic the motion, the better. All of the following techniques require that you focus your undivided attention on your intention and the sensations of motion as you drift off. Hold this image and feeling of motion as your last conscious thought. As you "fall to sleep," amplify the sense and feeling of motion in your mind's eye. Each of us resonates with a different form of imagery. In this chapter you will find a wide selection of simple and easy approaches.

Climbing

An ideal method for those who have difficulty with visualization is to focus your entire being on the physicallike sensations of climbing a rope or ladder hand over hand. If possible, actually climb up a physical ladder and memorize the sensations that you experience. There are several variations on this method. During my workshops I often pass around several lengths of heavy rope before we begin the technique so that everyone can memorize the physical sensation of the rope. Then we proceed to do the technique. As in all methods, it is important to maintain the sensation of motion as your last conscious thought. I have received several letters confirming that this method is particularly effective for the visually impaired.

Climbing Technique

Take several deep breaths and allow your eyes to close. Relax your body, starting with your toes. Stretch your feet and toes and then release completely. Feel the relaxation move up your legs. Tense your calf muscles for a moment and release. Keep breathing with full breaths. Tense your thigh muscles and then relax completely. Feel your body becoming loose and comfortable. Feel the warmth of your relaxation move up to your hips and pelvic area. Clench your stomach muscles and release. Take a deep breath and slowly blow it out. Loosen your torso and stretch your arms from your shoulders to the end of your fingers. Wiggle your fingers; clench your fists and release. Remember to maintain deep, comfortable breathing. Surrender to the relaxation. Move your head from side to side and let it fall to a natural and comfortable position.

Take another breath and clearly picture a thick rope hanging down from the ceiling and descending to just above your chest. In your mind picture this rope—a white, silky rope. You want to reach up and touch the rope. Feel the satiny texture with one hand. Move your hand gently up and down the rope. Notice the feel of each individual thread. Now place your other hand on the rope, and gently pull. Feel the tension as you pull. The rope will easily hold your weight. With both hands around the rope, slowly begin to pull yourself up. You can feel yourself begin to lift off the ground with ease. As you feel your ethereal upper body move smoothly and slowly upward, you move your bottom hand up and above your other hand. You are pulling yourself up hand over hand. Your hips are lifting from the ground. You are weightless. As you move hand over hand, your awareness is now separating from all form and limits. As you move higher, your feet have just lifted from the ground. As you pull yourself higher and higher, your feet are now completely in the air. You are comfortably moving up the rope into beautiful, fluffy clouds. Moving hand over hand, you are weightless as you rise toward the soft clouds.

Continue to effortlessly pull your weightless body up through the clouds into a beautiful blue sky. As you move hand over hand up to the sky, you feel lighter and lighter and you begin to float. You no longer need to touch the rope. It begins to fade away, and you gently release the rope with each hand. You are free to float upward and away from all physical limitations.

I started using the rope-climbing technique because I own a sailboat and the feel of rope is very real to me. I don't picture scenes or objects well, so I find this to be the most effective way to lift up and out of my body. Sometimes I feel a weird sensation of falling or sinking. Now I know that this is an indication that I'm out or about to separate from my body.
—BENNIE M., ANNAPOLIS, MARYLAND

Floating/Balloon

There are several variations of the floating/balloon technique. You can imagine yourself in a hot-air balloon gently rising up and drifting along the air currents. Or you can picture your body as a balloon filling with helium. Sense and feel that your entire body is expanding and becoming lighter and lighter. Vividly feel your awareness rising slowly into the air as you allow your body to drift off to sleep. Any sustained image of floating upward can be effective.

On our twentieth anniversary my husband and I took a hot-air balloon ride. It was such an exhilarating experience that I often use the memory as a method to initiate out-of-body experiences. I picture every aspect of the balloon flight. I feel myself climbing into the basket, casting off the lines, and floating upward higher and higher. It's a wonderful feeling of freedom. —F. G., FLINT, MICHIGAN

Rocking

Visualize that you are sitting in a favorite rocking chair, gently rocking back and forth. Hold this rocking motion as your last conscious thought and sensation as you drift off to sleep.

I woke in the morning and drifted back to light sleep. In my mind I could feel my body rocking to and fro, and a strange tingling sensation filled me. The tingling sensation was extremely pleasant, and I persisted rocking in my mind. At some point I became aware that I could "see" in the room and tried to pull away from my body. I don't know why I felt that I could escape from my body, but it seemed logical at the time. I felt as if I was stuck to myself, and it took a great deal of energy to pull away. Eventually I was free of my body and turned to see my "real" body still in bed. The thought of my awareness of not being in my body was terrifying, and I thought I might have died. My fear slammed me back into my body as I tried to call to my husband, who was in the house getting ready for work. My body felt like it was out of sync with itself and seemed to be vibrating out of control, which increased my fear. It felt like I was riding in the back of a pickup truck on one of those washboard dirt roads. Finally I awoke. I no longer felt any of the fear. And that began my search for more information on OBEs. —JUNE L., ATLANTA, GEORGIA

Rolling

Rolling is an easy method that can be done in various ways. One well-known approach is to imagine and feel that you are floating peacefully in a beautiful, calm lake. Completely relax, and enjoy the sensations of floating free. At first enjoy the floating sensations; then slowly feel that you are rolling gently back and forth. Any focused imagery that involves rolling can be effective. This is an excellent method for initiating separation from the body whenever you are experiencing the vibrational state. I often recommend this procedure to those who experience the odd sensation of being stuck or somehow inhibited during separation.

I've had only one out-of-body experience, and it was semi-spontaneous. I was reading a book on OBEs, and was visualizing myself rolling over in my body, when the mailman interrupt-

ed me. That night I awoke to the same experience I had been visualizing. My thoughts were something like "Oh shit!" as I began to roll 180 degrees and then I floated up to the ceiling. Startled, I tried to go back to my body and did, but I went too far, down to the floor, while my head and feet were in the proper position. I heard that you should try to move your physical finger as a method of getting "back in." I did that, and it worked like a charm. —Nick B., Jersey City, New Jersey

Rotating

While lying down and completely relaxing, imagine that you are becoming lighter and lighter and then slowly rising. Then imagine that you are beginning to slowly rotate at your stomach axis. Vividly feel yourself becoming weightless and turning above your physical body. Hold this as your last conscious thought as you fall asleep.

When I was a teenager, I frequently had those experiences of being lifted from my body, and I playfully practiced rotating around my axis. Sometimes I was being pulled with a lot of force and speed from my feet. Before I really started floating I would hear a lot of voices, as if ten radios were blasting at a high volume with all kinds of different people talking. One time when I was in the middle of being lifted and feeling and hearing vibrations, I looked down at my chest—in my sleep— and saw a very bright white light coming from under my sheets. —Paula T., Asheville, North Carolina

All of my OBEs began when I was resting in bed but not sleeping. They all began with a sense of heaviness, which progressed into a rapid spin. At a high rate of spinning, I am released from my body, and can float or fly at will. I can usually move freely about my house, have occasionally elected to leave my house, and have even flown away several miles. —D. C., Casper, Wyoming

Swinging

Clearly picture yourself as a child again, playing on a swing as you move back and forth. Feel all the sensations of motion as you kick your feet and go higher and higher. Enjoy the feeling of swinging, and allow yourself to go even higher as you drift off.

The first out-of-body experiences that come to my mind are from my childhood. When I was around ten years old, I liked to "swing," as I called it. I was lying on a couch, and although I was motionless, I could feel as if I were swinging. It was as if the couch were hung on ropes, like some seats in gardens.
—DOUG S., MERIDIAN, MISSISSIPPI

Whirlpool/Whirlwind

The whirlpool/whirlwind technique was frequently used by a French author, who wrote under the pen name Yram, to initiate his out-of-body experiences. Imagine a vortex of water or wind, and feel this motion rising from the area of your chest or brow. Feel your entire self-awareness in the vortex, moving slowly around. Sense and feel the whirlwind moving your awareness up and away from your body.

I am fascinated by natural weather events, so once when I was starting to meditate I pictured myself inside a tornado. It started small, but by the time I was fully into it, I was twirling inside a huge twister. I felt myself being pulled upward so fast, I felt like I couldn't breathe. I asked for clear breathing and I moved farther upward. —PETE F., NASHVILLE, TENNESSEE

Elevator

Visualize yourself inside an elevator and vividly feel that you are moving upward or downward. To enhance this effect, imagine the numbers of the various floors changing as you move. As much as possible, hold this image and sensation of motion as your last conscious thought as you drift to sleep.

Elevator Technique

You are relaxed and ready to accept new ideas and thoughts. You feel open and free, fully protected from any outside influence. As you lie in total relaxation and comfort, your mind is clear and free from worry. You are totally focused on your breathing and relaxation.

As you relax, think of a tall building with a large lobby. You step inside and cross the lobby, moving toward the elevator. Select an elevator, and see the door slowly open. Take your time and enter, then press the button marked for the twentieth floor. As you lean against the cool wall of the elevator you watch the floor numbers climb as you move higher and higher. The light shows the first floor and then the second. You feel the elevator moving slowly but steadily higher and higher—to the third floor, then the fourth. You are now moving more quickly to the fifth, sixth, and then the seventh floor. You can feel the movement and watch the numbers rise as you go higher and higher. You clearly see the eighth and then the ninth floor. The motion is steady as you feel the elevator moving higher and higher.

You pass the tenth floor and then the eleventh. The twelfth and thirteenth are now below you as the elevator moves with constant speed toward the higher floors. The numbers show you've passed the fourteenth floor and are moving toward the fifteenth, then the sixteenth. You are higher than before; the motion is comforting and secure. The floor below you is getting softer as you approach the seventeenth and then the eighteenth floor. You begin to feel as though you are floating to the nineteenth floor. Your feet are off the ground now as you reach the twentieth floor and the door slowly opens to a warm, inviting sensation of floating free.

Floating

Imagine yourself floating in a body of relaxing, warm water. Then visualize that the water level is rising and you are moving upward. There are many variations of this method, including floating in a large cylinder pool or the ocean.

Floating Technique

It is a warm, beautiful day, and you can clearly see a small pond before you. It is clean and clear, fed by a bubbling spring. You walk closer and see that there is a soft sandy bottom. Stick your toes in and feel how warm and bubbling the water feels. It swirls around your ankles, and you step in and the water is as high as your waist. The water feels clean and clear as the warmth swirls around your legs and hips.

You know that you can lie back and the water will hold you like a soft, comfortable mattress. As your back lowers into the water, your legs float to the surface. You can feel the warmth and comfort; you can now feel yourself floating in the water . . . Your body is surrounded by the warm, relaxing water. Your head is comfortably pillowed in the soft, lapping water . . . You are weightless as the soothing water holds you steadily on the surface. You spread your arms, knowing that you are completely safe and protected . . . The warmth of the sun is keeping you comfortable.

You actually feel lighter and lighter until you feel weightless . . . The water cushions you, and you can barely feel it anymore. Your arms and legs are so light that they are barely there. Your torso has become weightless. You can't even feel your body . . . You can hear the gentle movement of the water, but you can no longer hear anything else . . . You feel the floating motion from within . . . The gentle rocking spreads throughout you and you are weightless . . . You begin to float above the water, from the very center of your being. You are slowly moving upward into the blue sky above you . . . You are absolutely weightless as you rise higher and higher into the warm and inviting sky . . . You are safe and protected, moving higher and higher to the heavens.

Bouncing

As you relax, imagine that your awareness is taking the shape of a ball. Simply imagine that you are bouncing like a ball as you fall to sleep.

During one of my OBEs I was bouncing like a basketball and jumping up and down. At first it was very interesting and the view of the physical things and environment was exciting. As I jumped higher and higher I could see more and more of the surrounding neighborhood—sidewalks, streets, trees, houses, and so on. But then as the altitude became higher, several hundred feet above the earth, I became afraid of the height. One thing I do remember is that I could not control the jumping elevation. With each bounce I went higher and higher beyond belief. —LINCOLN G., BECKLEY, WEST VIRGINIA

Exercising

If you enjoy exercising, the visualization of sit-ups or leg lifts may be ideal for you. As you drift to sleep, imagine your upper body sitting up and out of your body. Repeat this as you fall to sleep.

Extreme-Motion Methods

In your mind's eye, clearly see and feel yourself enjoying the sensations of skiing or snowboarding down a mountain. Allow yourself to enjoy your favorite location. Imagine the beautiful surroundings: the snow-covered mountains, the ski lift, the lodge. Become immersed in this picture and feel the cool enjoyment of a perfect day on the slopes. As your body drifts to sleep, feel that you are moving rapidly down an extreme slope through perfect powder.

Any visualized form of continuous, intense inner motion can be effective. Feel free to experiment and create your own method. Other variations include any form of flying, falling, or skydiving, as well as any form of rapid or high-speed motion such as running or biking, motorboating, motorcycling, jet-skiing, diving, water-skiing, or going down water slides.

MEDITATIVE PRACTICES

I often meet people at my lectures and workshops who tell me they have incorporated out-of-body techniques into their daily practice of meditation and yoga. They recognize that OBEs provide a powerful opportunity to experience a profound spiritual adventure.

My intention in this section is to provide an effective but brief overview of the various meditative practices used around the world. Some of them are not thought to be directly related to out-of-body exploration. For example, many view the various forms of yoga, meditation, and breath work as being distinctly different spiritual practices. Yet experience teaches us that they share many elements. When we examine them closely, we discover that all of them share a commonality of inner shifts of consciousness. They all guide us to experience altered states of consciousness that lead in the final analysis to a transcendence of awareness beyond the body. Out-of-body states of consciousness are a universal spiritual experience. That is why this information is relevant to all of us on our spiritual path.

The connection between meditation and out-of-body experiences is ancient. It is not uncommon for out-of-body experiences to spontaneously occur during deep meditation. In the OBE survey conducted by Twemlow, Gabbard, and Jones, 27 percent of the 339 participants reported that they had been meditating immediately before their experience.[1] I have received many letters from people that detail a meditative state of mind immediately before their out-of-body adventure. In fact, this is so often the case that I often recommend using meditation as a preliminary relaxing and conditioning procedure before beginning an out-of-body technique. It is an effective method for creating the ideal state of consciousness for out-of-body exploration—the body asleep and the mind awake. After you are completely relaxed and in the meditative "zone," begin your out-of-body exploration method.

THE VIBRATIONAL STATE AND MEDITATION

It is important that those practicing meditation and yoga learn how to recognize and respond to the vibrational-state phenomena that are so often the prelude to an out-of-body experience. Different elements of the vibrational state such as floating, sinking, spinning, and high-energy sensations are often reported during deep meditation and yoga. The manifestation of any vibrational-state phenomena is a clear indication that an out-of-body experience is imminent. Unfortunately, this important topic is often glossed over or ignored completely by some yoga instructors and authors. Some assume that out-of-body experiences are simply a psychic development or power of the mind. As such they are considered a side step in our spiritual development and to be avoided. This narrow view of out-of-body experiences is not only inaccurate but also extremely detrimental to the ultimate goal of self- and God realization.

I strongly believe that the practitioners of meditation and yoga would be wise to learn about the benefits and purpose of vibrational energies and out-of-body states of consciousness before they dismiss those subjects as simple disruptions. Lack of knowledge concerning these powerful energy phenomena and the resulting transcendence from the body can only slow the progress of the spiritual seeker. It is vital that we recognize that out-of-body experiences are a natural and direct path to the ultimate goal we all seek.

I have experienced numerous OBEs since I started meditating just over a year ago when I was seventeen. The most vivid memory is that of visiting my best friend in his sleep, or perhaps running into him somewhere out there . . . But we were in a familiar place, and the more I think about it, the more it seems that I went to see him. We talked for some time, planning the next time we would see each other, talked about his family, our friends, and so on. At first, when I came out of meditation, I thought I had dozed off and had had a dream. The phone rang, and it was him. He started telling me about his "dream," and when he started to quote the "me," I interrupted and said the exact thing he was about to say. I don't know how long we sat there in silence, but it seemed like at least five minutes. We talked about it, making sure it was no coincidence. It wasn't. Everything we remembered was the same. —G. C., VIA E-MAIL

Many yogi masters have stated that they experienced profound out-of-body journeys while practicing yoga. In the higher initiations of yoga the ultimate goal is to experience a mystical spiritual union with God by essentially withdrawing from the physical senses. This very process of withdrawing from the senses is a natural prelude to out-of-body adventures. In fact, one of the more famous systems of yoga, well known for stimulating profound out-of-body journeys, is Kundalini yoga.

Today, many yoga instructors understand and appreciate the integral connections between meditation, yoga, and OBEs. They are well aware that deep states of meditation can lead to profound out-of-body states of consciousness. Some masters and instructors of yoga openly embrace OBEs as an important step toward spiritual enlightenment.

It is important to recognize that the ultimate goals of yoga, meditation, and self-initiated out-of-body explorations are the same. All three offer an effective method for exploring and experiencing our spiritual essence. All three are time-proven methods of experiencing self- and God realization. As we evolve spiritually, this important connection will come to be embraced and openly encouraged by the modern masters of yoga and meditation. In the future we will see that out-of-body techniques and the higher-self method will be actively taught in advanced systems of yoga and meditation.

From 1995 to 1998, I was practicing Kundalini yoga. On several occasions I experienced a wave of heat and energy flowing

up my spinal column. It was extremely intense and wonderful at the same time. Many times I felt the energy sensations that you describe, and on three different occasions I experienced myself float up and out of my body. It was incredible.
—JOHN D., CHICAGO, ILLINOIS

Chanting and Mantras

The ancient methods of chanting and mantras are used worldwide to focus and clear the mind and raise the internal vibratory rate. Numerous religions and sects are well known for chanting the holy name of God. Throughout history many different cultures have developed individual styles of chants and mantras. Chanting is an integral part of spiritual ceremonies throughout the world. In the West these chants date back twelve hundred years to the Christian church of the Roman Empire. Good examples are the hauntingly beautiful Gregorian chants created by French monks. One of the more popular chants used today is the *om* sound. It is believed by many to create a profound vibration that helps us initiate expanded states of awareness. Repetition of the sound is thought to clear the mind and raise the vibratory rate, helping to initiate various altered states of consciousness and out-of-body experiences. In the modern out-of-body exploration method you imagine yourself actually becoming the *om* sound as it rises up and away from you. As much as possible, you become one with the sound as your body drifts off. This technique is especially effective and enjoyable when combined with the latest in psychoacoustic sound technology and quality headphones.

I have been going out of body since 1998 and have had about forty or so OBEs to date. They usually occur after I wake up early in the morning; I chant briefly and pull in energy.
—LILA M., BUTTE, MONTANA

Breath Control

There are different forms of breath control and deep-breathing techniques used to stimulate expanded states of consciousness. The term commonly used for the energy created by the use of these techniques is *prana energy, prana* being the Sanskrit word meaning "primal." The phrase is sometimes interpreted to mean "breath" or "vital force." The knowledge of this essential energy dates back to India's oldest and most revered spiritual texts, the Upanishads.

The control of our breath cycles is believed by many to be highly effective in initiating altered states of consciousness and out-of-body experiences. In the last twenty years, the work of Dr. Stanislav Grof has largely been responsible for reintroducing the many benefits of deep breath work to the West. Today's breath-control methods are practiced under many different names such as *connective breathing, circular breathing,* and *yogic* or *cross breathing*.

Several people have described to me spontaneous out-of-body experiences that occurred during an intense breathwork session. This is a powerful method for inducing altered states of consciousness and out-of-body exploration; however, it is not for everyone. I would recommend learning this process from an expert in the field, because it is not unusual for subconscious issues and even hidden traumas to surface. It is advisable to undergo this process with a trained breathing coach at your side.

If this method appeals to you, I suggest exploring the various approaches in detail. The last decade has seen the creation of some innovative programs that help direct you through an extensive series of breath sessions. These training programs are available online at various Web sites and via the rapidly expanding MP3 technology. The innate potential of directed breath work makes its exploration well worth your time and energy.

VISUALIZATION TECHNIQUES

The technique of creating an energy body, or duplicate, is believed to have originated in England over one hundred years ago. Using this method, you essentially create a subtle energy duplicate of yourself and then transfer your awareness into the manifested form. The created image is often a duplicate of the person's body, but it can also be a cloud or any shape or form you choose. There are many variations of this technique. Two such variations, which I call the Mirror Technique and the Rising-Steam Technique, require good visualization and concentration skills. I describe the Mirror Technique in my previous book, *Adventures Beyond the Body*. A brief description of the Rising-Steam Technique follows.

The Rising-Steam Technique

Imagine steam slowly rising from every pore of your body. See, sense, and feel this steam becoming more and more dense as it rises from your body. With every breath feel the steam slowly forming into a cloud above you. Take your time, and vividly imagine the cloud becoming a floating duplicate of yourself. Now feel yourself becoming one with the cloud. As much as possible, sense and feel that your awareness is transferred into the cloud. Clearly feel yourself floating free. Hold this image as your last conscious thought as your body drifts to sleep.

I had a really strange thing happen when I was sitting in the steam room where I work out. There was no one else in there at that time. After a particularly stressful day, I leaned back and focused on the steam rising from the rocks. Suddenly my body became numb and I heard a loud ringing in my ears. It was like a distant fire alarm. I closed my eyes, thinking, "I really need to relax so the ringing will stop." But instead I felt pulled through my own body and found myself in a corner of the ceiling. Even though I didn't see or feel my body up there, I could sense it. I was part of the steam, inside the warm droplets of moisture. I was so shocked, I immediately snapped back into where I was sitting. I didn't know how to explain this to anyone until I heard about out-of-body experiences on a radio show. That's when I realized that it must have happened to me. —H. L., HARTFORD, CONNECTICUT

ANCIENT TECHNIQUES

Fasting

Since the beginning of time, fasting has been an accepted spiritual practice. It has been used for inner cleansing, raising vibratory rates, and inducing mystical and spiritual states of consciousness. Many of the biblical saints and prophets were known to fast for lengthy periods of time. In the New Testament, Jesus is reported to have fasted for forty days and nights. The basic metaphysical concept behind fasting is that it loosens the connection between our dense physical form and our subtle spiritual bodies, allowing for mystical experiences and the separation of consciousness to occur.

Some people believe that the ideal physical preparation for out-of-body exploration is to fast for at least twenty-four hours before attempting projection. There are those who insist that their success rate increases substantially when they fast. Others believe that juice fasts are just as effective as a total fast. This is another area of personal choice. Keep in mind that your beliefs concerning this and any related topic will definitely influence your experience. In short, if you believe that fasting is essential, then you have made it so. Most people find that moderation is an effective approach. They eat light and avoid caffeine and alcohol. I believe that fasting may provide a benefit, but only you can decide if it can be realistically incorporated into your lifestyle. The question of food intake is part of my latest OBE survey, found in the back of this book, and I welcome your opinion.

Drumming

Drumming may be the oldest and most widely used method for initiating altered states of consciousness, trances, and out-of-body experiences. Almost every culture throughout history is known to have used some form of drumming during its spiritual ceremonies. In a sense, drumming is the first brain-wave synchronizing method. Specific forms of rhythmic drumming are known to create a frequency-following response in the brain, potentially leading the person to experience various altered states of consciousness. For this reason drumming is used during shamanic vision quests. Drumming is a proven and universal method to assist us in shifting our awareness from our physical senses to the inner realms of spirit. In my workshops I use specific drumming sequences to enhance the shamanic-inspired OBE techniques. Be aware that every person responds differently to different beats and rhythms. Through personal experimentation you will discover what is most effective for your journeys.

I am part of a spiritual exploration group that meets about once a month to share techniques and experiences. One month our leader invited a Native American shaman to perform a sacred ceremony for us. It was during the drumming session that I felt myself spinning uncontrollably toward the ceiling. As I looked down, I found myself—my body?—lying on a blanket, like it was in a trance. It was so scary, and I popped back right away. I wanted to sit up and tell everyone what had just happened, but I couldn't move. Was this the vibrational state? —RANDI K., MILWAUKEE, WISCONSIN

Shamanic Techniques

A shaman in the traditional sense is a priest or priestess who functions as an intermediary or conduit between the physical world and the spiritual dimensions. The term *shaman* comes from a Tungus word meaning "between the worlds." In various cultures around the world shamans are known for their ability to self-induce altered and out-of-body states of consciousness. In shamanic cultures various ceremonies and vision quests are used to expand perception beyond the limits of matter. One of the more widely used techniques is to relax and vividly imagine that you are shape-shifting into the image of a powerful bird such as a condor, an eagle, or an owl. This is often done to the backdrop of a rhythmic drumbeat as you let go and imagine that you are actually becoming the bird. As much as possible you become one with the bird and enjoy all the sensations of flying free. You clearly see and feel yourself soaring and gliding on the air currents high above a lush green valley. You can feel the wonderful sensation of pure freedom as you disconnect from the ground far below.

The key to this and all spiritual exploration methods is to really get into it. Completely surrender to the sensations, sights, and sounds of the soaring bird. This is one of my favorite techniques, and I often incorporate it in my workshops.

During the bird technique I experienced myself "flying" along the coast. I saw many homes. I then noticed that my body had changed. I looked and saw that my feet were webbed. My arms were wings . . . and my voice was nothing more than a screeching sound. I was a seagull. I swooped down along the water and felt the water on my feet. I had a "bird's-eye" view of the world. I was totally amazed! But I also knew how wonderful it felt to be a soaring bird. —Joan T., Carmel, California

Sometimes while on long car trips—my husband does all the driving—I have found myself, my awareness, sitting on top of the vehicle. But I usually snap back into myself as soon as I realize what is happening. One time when I found myself on top of the truck, I noticed an eagle flying right over the top of us. As soon as the thought occurred that it would be wonderful to fly with this eagle I was up there with it, looking down on our pickup, watching it moving along the highway. I thought it was so fantastic when I turned to watch the eagle alongside of me that my next thought was to join with the eagle and become one with it, and—wham!—I was instantly inside the eagle, looking through its eyes. The stretched-out wings were now my wings. This continued for a short time, because my next thought was that I had to tell my husband about this. In the next instant I found myself back in the truck, babbling excitedly to my husband about what had just occurred. —Beth Anne V., Yakima, Washington

Medicinal Plants

The topic of medicinal plants is, of course, controversial. I believe it's important to recognize that we often make judgments based on our current cultural ideas instead of objective information. For thousands of years native peoples in South America, North America, and Africa have used plant substances to induce mystical states of consciousness and out-of-body experiences. Some of these plants, such as mescaline and peyote, are well known. In the last decade the growing popularity of shamanism has introduced many people to the uses of plants such as the San Pedro cactus and ayahuasca, the extract of a South American jungle vine. Both contain hallucinogenic substances that are known to induce altered states of consciousness and out-of-body experiences. A number of shamans around the world use these kinds of plants so they can better see and interact with the nonphysical energy field of their patients. Many shamans are capable of shifting their awareness beyond their physical bodies. They use this ability to provide assistance and healing by interacting with and consciously altering the subtle unseen energies that influence the person who is ill.

It is important to recognize that the most important element of medicinal plant use is the clear spiritual intention behind the usage. All of the ceremonies I have attended that incorporated the uses of plants were of a highly spiritual nature. The focus of the group and each individual was on personal and spiritual development. As a result, the experiences were uplifting and positive.

The use of medicinal plants is a personal choice, and I am well aware that this form of inner exploration is becoming more popular. However, keep in mind that the use of any external substance can become a crutch. Because of this, I would like to provide a few insights that may be useful. First, be aware that only natural plant substances are used in authentic spiritual ceremonies. The use of artificial, man-made substances such as LSD is considered dangerous and toxic to the body and the mind. The universal shamanic viewpoint is that the ingested plants are alive and possess consciousness. The plants are considered ancient, wise, and directly connected to nature; as such, they can provide powerful inner teachings beyond the human experience. In a sense there is an inner merging of two separate states of consciousness.

During a trip to Peru, I participated in several sacred ceremonies that involved ayahuasca. About two hours into the ceremony, I felt and heard an inner rumbling like a freight train moving through my body. I saw visions of my past and my possible futures. Then I was suddenly flying like a bird. It was incredible. As I lifted higher and higher, my thoughts were crystal clear. My body was far below me. I felt a sense of motion and was in a new surrounding of radiant colors. Globes of color approached me and spoke to my mind. It was real in every sense of the word. I learned things about myself that are impossible to describe. It was an unforgettable experience. —ART F., GREENVILLE, SOUTH CAROLINA

If you are drawn to the use of medicinal plants in your explorations, it is extremely important to focus on your spiritual intention and goals before and during your journey. Medicinal-plant journeys are powerful and should not be taken lightly. Be prepared, for it's not uncommon for subconscious issues to surface. Immediately before your journey, meditate on your spiritual intention and consider writing down your primary goals. In preparation, I would highly recommend learning to use consciousness focusing and control techniques, such as the "Awareness now!" or "Clarity now!" affirmations, when required. I am also a strong advocate of implementing the higher-self method when the conditions are appropriate. I would also recommend reading the "Keys to Control" section in chapter 7 of *Adventures Beyond the Body*. In short, be as psychologically prepared as possible to have a profound inner journey.

BRAIN-WAVE STATES

Researchers have found that different states of consciousness are related to specific brain-wave states. The frequency—

cycles per second—of our brain waves changes in accordance with our mental state. Keep in mind that some of these states will overlap, depending on the individual.

- Beta state (13+ cycles per second): Concentration, waking active consciousness, spiritual affirmations and intentions
- Alpha state (8–12 cycles per second): daydreaming, meditation, light trance states
- Theta state (5–7 cycles per second): lucid visualization, start of vibrational state, deep trance states, hypnosis, deep meditation
- Delta state (0.5–4 cycles per second): healing, dream conversion and awakening, deep sleep

Beta waves characterize our normal waking consciousness. Our eyes are open; we are mentally focused and are directing our attention to the world around us. Whether we are at our jobs or working on a home project, we are producing beta waves (generally between thirteen and forty cycles per second). These are the most dominant waves in the brain and are associated with physical attentiveness, excitement, focus, and, at higher levels, even distress and fear.

As we slow down our brain-wave activity, we become more relaxed and inwardly focused. This is called the alpha state. This seems to be the brain's neutral or drifting phase, common to healthy, stress-free people. This is the meditative state that many achieve after some practice. Lack of significant alpha activity can be a sign of social or personal stress, disease, or other forms of discomfort.

When we become completely relaxed, and even sleepy, the brain shifts to a slower but more powerful state characterized by theta waves. Theta has been called the "twilight state," occurring between consciousness and sleep. This phase is generally punctuated with unplanned mental images or daydreams. It can be the launching point for out-of-body experiences and mystical states of consciousness. Theta opens the mind to subconscious material, sudden understanding, intuition, and creativity. This state can be esoteric and difficult to maintain. Researchers have difficulty analyzing this state because of the very short period of time people can hold it. Most subjects fall asleep before much data can be gathered.

When we are fully asleep, the dominant brain waves slow to become delta. These are even slower than theta, falling into a frequency range below 4 cycles per second. There is evidence that some people may maintain consciousness while in this state, which appears to be associated with very deep meditative, trance, and other transcendental states of consciousness. Dream conversion and awakening can occur in this state. It is known that while in the delta state our brains trigger a significant discharge of healing growth hormone.

SOUND AND THE SUBTLE ENERGY BODY

Sound has a profound impact on our subtle nonphysical energy body. Many modern forms of music such as rap and hard rock owe their popularity to the fact that they stimulate the lower energy centers of the body and initiate an immediate shift in consciousness. Certain sounds and tones are well known for their ability to move us. A good example is the song "We Will Rock You," by the group Queen. This song is played at practically every major sporting event in America because it effectively stimulates our subtle energy body. Often the reason we like or dislike a song is because of the impact it has on our spiritual energy body. For example, I dislike rap music because the driving bass beat stimulates my lower chakra and invokes uncomfortable sensations such as anxiety. It's wise to be aware of this impact, because music has been used extensively throughout history to manipulate the masses. In the 1930s Hitler used music in his huge political gatherings to stir the emotions of the crowds. Today it is used extensively in movies and advertising to arouse the emotions of the audience. The wild mosh pits seen at modern rock concerts are a living example of the power of music on the lower chakras. Music impacts all of us, so from now on pay close attention to how different songs influence your emotions and state of mind. Become aware of the subtle energy shifts you experience. This awareness will help you recognize the various nonphysical energy currents that flow through your etheric body.

I am seventeen years old, and I have had OBEs since I was about eight or nine. It seemed so easy to do it then, but my guess is that I was so young that my mind was less cluttered. I can still experience them, although now I use different methods. I use . . . music. Before my great-grandmother died, she told me, "Music is a key, a language that can take you to where your heart's desire seeks . . . You'll understand when you're older." And I think I understand now. My best OBE was when I went to a lake and confronted the Phoenix. There was another traveler there who told me that the lake was called K-yun-loa. It was very exciting; I felt every emotion. I could even feel the sensation when I touched the water of the lake, which was very warm. That is why I call myself Phoenix—because it was the greatest experience I have ever had. —PHOENIX, NEWPORT, RHODE ISLAND

Music can also be profoundly uplifting and positively influence our chakras and our entire subtle body. I know several artists and writers who swear by the benefits of music. Many believe that it helps stimulate the creative and healing energy flow within us. Music is also thought to be able to assist us in raising our internal vibratory rate and connecting with our spiritual nature. Music combined with binaural beat technology and other psychoacoustic mind technologies can provide a powerful method of initiating altered states of consciousness and deep relaxation, and can be the ideal prelude to out-of-body exploration.

On many occasions I have initiated an out-of-body adventure while listening to specially designed trance music. It is well documented that hypnotic rhythms and certain modern sound technologies can transport the listener from the beta and even the theta brain-wave state. We are only beginning to explore the potential benefits and applications that are available. In the near future I believe that specially programmed music combined with powerful psychoacoustic mind technologies will be able to initiate specific altered states of consciousness that can lead to out-of-body explorations. These tools for exploration are closer than you may think.

I am a musician, and a lot of my experiences have to do with music. The first major episode was like this: I was sleeping, and singing in my head "I Saw the Light," which is a song we do in my band. Then I heard a voice say, "How about 'I Saw the Soul'?" At that moment an extremely bright light "switched on" in my head, and my entire being was filled with an almost unbearable energy and my head felt like it was going to explode. The energy was too much for me to handle; I felt paralyzed and was finally able to wake up. When I did, my body was vibrating with energy for about two minutes. Needless to say, it really blew me away. —TAYLOR S., REDWOOD FALLS, MINNESOTA

TECHNOLOGICAL INNOVATIONS

In the last two decades, new inner exploration tools have evolved. These electronic devices are reported to assist and even guide us in experiencing brain-wave frequencies and states of consciousness beyond the normal waking beta state. It is claimed that this technology allows us to experience deep meditative states of consciousness without years of training. One of the most popular uses of this rapidly evolving technology is the development of sound and light synthesizers, commonly called *mind machines*. In brief, these devices allow the user to experience specific light and sound patterns that the brain will follow or entrain. By this I mean that the brain has a natural tendency to follow the rhythmic patterns that enter from the various senses. You experience this process when you become immersed in a musical beat or a drumming sequence. In a sense, our brain locks onto the beat and follows it. Our brain interprets patterns of light and sound as electronic signals. These electronic signals influence the brain and initiate corresponding patterns in our brain waves. This phenomenon is commonly called the frequency-following response (FFR). In short, specifically designed electronic patterns are proven to create a corresponding change in the brain-wave frequencies we experience, allowing us to effectively alter our state of consciousness. Many people report that with the aid of mind machines they can enter deep meditative states of consciousness in only a few minutes.

The benefits of this technology become obvious when you consider that two of the biggest obstacles to pursuing the spiritual path are quieting the mind and finding adequate time to practice the various methods. Whatever your path—meditation, yoga, breath work, out-of-body techniques—these two challenges are always present. Just imagine the benefits of being able to enter your ideal deep state of consciousness in a few minutes, at any time and in any place you choose. The potential is staggering. I believe we are at the dawn of a spiritual renaissance and that this technology will become one of the tools for personal and spiritual empowerment. I should temper this statement by emphasizing that external tools are obviously not essential to our development on any level. We are all naturally connected to God and the highest spiritual realms. We require no external assistance, electronic or ingested, to experience our true home. However, if there is a method or tool that will assist us in our goal of spiritual self-realization, exploration, and empowerment, we would be shortsighted indeed to disregard it. As I have stated many times, the evolution of consciousness is creating new openings and opportunities for the acceleration of spiritual development. It is up to us to recognize and appraise the opportunities when they appear. The use of external aids in any form or manifestation is a personal choice. Life is about the choices we make, and it is important that we be aware of the various tools and methods that are available for the exploration of consciousness and our spirituality.

During workshops I am often asked about the use of modern tools and substances. For over two decades I personally used no external tools or substances of any kind in my out-of-body explorations and spiritual quest. However, I always remained open to the evolving technology around me. After years of personal research and experimentation into the benefits of brain-wave and sound technology, I now know it to be effective when used properly. It is not some form of instant enlightenment, but rather an effective aid in our quest for personal and spiritual growth. When technology is intelligently combined with the proper spiritual intention, training, and mind-set, it is incredibly powerful. It assists us in accessing various altered states of consciousness that are an essential prelude to out-of-body journeys and profound spiritual experiences. It does not create the experience, but helps us to open up to our inherent mental and spiritual potential. I strongly believe that it is critically important to learn the higher-self technique and various methods for focusing and enhancing our state of consciousness during any kind of altered state and spiritual exploration. Having these methods at hand will help us experience and receive the optimum benefits from our inner explorations of consciousness.

The technologies and tools that are available to the public have grown extensively, and prices have dropped to the point where such tools are affordable for most people. When examining the various products, pay special attention to the quality and quantity of meditative programs that are included because these are likely to be the primary programs that you will use. Keep an eye on personal programmability and expansion capabilities. Also examine the programs that are available to be downloaded from the Internet. Most people who use mind machines eventually want expanded and custom programming capacity.

Examples of this technology are the various brain-wave generators, such as the Nova Pro, the Orion, the Mind Lab Pro, and the David Paradise. All of these devices claim to enhance relaxation, learning, and meditation. (Be aware that anyone suffering from epilepsy or a heart condition, or who may be mentally unstable, should not use light and sound machines.)

Another fascinating development is the creation of lucid dream induction devices that are specially designed to signal you when you enter REM sleep. The idea is to stimulate an increase in your conscious awareness or lucidity during dream states. One such device is the Nova Dreamer, developed by the Lucidity Institute. These devices determine when you have entered REM sleep and then proceed to signal you by flashing red lights or through audio signals. The basic concept is to make you aware that you are dreaming while you are still in the dream. People have told me that this technology helped them initiate out-of-body experiences. It is also used in dream awakening, or what I call a *dream conversion*.

During REM sleep, you are notified by a flashing red light or signal that you are indeed dreaming. Your new awareness of the dream state allows you to immediately repeat a mental command such as: "Awareness now!" This focused demand for mental clarity increases your awareness and can initiate the vibrational state and separation from the body. The potential for this kind of technology is exciting when you consider the fact that we enter REM sleep approximately six times every night. Thus we have six valid opportunities to explore expanded realms of consciousness and spirit every single night. Many people have told me that they prefer dream awakening because it seems to them a more gradual and natural approach to out of-body exploration. The dream awakening method is often reported to involve a less dramatic shift of consciousness. However, it does not always eliminate the vibrational-state phenomena, as many seem to believe.

It is important to recognize that it is not the technology that creates the out-of-body experience. The various electronic devices are tools used in conjunction with effective out-of-body techniques and instruction. The technology helps to create the initial internal conditions or psychological mind-set that will allow the out-of-body technique to be used effectively. Your success is often directly related to your ability to focus your awareness at the appropriate time. For example, imagine that you are dreaming, and the flashing red signal alerts you to this fact. At this point you become increasingly aware or lucid in the dream. The ideal next response would be to completely relax and mentally demand, "Awareness now," repeating your thought command until you experienced a shift or major enhancement in your awareness. (For more information about dream conversion, refer to chapter 6 in *Adventures Beyond the Body*.)

In the summer of 1999 I was experimenting with a popular light and sound machine. I was using one of the deep meditation programs while lying comfortably on my sofa. I used the program for about ten minutes and was amazed at how quickly I reached a state of total relaxation and then detachment from my senses. I then enjoyed an inner floating sensation. I completely surrendered to the floating and allowed my entire being to just float free. Without effort or motion I directed myself to the door by thinking, "To the door!" In a few moments I was floating effortlessly to the door.

I started out seriously doubting the various claims made by some of the manufacturers. However, after several months of personal experimentation I had to admit I was quite impressed with the results. Some of the devices are surprisingly sophisticated and well designed for inner exploration. Again, this is a personal choice, but I suspect that if you appreciate the rapid developments in modern computers, you will find this technology fascinating.

Virtual Reality

Other technology-related innovations include virtual reality and flight simulators. The rapidly growing popularity of computer and video gaming has created some unexpected results. I know a movie producer in California who had his first out-of-body experience after playing the video game "Pilot Wings" for two hours prior to going to sleep. He found himself suddenly aware of flying in a dream and was able to convert this awareness to a fully conscious OBE. I believe that the flying motion he experienced immediately before going to sleep triggered his subconscious mind to take action. The potential benefits of this kind of stimulation are immense. In the future, the use of simulation technology will be expanded to the point where it may provide a reliable method of OBE induction. I believe the rapid evolution of technology will continue to impact the group consciousness of our species in ways we can only imagine.

For many people OBEs are accessed at the slower and deeper brain-wave states such as theta. There has been a recent surge in the development of machines and techniques to access the various brain-wave states beyond beta. It was found that by using light and sound devices, different brain-wave states can be "entrained." However, after several years researchers discovered that some people still couldn't access these states. They found that a large number of people possess a form of fixed thought patterns and could not of their own volition consciously access the full range of the brain-wave spectrum. The various states that a person needs to access in order to experience altered states of consciousness and OBEs were essentially blocked.

In recent years a small number of light and sound devices have appeared that allow the user to select and customize program frequencies, creating the potential for accessibility to a wider range of brain-wave states. This technology offers the possibility that the "average" untrained individual can access those deep meditative and expanded states of consciousness that may have been subconsciously blocked for any number of reasons.

Self-initiated out-of-body exploration have historically been experienced by only a small percentage of the population. As a culture we are trained to be externally focused. We are not taught to quiet the mind and explore altered states of consciousness. In fact, most people have little understanding of the tremendous benefits experienced by exploring altered states of consciousness. Modern technology innovations are opening the door to new vistas of inner exploration for a larger percentage of the population.

The first OBE I had was the result of using brain-synchronization technology. I had been listening to the CDs for about a week when one night I decided that instead of following the tape instructions, I would just go to sleep listening. After about thirty minutes I felt the vibrations and told myself to lift up. At the thought of this I began to feel myself lift up very *smoothly. I opened my eyes and discovered that I was floating feet-first toward my ceiling fan. It felt like I was floating in water. I didn't try to move anywhere; I just floated there. Then I started to move down toward my bed, and I began going through it. I put my arms out on the surface of the bed as if to stop myself from falling all the way through. I stopped and looked at my arms and noticed that it looked like electric sparks and electricity were moving up my arms, crackling and popping! After that I began to lose the clarity that I had and woke up. One of the weird things I noticed was dark blobs floating in the room with me. I don't know if they were thought forms or what.* —HARRIMAN T., SPRINGHILL, TENNESSEE*

Sound Technology

Research over the past twenty years has established the effectiveness of audio technologies in enhancing our state of consciousness. Specific sound frequencies have a powerful effect upon all of us. The modern use of various sounds such as specially designed multiplexed binaural beats helps to synchronize the two hemispheres of the brain. Our brains create patterns or waves of electrical activity. Research has confirmed that different brain-wave patterns indicate specific mental states. Specially designed audio patterns influence our brain waves and provide opportunities to experience various focused states of consciousness. Sound stimulation can entrain brain waves and assist us in experiencing brain-wave frequencies beyond the usual waking state. Specific sound frequencies help to guide us from our normal waking (beta) brain frequency of approximately thirteen to eighteen cycles per second to the slower cycles of alpha and even theta frequencies.

Brain-synchronization music works for me. I burn jasmine, my favorite incense, and lie flat on the floor in the center of the room. The music begins to play, and I focus my attention on the beats until I find myself in the vibrational state. It's relax-

*ing and seems to send a message to my subconscious that I am ready to meditate and travel out of body. —*DEB V., PHOENIX, ARIZONA

Modern audio technology offers an exciting potential for the exploration of various altered states of consciousness. It is a proven and valuable tool for meditation, healing, and spiritual exploration. Today this technology is used for overcoming sleep disorders and countering attention deficit disorder, and is often used in a variety of self-improvement programs ranging from learning musical instruments to increasing self-esteem. This technology is especially helpful for individuals who have difficulty relaxing and quieting the mind during meditation and spiritual exploration. Audio technology plays an essential role in the mind machines discussed earlier in this chapter. Over the years I have received hundreds of letters affirming the effectiveness of this technology. I feel so strongly about this technology that I incorporate it in all of my workshops and audio programs.

OTHER METHODS FOR INDUCING OUT-OF-BODY ADVENTURES

Progressive Relaxation

Progressive relaxation is primarily a method for relaxing the body and mind. However, many have discovered that it is can be used effectively to induce deep trance states. Progressive relaxation is a popular induction method used in hypnosis, in healing, and in attaining numerous altered states. The basic premise is to tense each major muscle group and then completely release it. In this way, each muscle group throughout the body becomes systematically relaxed.

I practiced one of the techniques mentioned in the book that I call the "forgetting your body" technique. You start at your toes and work upward on the body, turning off the feeling in your toes, feet, ankles, and so forth until you have gone over the entire body. I practiced this for a year, frequently, as I was lying in bed prior to going to sleep. Sometimes I would get a spaced-out feeling or a mind-awake, body-asleep feeling. Then things began to happen. I began to have spontaneous OBEs while sleeping. —Tom S., Boise, Idaho

Hypnosis

Hypnosis is a proven tool for self-improvement and inner exploration. It has been used effectively in past-life regression and in the elimination of fears and phobias. In out-of-body exploration it is used to condition the mind to accept and embrace our multidimensional potential. It is also highly effective in creating the ideal pre-OBE mind-set: mind awake, body asleep. Hypnosis is a valuable tool in lucid dream induction and awakening. It is often combined with affirmations and rescripting methods.

Hypnosis has established itself as highly effective in removing subconscious blocks that retard our spiritual growth and thus opening the doors to our unlimited potential. It is commonly used for fear reduction and regression. As a certified hypnotherapist I am a strong advocate of the many benefits of individual, group, and self-hypnosis. For over ten years I have employed hypnosis in my out-of-body exploration and past-life regression workshops. For years I have conducted individual sessions and have witnessed the tremendous benefits people have derived from them. I highly recommend learning self-hypnosis from an expert hypnotherapist who is well versed in metaphysical principles and the spiritual benefits that are available. In *Adventures Beyond the Body* I provide more detailed information on the many benefits of self-hypnosis and provide an entire hypnosis script.

I had a hypnosis-induced OBE in 1974 when I was in college. I went to a dorm room that I had never visited and saw my friend "Steve" asleep on his left side. The covers were pulled

up to his ears, the window was half open...
dicular to his bed, right shoe toe facing...
degree angle, toothpaste cap off and...
all immediately verified by an observer...
body. —P. H., LEXINGTON, KENTUCKY

A woman I met during one of my out-of-body...
described a fascinating experience. Barbara was a
teacher in a rural school district that had experienced a re...
tragedy. A school bus carrying children home had a terrible
accident in which three of her students were killed. She had
been distraught about this event for some time, as she felt a
personal attachment to these young children. She recounted
this experience after I had led the group through a hypnosis
technique designed to create and release energy.

I was very upset about the bus accident. Three of my students
were killed, and the classroom never seemed the same after
they were gone. I had been thinking about these children as
you began your hypnosis session. As I fell deeper and deeper
into a state of relaxation, I felt like I was hearing voices—
young, happy voices, like those you hear on a playground at
recess. I willed myself to have clear vision and hearing. At once
I saw those students playing together not far from where I
stood. They seemed to recognize me right away and greeted
me by name. I was particularly confused as I somehow
remembered that they were no longer of this earth. An espe-
cially bright student, Jennifer, spoke directly to me and said,
"Please stop worrying about us, Mrs. P. We're really okay."
And each of them offered a similar phrase regarding their well-
being. It was as though a weight had been taken off my shoul-
ders. They faded away with the sound of their voices, and I
slowly became aware of our conference room again. Although
I will always miss them, as I'm sure their families do, I most
definitely know that they are safe and happy where they are.
—BARBARA P., ORLANDO, FLORIDA

d Tantra

Our culture tends to separate sex from spirituality; however, any cultures do not. I occasionally hear reports of out-of-body experiences initiated by an intense sexual orgasm. This appears to be a rather rare event, but it does occur. In the previously mentioned Twemlow study, 3 percent of the participants reported a sexual orgasm as an immediate prelude to the experience.[2] I have heard from several people that they can self-initiate an OBE by becoming one with their orgasm. At the point of orgasm they completely relax and visualize their full conscious awareness being ejected from their physical body. I have also received some interesting reports of prolonged Tantric methods initiating out-of-body experiences and mystical states of consciousness. The key to this practice is to become completely objective and release all association with the body. As much as possible, allow your entire awareness to become one with your orgasm. At the same time, encourage and feel your conscious awareness flowing away from your body. Completely surrender to the motion and bliss.

Affirmations

Affirmations have become one of the most widely used methods of initiating OBEs. The reasons for this are the method's simplicity, ease, and noninvasive nature. Affirmations can be repeated aloud or silently to yourself; they can also be recorded and then played continuously during sleep. Many people find it helpful to write down their affirmations in order to fix them in mind. The key is to maintain your affirmations as your last conscious thought as you drift to sleep. I highly recommend recording your own affirmations. When recording your voice, speak in a slow, relaxed manner, and play soft music in the background.

As a student of astral projection, I began my attempts with affirmations such as "I want to leave my body" and "I will travel out of body." I could only get to the point where I heard

loud noises and felt a tingling sensation in my legs. After read-
ing more on the subject to see what I was doing wrong, I
learned that you must be insistent about what you want. So I
changed—upgraded—my affirmations to "I demand to leave
my body" and "Now I do leave my body." Since then, I've
been able to go beyond the vibrational state. —Dan F., Fort
Worth, Texas

Interrupted Sleep Patterns and Sleep Depravation

One of the most well known and effective methods for initiating an out-of-body experience is to alter your sleep pattern.
Interrupting your sleep pattern has an immediate impact on
your REM cycles.

I could not sleep for three days. I didn't feel tired, nor did I
show any signs of losing sleep.

At 2:50 A.M. I "seemingly" woke up after getting to sleep—more
like blacking out, I think. What woke me up were four evenly
paced knocks on the door—an illusion, I think, to remove me
from my body. I thought, "I finally got to sleep and she wakes
me up!" I tried to move in order to get up to answer the door,
but I couldn't move. (I was lying facedown on my pillow, with
my hands under my pillow.) I thought I was paralyzed. Trying
to think logically how I might revive my body, I thought that if I
could just concentrate on only moving my fingers, I could start
to limber up. As I tried to do this, I suddenly was able to see my
hands through my pillow. Then I felt a sort of jerk from my
head to my feet and I was floating in the air. As a reflex action, I
started to move my feet toward the floor as if to sit up and then
stand up to get up to answer the door, but my feet never made it
to the floor. I floated to the middle of the room and turned 180
degrees in a counterclockwise direction. After this turn, I gained
control and then became aware that I was astral-traveling! I
looked normal and seemingly even more real than I did when I
was in my body! It even seemed as if I could see new kinds of

colors. I could look through the wall to the outside or look at the wall if I wanted to. I also saw what looked like small stars of light flowing out of the earth—perhaps the magnetic lines of force of the earth! I looked down and could see my "spirit" hands and legs. I was afraid to look at my physical body for fear that it might mean I was dead. As I looked toward the bed, I saw a dark area where my body would be. I was amazed that I didn't have to see something if I didn't want to.

I thought of answering the door again, but as I tried to do so my hand passed through the doorknob just like it passes through air. —LONNIE A., HUNTSVILLE, ALABAMA

Chakra Techniques

Nonphysical energy activation and motion is effective in initiating out-of-body experiences. One of the classic methods is to activate the unseen energy centers of the etheric body. When the chakras open, massive quantities of pure energy pour into our etheric body, creating a dramatic expansion of the nonphysical body. It also appears that this energy flow and expansion is the cause of the sounds reported during the vibrational state. The buzzing, humming, and roaring are the direct result of this energy flow. Chakra activation and breath control are becoming well known as effective methods for initiating OBEs. The following is an example.

The out-of-body experience I will share with you occurred when I experienced breath work under the guidance of a skilled therapist. She had advised me that she might be placing her hands on the chakra areas while I was undergoing the work. We prayed before the experience, and I allowed myself to go with the process.

In this experience you are in a deeply relaxed, altered/meditative state. I was lying on a mat on the floor, with a blanket/quilt

over me. There was music playing, and I was led into a deeply relaxed state through suggestion, music, and breath work.

The therapist reached her hand under the blanket/quilt to place it on the second chakra area. At that moment intense fear rose up within me. I have some memory of an incest experience from my childhood. At that moment "I" shot from my body and was across the room crouching down in the corner area, watching what was taking place. I wanted to scream and tell her to stop.

I remember clearly being in the corner of that room, watching the experience of what was happening to my body. I saw my body lying in the center of the room. I saw the therapist and her movements during the course of the work. I heard her voice and saw my body as witnessed from the corner of the room. As the experience was coming to an end and I recognized that it was safe, I rejoined my body. This was a very real, powerful experience for me and a clear demonstration of the fact that we are not our bodies. —Charlene M., Lawton, Oklahoma

ALTERED STATES AND TRANCE INDUCTION

I believe that it is important to recognize that altered states of consciousness and trance induction in all of their various forms can initiate the emergence of suppressed subconscious issues and blocks. As we open to and explore our multidimensional nature it is normal that we access and experience the stored energies and memories of our subconscious mind. For the vast majority of people this is not a problem but is instead a clear indication of our personal progress and spiritual growth. In general, it is not unusual for us to uncover a past trauma or psychological block in some manner in order to resolve it. For example, many people report a new awareness or glimpses into their childhood and even their past lives. It's also common to tap into our many hidden talents and abilities.

Be aware that uncovering subconscious issues and energy blocks is the normal result of our spiritual growth. The more we open to our true potential, the faster our subconscious issues will surface so they can be recognized and resolved. This is true for all methods and paths of personal and spiritual development.

I believe the path of soul is clear. Each of us must decide either to travel our inner path and experience a profound spiritual adventure, or remain imprisoned by the limits of matter and beliefs. As the new millennium opens, make a total commitment to yourself to explore beyond the confines of the body and experience the absolute freedom of your spiritual essence. The path of soul awaits. It is up to you to take action.

1. Twemlow, Gabbard, and Jones, "Out-of-Body Experience Phenomenology," 21.
2. Ibid.

11

Overcoming Challenges That Confront
the Out-of-Body Explorer

*I have experienced sleep paralysis consistently for the
last fifteen years. I have had multiple out-of-body
experiences, with a dramatic increase over the last two
years. The experiences contributed to overcoming my
fears. It wasn't until I embraced the idea of spiritual
evolution that my experiences changed from being
plagued by pure terror to enlightenment.*

LEIGH T., BUFFALO, NEW YORK

There are a variety of challenges that face both the experienced out-of-body explorer and the novice. They can range from visual problems and unusual sounds to simple overexcitement that keeps the experience from developing. Some people have difficulty maneuvering through a perceived "negative" experience or cannot successfully interact with a nonphysical entity. Research shows, however, that by far the biggest challenge is overcoming fear. Many fears are directly related to vibrational-state phenomena that occur at the onset of the experience. This chapter will provide you with ways to overcome these obstacles so that you can become an effective spiritual explorer. The more we know about what is happening to us, the more effective we will become. Let us begin by examining fear.

FEAR: THE GREATEST CHALLENGE

Fear is the major obstacle to our achieving our true potential. It is like an invisible barrier that hinders us from reaching our personal best. Fear brings with it the insidious energy of anxiety, causing us to feel uncomfortable and even threatened when we attempt something new or set out into uncharted territory. Fear seduces us, encouraging us to remain the same, to stay in our comfortable box.

How do we defeat this powerful enemy? There are many approaches, but the harsh truth is that fear must be faced head-on. Fear must be confronted to be defeated, or it will manifest itself again and again. One of the great benefits of out-of-body exploration is that it provides a powerful opportunity to effectively confront and dissolve the unseen energy source of our personal fears and limits. When we leave our body, we are consciously interacting with and exploring the subtle energy substructure of our psyche. In a very real sense this gives us the ability to confront and remove the energy origin of our fears and dramatically accelerate our personal growth.

FEARS RELATED TO THE VIBRATIONAL STATE

The first step to conquering our fears is to master our response to vibrational and trance states (fig. 9). Each out-of-body experience offers us a tremendous opportunity to overcome our fears and grow spiritually. Many people state that if they had understood what was happening to them, they would have reacted to the experience differently.

One night as I was just about to doze off, I began to hear a light buzz in the room. This buzzing sound started off low, but quickly became louder in my ears. Not only that, but I also felt my body somewhat paralyzed. Whenever I attempted to move my limbs, it was as if I was doing so underwater—extremely difficult. My immediate reaction to this entire experience was intense fear and panic. I fought it off as much as I could, and

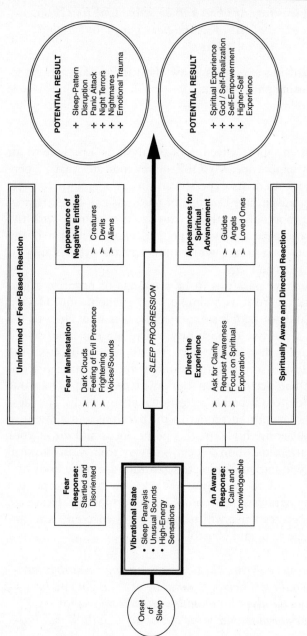

Fig. 9. Different Reactions to an Out-of-Body Experience

The outcome of an out-of-body experience and the vibrational state is dependent on our mind-set and response. Fear can create a negative experience, while a positive, spiritually focused reaction can manifest a self-empowering experience. WILLIAM BUHLMAN

eventually I was free. If I had known at the time that this was just a prelude to an OBE, I would have gone along with it.
—PERRY Z., SOUTH BEND, INDIANA

The following examples show the variety of reactions to vibrational-state phenomena.

Paralysis

People often report a feeling of paralysis as a prelude to an out-of-body experience. My OBE survey indicates that 72 percent of the respondents experienced this as a prelude to their out-of-body adventure. Feelings of paralysis can be extremely frightening, especially to those who are not familiar with the out-of-body experience. Some people report feeling a heavy weight upon their torso, while others relate the inability to move their arms and legs.

Many perceive paralysis to be a strange or negative event, while others regard it as a simple sleep phenomenon. Having read thousands of people's experiences, it is now clear to me that this is a positive opportunity to explore our inner self, a clear indication that we are close to full separation from the body. Paralysis is the natural result of the transition of consciousness that occurs when our awareness shifts from our physical body to our higher vibrational energy body. The ideal response is to calmly surrender to the paralysis and allow it to saturate your entire body. At this point, focus and direct your undivided attention upon a location away from your physical body. This will initiate complete separation from the body and immediately end the paralysis. When you fully accept and embrace the paralysis, it becomes an important ally. However, any fear-based response will turn the experience into a frightening struggle to obtain control over the body.

When I was eleven years old I had a recurring event that terrified me. I would awaken in the middle of the night and be vibrating and paralyzed. I would try to scream out for my mom but no sound would come out of my mouth. It was hor-

rible. Finally, after several minutes of absolute terror, my voice would work again and I would scream for my mom. She would rush in my room and comfort me, saying, "It was just a nightmare. It wasn't real. It's only a nightmare." I would try to explain to her that I wasn't dreaming, that it was real, that I couldn't move or talk and my whole body was tingling and numb. I was so scared I couldn't go back to sleep. Generally she would let me get into her bed. For some reason it never happened in her bed, only in mine. For over a year I was afraid every time I went to bed. —TODD S., VIA E-MAIL

A teenager came up to me after a lecture I'd given in Michigan and shared her experiences.

When I was younger, around fourteen or so, I would be shaken awake by a strange internal rocking and loud roaring sounds. Then I would be numb and sometimes unable to move. When this happened I was overwhelmed by a surge of fear. It's scary when you can't move and you don't know why. After reading your book I realized I was in the vibrational stage and I could just float out of body if I wanted to. So far I haven't, but now I know what's going on. Next time it happens, I'll be prepared and I'll know what to do and how to handle it. —JESSICA M., BLOOMFIELD, MICHIGAN

Unusual Sounds

Strange sounds are often reported as a prelude to separation from the body. The sounds are often combined with paralysis or electrical-like sensations and can be startling and even shocking. The vibrational-state noises are the direct result of the energy flow created by an opening of one or more of the primary chakras. Nonphysical energy rushes through the opening and expands our subtle ethereal body. This inner energy process can create intense and startling sounds and initiate the beginning of an out-of-body experience. The reported noises include buzzing, roaring, humming, footsteps, and thumping, as well as electrical, enginelike, and musical sounds of all sorts. The following are a few examples.

I woke from a dead sleep because of an intense and terrifying buzzing sound in my head. The sound and fear continued even after I was wide-awake, and I had to desperately fight it off as it increased in intensity. I have always wondered what the heck was going on and thought about it often, worrying that I had some kind of medical problem. —GIGI L., LONDON, ENGLAND

In the last few months I've been getting a loud buzzing sound in my head after being up very late at night. It lasts for about five seconds. I believe it would last much longer, but it scares the hell out of me so much that I jump awake, almost jumping right out of bed. This happens about three or four times a week. I wake up trying to figure out what happened. The first time it happened, I thought I was dying. It was weird. —MARY S., MANHATTAN, NEW YORK

When I was a kid, my mother always made me take afternoon naps for two hours. I was bored out of my mind and amused myself by pretending that the toys in my room were waging wars of galactic proportions. That is when I realized I could hear a deafening roar in my head. If I lay absolutely still, after a few minutes the sound would flood through me, drowning out everything else. However, as soon as I tried moving, it vanished. I soon discovered that I could bring the sound back. I don't know why I liked it so much—maybe because it sounded so large and awe inspiring. —JACK M., SACRAMENTO, CALIFIORNIA

Intense Vibrations

Vibrations are a common element of the separation process and one of the most dramatic. They can vary from an intense inner earthquake to a mild electrical sensation. My ongoing

Web-based survey indicates that 56 percent will experience them. During my own experiences, internal vibrations occur over 90 percent of the time; sometimes they are overwhelming; at other times they are mild. It is common for a variety of vibrational-state phenomena to occur simultaneously.

I've had what is called the onset of an OBE. I've had paralysis and an incredible vibrating and buzzing sensation. Every time this happens, I've tried with every bit of energy I have to stop it. I have this experience one to five times per month. I'm afraid to death of "letting go" for fear that I will die.
—LUCY Y., SAN FRANCISCO, CALIFORNIA

In my experience I was already sleeping. I thought I had awakened, but I instantly realized that I could not move. I tried to call for my dog, who I knew was at the end of my bed, but I couldn't speak. I tried to look for him, but still could not move my body . . . Instead, I saw my whole room in a swift circular view, like I was standing and spun around on my toes! Then suddenly I started to feel like my insides— my soul, I guess—was shrinking. I thought I was suffering a heart attack. I thought to myself, "This is it, I'm dying." I felt a shaking sensation and thought maybe I was having a seizure. The shaking seemed violent. The sensations stopped suddenly and I was back. I was covered in sweat. —S. D., GRAND HAVEN, MISSOURI

The inner vibrations and sounds are created by the same process: the opening of the primary energy centers, or chakras, within our nonphysical body. This inner opening and subsequent energy flow can manifest itself in various ways. It initiates a tremendous flow of energy into our subtle body, creating an intense inner disturbance. After we complete the separation from the body, the inner energy flow and the expansion cease, causing the vibrations and sounds to stop as well.

FEARS RELATING TO STRANGE SENSATIONS

Because the nonphysical body is weightless, it is only natural that we would be subject to strange sensations as part of any out-of-body experience.

Being Touched and Pulled

According to my OBE survey, 33 percent of people experience being touched or lifted. This phenomenon can be unexpected and frightening to many. Touching experiences that have been reported range from highly sensual encounters (see chapter 1, "Meetings and Messages Beyond the Body") to the presence of another person or animal on or near the bed.

I have about eight near-OBEs each month. I have not been able to induce them; they just happen. I never feel a vibration; I feel a pulling sensation, as if something is pulling me out of my body. This makes me feel out of control, causing me to panic. As soon as I start to panic, I go back into my body. I had the worst one on the night my friend died. I had just fallen asleep; then I woke up feeling myself being pulled away from my body. At the same time this was happening, my deceased friend was in my room calling my name and asking me to come with him. At that point I had a panic attack, thinking that if I left my body I would not be able to return. I might add that several times when this happened I did not return back into my body all the way because there was some force pulling at me as I was trying to get back into my body. It was kind of a struggle, like pulling on two ends of a rope. I always get the feeling that there is something not human trying to pull me out of my body. —SAM K., ROCKFORD, ILLINOIS

I've had mostly spontaneous experiences that involved floating and spinning, but one experience really stands out in my memory. I was a little bit stressed out due to my upcoming finals, and I decided to take a nap after an intense round of studying. I started hearing a sound next to my head—like a jackhammer

was going in the next room. I opened my eyes, I thought, and saw that there were some shadowy figures at the end of my bed. I thought they were my roommates, but I found out later that my roommates had gone out for pizza. I felt a tingling in my feet, and it was then that I realized the people/ghosts were pulling at my toes. They were tugging at my feet, trying to get me off of the bed. "Man," I'm thinking, because I can't speak, "get off, get off my feet." I want to start kicking, but I can't move. Finally they faded away and I looked to the end of the bed and saw that there was a blanket covering my feet.
—JERRY C., BERKELEY, CALIFORNIA

Two primary scenarios can cause this sensation. One is the presence of someone actually touching or lifting you; the other is our mind's interpretation of energy movement or shifts occurring within our subtle energy body. The key is to relax as much as possible and allow the process to precede, then focus your complete attention away from your body.

Sinking

The sensation of sinking is widely reported. This phenomenon is more common than expected and often evokes a fear response because of the unusual results. It is not unusual for out-of-body explorers to sink through their bed or even the floor. The key is to remain calm and mentally ask for awareness and control. We must remember that when we leave our bodies, our physical surroundings are no longer the prevailing reality.

It seemed to happen when I would be napping and I would awaken with the feeling that I was sinking away and was about to lose consciousness. I would be so scared, for it was such a strange experience. It got to the point that I was almost afraid to lie down in the afternoons, for that was always when it happened. I even considered this to be some type of seizure, but after about eight of these experiences they ceased, and I have had no more. —PAT N., VIA E-MAIL

Floating and Other Movements

The experience began happening to me at around age nine-teen. I am now thirty-two. Until this week, I had no idea what I was experiencing. The experiences frightened me, and I never spoke of them to anyone. What usually happens is an intense buzzing in my ears, followed by a vibrating sensation. I am incredibly aware of the sounds in the room around me—TV, radio, and so forth. It's at this point that I realize I cannot move. I try very hard, over and over, to just move my arms, but I am unable. I also get a floating feeling, as if I am floating on my back in rippling water, floating back and forth, head to foot. Every once in a while I will actually flip completely over in a backward somersault. But as the humming/buzzing gets more intense and I can no longer ignore the paralysis, I get frightened and insist I wake up. It takes a great deal of concentration to wake up, and when I do, the buzzing may remain in my head for a minute or so after the experience and I'm quite tired. —PHIL G., BOSTON, MASSACHUSETTS

When we leave our bodies, we are operating in a subtle body and environment that is controlled by our thoughts. It is important to recognize and take control of our thoughts in order to receive the maximum benefit of our experiences.

FEARS RELATED TO PERCEPTUAL ABILITY

Darkness

Many people report being afraid of the dark during their OBEs. This is especially true of beginners, who are already uneasy with their new adventures.

I have had one OBE, which occurred when I was about thirty-five years old. I was lying on my bed in the afternoon, about to drift off to sleep, when I experienced violent shaking. I thought I was having a seizure. Then I found myself floating near the ceiling, looking down at my body. I tried to will myself to move down, because I was close to the ceiling fan and was afraid of being hit by the blades. The next thing I knew, I was diving through the floor and found myself in the basement. It was dark and I became afraid. I immediately went back up through the floor and jumped into my body. I sat upright with a jolt. —F. B., Tulsa, Oklahoma

The simple solution to any vision issue is to demand an improvement: "Clarity now!" In addition, you can practice the OBE techniques during the day until you build your confidence. Generally, during my nighttime experiences I have noticed that the surroundings are never completely dark but appear illuminated, as from the silvery glow of a full moon.

Poor Vision

Poor visual perception is a commonly reported problem upon separation. We as soul, or pure consciousness, possess no eyes or ears; we manifest our perception capabilities based on our expectations.

At the beginning of my out-of-body experience I was thinking I should go to the door when I first felt the vibrational state. Problem was, I couldn't find the door. I couldn't see it or even remember where it was. Very frustrating. So I repeated, "I must see the door, I must see the door." Then it appeared very clearly before me and I went through it. —Tina M., Dover, Delaware

Visual distortions, vision reversals, and aberrations of the immediate environment are commonly reported. It is not unusual for the observed environment to be different than the physical. For example, a room may appear to have changed; the furniture, doors, and windows may be in different locations and may not even be present. Two forces are at work here. First, we must always remember that when out of body we perceive with our mind. Our natural state of perception is 360 degrees. I have noticed that during out-of-body experiences I can see behind me with surprising clarity. This can be strange and somewhat disorienting at first. Second, the nonphysical reality we observe when out of body is the energy substructure of matter, not matter itself. We are observing the reality of a different dimension, so although the environment may appear similar, it will not always appear the same.

I have found that poor visual perception is primarily caused by a lack of awareness in the energy body we are experiencing. The solution is to transfer more of our consciousness by demanding it. A simple, direct command such as "Awareness now!" can be effective. If you prefer, you can demand a specific perception enhancement, such as "Vision now!" Repeat this demand until you obtain the state of awareness that is ideal. Always remember that you create the quality and mode of your perception, so expect and demand the very best and it will manifest itself.

Voices

Hearing voices or hearing your name spoken aloud is generally regarded as the result of the presence of nonphysical loved ones or residents in the immediate area. On several occasions I have clearly heard my mother call my name during and after separation. After full separation, I looked around but could not see her.

I remember floating up toward my ceiling light at night while a female voice or voices called my name. It was the strangest thing I have ever experienced. —RICH N., NORFOLK, VIRGINIA

Many people report hearing a group of voices during their OBEs. This often occurs while they are in the latter stages of the vibrational state and before they have separated completely from the body. It is not uncommon for the overheard discussion to be centered on the subject's openness or receptivity to consciously go out of body. I believe that the voices are generally nonphysical residents or guides that are attempting to assist in, communicate, or even observe the separation process.

During my experiences it was hearing some "people" talking about me that was the scariest. They were debating about

whether I was ready. I kept thinking, "Ready for what? Are they going to do something to me?" I started freaking out, and then it stopped. I had to wonder if I was dreaming the whole thing, but it sounded so real. —P. R., VIA E-MAIL

Out-of-body explorers also report hearing negative or threatening voices that seem intent on frightening them. The other dimensions are inhabited by many different beings; some are helpful and some are mischievous. The question arises: Is the explorer actually experiencing an actual reality, a mischievous nonphysical resident, or do the voices emanate from the vibrational state phenomena or an internal, fear-based event manifested to block the exploration? Each person must make their own judgment. The important point to remember is that sounds and voices cannot harm us. Generally, when full separation from the body is achieved the reports of threatening voices cease.

I started to float up, and suddenly I could hear a growling voice calling my name. I was terrified and struggled to get back in my body. —RITA K., RIVERHEAD, NEW YORK

Entities

Seeing or hearing nonphysical entities when you leave your body is to be expected. My survey revealed that 22 percent of the participants reported seeing or feeling the presence of a nonphysical being. In addition, 24 percent reported seeing, hearing, or speaking to a deceased loved one. As we understand more about nonphysical contact, the fears we associate with this type of encounter will diminish.

Every time I have an out-of body experience there are beings all around me. This startles me, because they are often talking about me like I'm not even there. I can't see them very well, but I can hear every word. This is the one thing that really scares me. —ANDY B., MADISON, WISCONSIN

We live in an ocean of energy that is filled with life. If we are going to be effective explorers when out of body, we must learn to remain calm and explore the opportunities for contact when they arise. In general, nonphysical entities that are attracted to you probably know you from this life or one of your previous incarnations. During out-of-body experiences it is common to communicate with deceased loved ones, and for many this is their most memorable out-of-body experience. Instead of being negative experiences, these encounters are often life-changing, positive verifications of our immortality. Each encounter is a wonderful opportunity to learn and grow. However, it is our approach, together with the way we respond to the encounter, that determines the outcome.

In addition, there is a tendency for lost and bewildered souls to be attracted to conscious spiritual travelers. This is especially true of those who project to the astral plane. Be prepared for this kind of contact, because eventually it will occur. The best approach is to remain calm and provide as much assistance as possible. These souls will often ask a lot of questions and be reluctant to listen to advice.

Nonphysical beings that are unknown to us are attracted to us for three primary reasons. First, they have lowered their vibrational rate by focusing their attention on form and matter as the only authentic reality. Second, they are often so attached to matter that they refuse to accept the higher-dimensional environments and inhabitants as a valid reality. Third, it is common for the vibrational signature or density of out-of-body explorers to be closer to the energy frequency of the denser astral dimension than the higher realities. In other words, when we leave our bodies we are often visible to wandering or lost souls who are still obsessed with the physical reality. These beings are normally not a threat; they are generally confused and in need of assistance or attention. The best response is to instruct them to "go to the light" and direct them to the various dimensional portals that interconnect the different realities. Be aware that these portals can appear to us as any system or device of movement from one energy level to another—stairs, ladders, ramps, elevators, and so forth. More advanced out-of-body explorers have been known to escort lost beings to the appropriate energy level. Emanuel Swedenborg's spiritual travels provide some well-documented examples of this process. (For more information, refer to chapter 8, "A New Vision of Death and Dying.")

FEELING THE PRESENCE OF A THREAT

It is common for out-of-body explorers to experience a presence in their surroundings during and immediately after separation. Our society and culture is overflowing with fears related to the separation of consciousness from the body. Many still equate the entire experience with death. Because of the many unknowns associated with out-of-body exploration, our anxiety and fear are sometimes elevated during separation. For many, the flight-or-fight instinct seems to kick in at the slightest sound or movement. In addition, many report that their vision is poor, and that causes them to feel somewhat vulnerable. This combination is the recipe for a perceived negative experience.

When I left my body I felt tingly—almost like wind could blow through me instead of having to go around. When I walked around my bed there was a ghostlike entity, more than a glow. I could see vague details—head, shoulders, arms. I felt angry that she was in my room. It was like she was lost, looking for something but it was hopeless. I started hitting at her. At first she didn't even notice; my arms just went through her. And then she was startled—like she was shocked that I saw her. She seemed so sad, and went to hug me. She stepped right through me and was gone. I didn't know her. —SHEILA P., LORDSTOWN, OHIO

I had been napping and tried to awaken and felt unable to move. It felt like a large powerful animal was on me, making me unable to move. I couldn't open my eyes and felt like a dead weight. I struggled to speak, but couldn't. —YVETTE C., NICE, FRANCE

INTERACTION WITH A NONPHYSICAL BEING

Interactions with nonphysical beings are commonly reported. I can personally relate to the shock and fear of seeing a strange or unfamiliar entity in your room during an out-of-body experience. It took me many years to accept this event as a normal experience. It is important that we remain as non-judgmental as possible when encountering nonphysical beings. Generally they are simply being curious.

The solution is to be as prepared as possible. Reduce your fears by learning effective spiritual protection methods such as the globe technique and the armor technique, both of which I describe later in this chapter. In addition, improve your non-physical perception and vision by using the "Awareness now" method. The more experience you gain, the more confident you become. Eventually you come to realize that you are a powerful, immortal being that cannot be harmed by any thing real or imagined.

REALITIES OF NONPHYSICAL CONTACT

- The unseen dimensions consist of energy and are inhabited by billions of different forms of life.
- Consciousness uses different forms for expression. There is no limit to the variety of possible forms available. The humanoid form is only one of many.
- A truly evolved life-form is not limited to a simple shape or form of expression. Nonphysical beings can change their outer shape and mode of communication in order to achieve their desired goal.
- You can demand to experience the true essence of any being you encounter.

When encountering nonphysical life forms, it is important to remember to look beyond shape and form. Form is simply an expression of consciousness. Don't be fooled by the facade; always ask to experience the essence of the being. For over two decades I have used a direct question to accomplish this:

"What do you represent?" or "Show me your essence." In a sense, I challenge the being to exhibit its true self. If it is showing a facade or pretending to be something it is not, it will often disappear or change its form once I question it. Things are often not what they appear, so assume nothing.

This ability to change form should not be considered negative or a trick; it is simply a practical way to communicate. Often a specific form may be more effective. For example, a guide may appear as a child or woman. This is often done to present a nonthreatening appearance. I have heard many stories of nonphysical beings appearing as gentle monks or little old ladies. This makes sense, since an unknown six-foot-tall stranger standing by your bed may not be an ideal guide for the average person.

Eventually we must come to realize that having an out-of-body experience and being surprised to see other life-forms is like diving into the ocean and being shocked to see fish.

In addition, it is important to understand that when we leave our bodies, we are no longer in "our" space or room. We have entered another dimension of reality, and we must be prepared for contact, because it will occur.

EMOTIONAL EXTREMES

Excitement

Excitement is a substantial block for many and is to be expected at the onset of the vibrational state. It is normal to suddenly feel or hear the initial vibrations and sounds and spontaneously begin to get excited.

After doing some deep meditation techniques for about forty-five days, I finally felt the full vibrational state for the first time. I could feel myself floating toward the window, and I started thinking, "Oh, my God, I'm going to start flying!" I got so excited that I slammed back into my body and lost the feeling. I'm working on control now. —LARRY T., NORTHVILLE, MICHIGAN

The very act of focusing our attention on vibrational-state phenomena will often abruptly end the entire experience. Our attention upon the physical-like sensations can shut down the energy flow and expansion process that occur during the vibrational state. The solution is to remain as calm and detached as possible and completely surrender to the sounds and vibrations that are so often the immediate prelude to separation. I know how challenging this can be. As much as possible I allow any excitement to wash over me and I focus my complete attention on a separation target—for example, the front door—or the sensation of floating. I don't analyze the energy process; I simply surrender to it and allow it to expand throughout my entire consciousness.

Panic Attacks and Night Terrors

The sudden onslaught of intense vibrations and loud sounds combined with paralysis can create a massive wave of fear surging through your mind. The instinctive and overpowering feeling of flight or fight seems to explode within and you desperately want the strange vibrations and sounds to stop. The sounds and vibrations are, of course, the classic hallmarks of the vibrational state, and for many the flight-or-fight response is the most difficult issue to deal with.

I am a fourteen-year-old male. I want to tell you about "jerk-awake": It does not happen much, but when it does it is like a boom! Then I get scared and fall asleep again. The sleep paralysis is scarier than hell. I can't stand that happening. It happens a lot. I can't move, I can't talk, I know I'm in a dream, and I try to yell for someone but I can't talk. The other night I had a panic attack, the first one I have ever had! I was so scared I couldn't get my mind off it. I tried to sleep in my brother's room but then it got worse, so I came to my mom's room and talked about it and fell asleep. —KEN M., CASEVILLE, MICHIGAN

I am a male nurse who has had what the medical community classifies as night terrors. I have had almost unbearable fears

at night for most of my life. I had gone to sleep labs, but nothing seemed to help my situation. The very first night I went to bed after reading Adventures Beyond the Body, *I had the most beautiful night of my life. It was then that I realized that the vibrations and sounds should be welcomed, not feared, for they are the first stages of a beautiful adventure. Now I demand what I want out of these episodes. The only problem I have now is not being able to get those sounds and vibrations to come more often.* —MARC P., HAMBURG, GERMANY

Our knowledge of the vibrational process will help reduce our level of fear and expand our ability to get the most benefit out of our experiences. We have to remember that the intense vibrations and sounds are an essential element of the natural energy expansion process. On occasion when I experience a fear-based issue I remain as calm as possible and simply repeat an affirmation, such as " Now I separate from my body!" The most effective solution to vibration-state fear is to separate as quickly as possible. The faster we move from the physical body, the sooner the vibrational phenomena will cease. Unfortunately, many remain uninformed and continue to linger in the vibrational state, and their fears become prolonged and magnified. The best approach is to train yourself, at the first sign of the vibrations, to spontaneously direct your complete attention away from your physical body.

BECOMING AN OBJECTIVE OBSERVER

The key to managing all of the above issues is to become a completely dispassionate explorer. As much as possible, be an objective observer of reality. When out of body you are the ultimate explorer of consciousness. The unseen universe is an ocean of thought-responsive energy, and we absolutely influence and mold the fluid-like energy around us with every thought we create. This neutral mind-set is important, because to be effective you must remain balanced and at ease in the face of tremendous energy change. In addition, the reality you experience is constantly influenced and interpreted by your subconscious mind. Be aware that your thoughts both conscious and subconscious can have a powerful impact on your surroundings. Don't blindly accept the shape and form that you observe as reality. Often, what you perceive is but the outer vehicle or facade of consciousness. For example, none of the people you encounter during an out-of-body experience actually have a body. The various humanoid forms we see and experience are projections and vehicles of their consciousness. Some of these entities are conscious of their projection, but most are not. This principle applies to all levels of the universe.

NEGATIVE EXPERIENCES

I believe that our life experiences are neither good nor bad. We place meaning on everything we do. Look back at your life: How many times has a perceived negative experience propelled you to dramatically grow or change in unexpected ways? The same applies to out-of-body experiences. Many times out-of-body and near-death experiences act as an abrupt spiritual call to action. Sometimes we need to be shaken from life's daily physical routine in order to grow. Each experience is a tool of learning and evolution.

There is increasing evidence that so-called spontaneous OBEs are actually highly planned events orchestrated by a higher aspect of our psyche. Our higher self or soul creates them for a specific purpose; often the experiences initiate a dramatic shift in consciousness and perception, opening us to new levels of personal growth. Dr. Raymond Moody, Kenneth Ring, and Dr. Melvin Morse have clearly documented that near-death experiences can provide a wide spectrum of life-changing benefits. The same benefits can be derived from out-of-body travels.

HOW TO OVERCOME CHALLENGES

Another method of avoiding a fear-based issue is to raise your vibration rate immediately after separation from the body. Most out-of-body experiences occur in the denser regions of the nonphysical universe. During a typical experience we shift our consciousness from the outer physical body to our next inner vibrational vehicle of soul. In other words, we end up experiencing what many people call the lower astral plane.

I am fifteen, and I had an OBE when I was ten. Being interested in the paranormal, I knew what it was, but I had a fear of demons. I was on the brink of sleep when I felt myself coming out of my body. I was partly out, but then I started screaming and "pulling" myself back in. I would like to try it again if at all possible. But those with bad experiences with OBEs are on a lower astral plane, which comes about from negative feelings about the OBE. If you find yourself in that situation, think positively and you should end up going to the higher astral plane, which is where you have good experiences. —JASON T., AUSTIN, TEXAS

PROTECTION

Take a moment to contemplate the fact that you are the creative force of your experiences and your life. You direct the events in your life with your thoughts, choices, and actions. In the subtle nonphysical dimensions, this truth is magnified and accelerated. Your fears can manifest a fearful experience, while your positive or neutral thoughts and expectations will orchestrate a positive or neutral experience. This energy principle is reflected in the physical world as well. If you are looking for and expect negative events or people in your life, you will find them at every turn. When you scan for positive events, you will begin to notice them all around you.

THE REALITIES OF SPIRITUAL PROTECTION

- We are immortal. We are powerful creative spiritual beings. We mold the energies around us both positive and negative by the use of our focused thoughts.

- We are far more protected than we are aware of. Each of us has a variety of spiritual guides, friends, and helpers who are always available for assistance.
- We are each connected to God. What better protection is there?
- When we ask for spiritual protection, it is given. However, we generally must make the request to receive it.
- Spiritual guides will not interfere with our personal development. They do their work as stealthily as possible.
- Our personal fears are the real enemy and block our spiritual growth and evolution.
- Sending love to a manifestation of fear will cause it to dissipate and disappear.

Spiritual-Protection Methods

The best way to feel secure when exploring a new energy dimension is to be aware of our personal creative abilities. Keep in mind that that obstacles and perceived threats are often manifestations of fear that are molded by our subconscious mind. Eventually we must take responsibility for our experiences on every energy level of the universe, for this is the beginning of true personal empowerment. Sending the energy of love to the manifestations of fear is always effective. The following is a brief overview of spiritual-protection methods commonly used today.

The Protective Globe Technique

Visualize an energy field of white light surrounding you, a protective globe of brilliant, glowing white light. The energy field is completely around you and warms you with the glow and light. You know that this light protects you from anything negative or harmful. You are surrounded by a protective, powerful energy field. No harm can pass through this beautiful, positive, glowing light. Vividly picture this globe of light surrounding you as you remain completely safe and protected. Repeat this visualization as often as you like.

The Spiritual Armor Technique

Imagine yourself protected by a glowing suit of armor or shield made from light. This armor or shield shelters you from any perceived negative force. The modern interpretation of this classic protection method is to visualize an impenetrable force field surrounding you.

The Higher Energy Level Technique

My favorite method to avoid astral entities, obstacles, or any fear-based manifestations is to completely remove myself from the environment. This is achieved by directing your awareness to a higher vibrational reality: "I move inward now!" This must be a focused demand for immediate action: "I move higher now" or "Higher self now." Any command directed to a different location can be effective.

Creating an inner shift of consciousness when out of body is essential in order to move from the denser areas of the astral plane to a higher dimensional reality. If you desire to communicate with more-evolved spiritual beings or explore the inner dimensions beyond the astral, you must be prepared to raise your internal vibrational rate. This can be achieved by doing the following technique.

Controlled Interdimensional Movement

Immediately after separation, move away from your physical body and become calm and centered. If necessary, request that your complete awareness or clarity be present: "Awareness now!"

While out of body, firmly demand to experience the next inner energy dimension: "I experience the next inner level/

dimension now!" Or pinpoint whatever interdimensional area you would like to explore. The immediate result will be perceived as an intense inward or upward motion that will last for several seconds. Remain as calm as possible; the sensation of motion can be intense and disorienting if you are unprepared for it. It is similar to being pulled or drawn inward through layers of energy and color into a new environment.

After your inner motion has ceased, immediately center yourself by requesting that your complete awareness be present: "Awareness now!" Be prepared: Your new surroundings and viewpoint will be completely different.

A more aggressive approach is to go beyond defense and become proactive. Since we mold nonphysical reality with our focused thoughts, we can create any weapon that we feel is appropriate to the situation. The following are a few examples.

The Light Device Technique

Imagine a powerful lightning bolt or flashing sword appearing in your hand. Create something that you can easily feel or identify with. For example, if you are an artist, use a paintbrush of light. An avid reader might open a book of light; a gardener could use a hose and spray the room with light. The key is to select something you can visualize without a lot of thought. Absolutely know and feel the energy of this and it will become manifest.

The Explosive Light Technique

This technique provides a highly effective method for clearing a room of uninvited guests. Imagine a grenade in your hand that when thrown will explode with a powerful burst of pure light, removing any potential threat.

Any thought-created device, weapon, or shield will be effective. The key is your personal acceptance of your creative abilities. Self-doubt and fear are our greatest enemies. When doing any of these methods, trust the creative power of your soul to make it real and it will be so.

REQUESTING ASSISTANCE

Whenever necessary, request assistance from a spiritual guide or angel. The assistance can manifest itself in many different forms. Often there is a feeling or sense of an unseen protective presence. This assistance may also take the form of invisible helping hands, advice, or an instant change in our reality.

I had numerous OBEs. All of the experiences are similar. I usually went to sleep around 4 A.M. After falling asleep, I became aware of a roaring sound. It sounded exactly like a train was traveling through my apartment. Then my body went into uncontrollable jerking. I would describe it as a convulsion, although it was not uncomfortable, just weird. After going through this the first time, I would yell when it occurred, out of sheer excitement. I don't know if this was an audible yell or my spirit just yelling. Then my spirit moved out of my body and I was flying. I never looked down to see my body or looked around the room. I remember flying fast and high. I noticed there was always this first layer of "muck" to fly through. I always thought of it as disgruntled spirits hanging around. When I flew through that layer, I always asked for God's protection as a safeguard. Then I was flying through a clear, beautiful sky. I was always driven to fly to the same place. I refer to it as the land of color. It is a place where the air sparkles. There are rays of color bands and a feeling of magic that is impossible to describe. Returning to my body was similar to leaving—the roaring train and my body jerking uncontrollably. —ISABELLE F., EL PASO, TEXAS

CONFRONTING MANIFESTATIONS OF FEAR

It is important for spiritual explorers to understand that the mind-set and expectations that we hold and project determine the energy manifestations we receive. Manifestations of energy, regardless of form, are molded by our own subconscious thoughts and fears. When I encounter a fear-based environment or manifestation, I look to myself, not the surroundings, for the solution.

The Power of Confronting Your Personal Fears

Each day we are confronted with decisions and choices that we must make. These decisions determine the course of our lives and the results we experience. If you examine the lives of self-empowered people, you will notice one overriding attribute they all share: All of them had to confront and overcome their personal fears and limitations to reach their goals. Every fear and anxiety in our life is an obstacle for us to overcome, a personal barrier that separates us from our desired spiritual goal. Life itself can be viewed as a school in which we are presented with a series of obstacles that we must eventually confront and overcome. How we react to each challenge will determine the personal growth we experience during our lives.

The fears and limits we experience in our physical life are the dense outer manifestations of our internal fears. In effect, our personal fears will manifest themselves as nonphysical confrontations or barriers such as perceived evil entities or life-threatening activities. These fear-based energy manifestations can restrict our freedom, mobility, and spiritual empowerment.

For example, during the third year of my out-of-body explorations I experienced a large, heavy object pressing down on me immediately after separation. I perceived the object to be an enormous ornate gold-leaf mirror. It was so massive that I was pinned under its crushing weight. I began to push against the mirror with all my strength. An intense feeling of despair flowed through me as I tried again and again but the weight of the mirror continued to crush me. In desperation, I focused all of my attention, all of my energy and strength, on moving this pressing weight and screamed out, "I have the power." Instantly, I experienced a surge in my personal strength and easily lifted the mirror and tossed it aside.

At that moment, I experienced a powerful new sensation of freedom and mobility I had never known before. I was as light as a feather and able to go wherever I pleased. For the first time in my life, I felt completely free, completely in control. I was able to move, perceive, and comprehend at an accelerated rate. I somehow knew that I had opened a door to new levels of personal possibilities and growth. Each fear and limit we experience presents an opportunity for learning and growth. Our recognition of this can assist us in confronting each new challenge.

The Many Manifestations of Fear

When we are out of body, fear often manifests itself as form. This energy can take the appearance of any form imaginable, such as an obstacle, a creature, a challenge, or even a devil. I have seen and heard countless confrontation scenarios; examples include a crashing plane, a sword fight, a fire to be fought, hand-to-hand struggle with all types of deadly enemies both human and nonhuman. The outer manifestation of the fear is often unimportant. What truly matters is our positive reaction and response to the inner fear that it instills. An empowered, fully conscious confrontation is the key to removing our fear.

One of the greatest benefits that out-of-body exploration offers is never discussed: the ability to confront and eliminate the unseen source of our fears and limits. I propose a direct approach. This of course is not recommended for the timid or inexperienced explorer. When you feel that you are emotionally and spiritually prepared, you can request an acceleration of your spiritual development. Often this manifests itself as a confrontation with the energy essence of your personal fears and limits. When a fear-based image or energy appears before you, stand your ground and forcefully demand that this manifestation of fear be gone forever from your life. Project unconditional love to any fear-created phenomenon and it will dissolve and disappear before you.

Fear-Confrontation Experiences

What I have found interesting is that veteran out-of-body explorers seem to have spontaneous fear-confrontation experiences. I had three such experiences in the '70s. The first was the huge mirror crushing down upon me. Then a year later what seemed to be a beast attacked me. During the third experience I was confronted by a giant sloth with the face of a dog. These confrontational experiences proved without a doubt to be some of the most transformational events in my life. It's difficult to express in words, but I felt a massive weight lifted from every level of my being. With each experience I felt a new, expanded sense of freedom and empowerment I had never known before. When we hold firm and face our personal fears we open the door to excelled learning and spiritual growth.

The following are a couple of examples of confrontations that can occur when we are out of body.

*In my last OBE I was in my friend's house, walking through the living room. I noticed that the room was full of snakes. They were everywhere—on the furniture, on the stairs, and even across my feet. In life, I am deathly afraid of snakes. I saw my friend coming from the kitchen when a snake attacked me from a table and bit me on the arm. I froze for a few moments and then asked my friend, "Are these snakes poisonous?" He thought about it and said, "Not if you don't believe they are." With that the snakes all dissolved away and the bite mark disappeared. At that moment I found myself back in my body. I couldn't move my arms and legs. At first I thought it was the result of the snakebite, and then I remembered that it had all faded. I felt energized and powerful after that, like a burden had been lifted from me. —*ROGER D., FT. WALTON BEACH, FLORIDA

I went to sleep reciting affirmations about traveling out of body. I found myself next to my husband on what appeared to be a crystal cliff. There was a waterfall next to us that had diamonds flowing instead of water. I couldn't see a body on either of us, but I knew it was him. We grasped hands—or what my mind conceived as hands—and decided to jump to the next plane. We had jumped off this cliff before to explore other worlds. It was just recreational. We didn't speak to each other. We just knew what we were doing.

As we jumped, there was a point where we realized that this jump was much longer than the others we had done. We continued to hold hands as he said affirmations and I prayed that we wouldn't get hurt—which was weird, since we didn't have bodies. As we kept falling, we stopped being afraid and it started to become more and more fun. We rolled and tumbled in the air, laughing, and about twenty feet before we stopped, we slowed down and "landed." Although our perception of feet never felt the ground, we just stopped falling. There was a square, glasslike structure that housed a guide—like a river guide or mountain guide—and we were so excited as we directed our thoughts to him: "We just jumped 950 feet. It was so cool. We've never jumped 950 feet." He acted like it was no big deal, like others did this all the time.

When I woke up, I told my husband about the feeling. It was exhilarating, and more exciting than anything I have felt on this earth. In this life I am petrified of heights, but after this experience I'm not as frightened as I once was, because it was so much fun. This was totally out of character for me.
—DENISE C., PORTSMOUTH, VIRGINIA

ACCELERATING OUR PERSONAL EVOLUTION

Each exploration beyond matter gives us a unique opportunity to expand our knowledge and to experience our true spiritual essence. The challenges we experience are important steps in our continuing spiritual unfolding.

The key is to be proactive. Spiritual development is not a stagnant process. Accelerating our spiritual evolution is about personal growth and change. We must eventually break the chains of fear that bind us or remain imprisoned within the dense realities of form and matter. If you have the courage, this is your opportunity to be free.

Conclusion:
The Courage to Be a Spiritual Explorer

In *Adventures Beyond the Body* and in this book I have detailed some of the qualities of an out-of-body explorer. After twenty-nine years of personal exploration, it is clear to me that what a spiritual explorer requires most is courage. It takes courage to flow through the intense energies of the vibrational state while remaining calm and focused. It takes courage and self-reliance to step beyond our physical limits and the prevailing norms of our society and culture.

Out-of-body experiences reside at the cutting edge of human exploration and evolution—individual journeys of consciousness to the very core of our spiritual essence. You will experience a powerful opportunity to confront your inner fears and transcend all the comfortable beliefs that others cling to. You will see and experience things that are alien to others, things that earthbound beings could not even begin to conceive of. As you grow, you will lose interest in old dramas and relationships that no longer serve your spiritual quest. As you become increasingly directed by your conscious connection to soul, the priorities and beliefs of others will become less and less important. In the end, your burning need for spiritual self-knowledge will propel you forward and you will never be able to go back to being dependent upon the prevailing beliefs around you. Eventually you will find that all beliefs are anchors to illusion and that you must break free in order to experience the truth of your existence. Only by letting go of all physical and mental anchors are you free to discover the truth of what you are. The authentic path to your soul is the practice of consciously journeying beyond the body to the true source of your spiritual essence.

When we transcend the body we become the ultimate explorers of consciousness and open the door to the answers to our existence. It is our destiny to evolve beyond the dense forms we see around us and experience our spiritual self. This will occur. The only real question is when.

Survey Results

The results given here reflect the input from over sixteen thousand people who responded to my Web-site survey. The varied origins of the respondents attests to the universal nature of out-of-body experiences.

COMMONLY REPORTED PHENOMENA ASSOCIATED WITH OUT-OF-BODY EXPERIENCES

(based on 16,185 responses obtained from 32 countries)

1. Experienced a jolt or jerk awake: 98%
2. Heard buzzing, humming, or roaring sounds: 85%
3. Felt floating, sinking, or spinning sensations: 82%
4. Experienced flying in a dream: 81%
5. Experienced sleep paralysis: 72%
6. Had vibrations or high-energy sensations: 56%
7. Saw through closed eyelids: 49%
8. Experienced a panic attack—an overwhelming surge of fear created by strange vibrations or sounds: 46%
9. Heard voices or footsteps: 37%
10. Had a sense of being touched or lifted: 33%
11. Saw, heard, or spoke to a deceased loved one, either family or friend: 24%
12. Saw or felt the presence of an unknown nonphysical being: 22%

COMMONLY REPORTED FEARS

Fear of the unknown: 5%
Fear of the inability to return to the body: 4%
Fear of seeing a nonphysical being: 3%
Fear of death: 2%
Fear of paralysis: 2%
Fear of possession: 2%
Fear of becoming lost: 1%
Fear of experiencing evil: 1%

Eighty-six percent of respondents reported that they had no fears. A few of the participants experienced multiple fears. Many people stated that their fears were dramatically reduced after several experiences.

AVERAGE AGE OF FIRST OUT-OF-BODY EXPERIENCE

The average age for the first OBE is between four and twelve. The rate at which the experiences occur often declines during the early teenage years.

AVERAGE NUMBER OF OUT-OF-BODY EXPERIENCES REPORTED PER PERSON

(based on 9,360 responses)

2–5: 41%
1: 36%
6–19: 13%
100+: 7%
20–100: 3%

Additional information about out-of-body experiences, the vibrational state, and a comprehensive survey is available in this book and in my first book, *Adventures Beyond the Body*. If you would like to participate in my continuing survey, please complete the survey or visit my Web site at www.out-of-body.com.

Out-of-Body Experience Survey

According to some estimates, over 30 percent of the population will experience their consciousness separating from their physical body. This can be due to illness or injury, or may simply be a spontaneous event occurring during sleep. The purpose of this new survey is to obtain more information about what occurs and is observed during an out-of-body experience. Your participation will help to expand our knowledge of ourselves and our universe. Out-of-body experiences are exciting because they provide personal proof of our immortality, firsthand observations of the nonphysical universe, and a glimpse of our future spiritual home.

Please respond via mail to P.O. Box 515, Bel Air, Maryland 21014, or through my Web site: www.out-of-body.com.

Please answer any or all of the questions in as much detail as necessary. Your comments and opinions are very important in gaining knowledge about this elusive subject. Feel free to add any information you believe would be helpful.

Name _____   E-mail address _____
Address _____   Sex   M or F
Age _____

Please describe in detail your out-of-body experience. (Was it spontaneous or self-induced?)

1. What was your state of mind immediately before the experience? Were you sleeping, dreaming, relaxing, etc.? If sleeping, exactly how long were you asleep before the experience began?

2. How old were you when you had your first experience?

3. How did your thought processes compare to what they are during your normal physical state of consciousness?

4. How do you perceive the nonphysical environment when out of body? Do you experience all five senses? Which senses do you normally experience when out of body? How do your vision and other senses when out of body compare to your physical senses?

5. What OBE induction technique is most effective for you?

6. What is the single greatest impact that these experiences have had on you?

7. Have you ever observed your physical body while you were separated from your body? Please describe in detail its colors, density, luminescence, shape, size, etc. How does it differ from your physical body? Are you wearing clothing?

8. Have you ever moved through walls or physical objects while out of body? Did the environment change during or after the movement?

9. Have you ever communicated with someone while out of body? Please describe your method of communication. Was it verbal or telepathic?

10. Please describe the nonphysical environment that you observed. Are your surroundings generally the same as your physical environment, or do you observe a different environment? Please describe.

11. Have you ever consciously altered the environment that you experienced? Please describe.

12. Do you see, feel, or sense another being with you during your OBEs?

13. Have you ever had a physical or emotional healing as a result of an OBE? Was the OBE spontaneous or self-initiated?

14. Have you ever consciously altered the shape, substance, or density of your body?

15. Have you ever observed the nonphysical energy centers (chakras) of yourself or another person during an OBE?

16. Have you ever been able to move a physical object while out of body?

17. Have you ever had any kind of sexual contact or experience while out of body?

18. Have you ever encountered a nonphysical animal? Could you communicate with it?

19. Have you ever observed a nonphysical vehicle, craft, or technology of any kind?

20. Have you ever encountered a child, an adolescent, or a person who appears to be older than sixty? Please describe in detail.

21. In what area of your body or chakra does the vibrational phenomenon begin? Is this consistent or does it change?

22. Does any part of your nonphysical body change in any manner when you look at it?

23. Have you ever encountered a nonhumanoid or alien-looking being during your experiences?

24. How long do the vibrational state phenomena—vibrations, sounds, paralysis, etc.—continue before separation from the body? Do the vibrations and sounds change or cease after separation is complete? Are the phenomena the same or different during different experiences?

25. Have you observed any kind of attachment or cord connected to your body? At what area or areas of the body is it attached? What is the shape, diameter, color, density, etc.?

26. How does your food or liquid intake affect your ability to have OBEs?

27. Have you ever observed what is generally referred to as thought forms? Please describe in detail.

28. Have you used any form of technology (light and sound machines, brain synchronization programs or music, etc.) to help you initiate an out-of-body experience?

29. Have you ever felt like you were attacked by a nonphysical being? Please describe the experience.

30. Have you ever had a Kundalini experience? Please describe. How did the experience compare to the vibrational state or an OBE?

31. Did you ever receive information or insights of any kind (past life, future, problem solving, etc.) during your experience? How was this information communicated?

32. Have you ever had a profound spiritual or higher-self experience during an OBE? Please describe in detail. Was the experience spontaneous or self-initiated?

33. What is the largest obstacle or challenge that you confront during your OBEs? If none, please so indicate.

34. What is the most significant benefit you received from your OBEs?

Observations and Insights Obtained from Out-of-Body Exploration

I n *Adventures Beyond the Body* I presented an out-of-body experience survey and a list of questions concerning our existence beyond matter. The following observations are the result of thousands of survey responses and information obtained from decades of inner exploration gathered from individuals around the world. Many of the following observations are not new revelations; instead, they are a confirmation of realities that are yet to be embraced by various modern cultures.

STRUCTURE OF THE UNIVERSE

The universe is a multidimensional continuum. The entire physical universe is the relatively small outer epidermis layer of the immense unseen universe.

The inner, unseen energy universes such as the astral and mental dimensions are expanding. This expansion creates the observed motion of the outer physical dimension.

As we explore inward, each dimension we experience is progressively less dense and more thought responsive in nature.

All dimensions exist simultaneously. However, they are invisible to one another because each individual dimension functions at a distinctive vibrational rate and density. The various dimensions can be viewed as multiple holographic projections existing at different frequencies.

The denser dimensions such as the physical and astral are designed to be training grounds for developing consciousness.

There are countless nonphysical realities or heavens. Many exist as consensus realities created by the thoughts of large numbers of beings. Uninhabited areas often appear as voids in space.

The tunnel phenomena so often reported during near-death experiences is the opening of the energy membrane that separates the physical and astral dimensions. Innerdimensional entry or transition points may appear to us in various forms such as doors, windows, stairs, portals, and ramps.

The physical and astral dimensions are designed to be dense training grounds for souls.

The ultimate expressions of "heaven" exist beyond all form or thought.

The universe is conscious.

The creative energies of consciousness create the various dimensions. Each dimension is an expression and extension of consciousness.

THE NATURE OF REALITY

Soul is the essence or core of consciousness. Soul exists far beyond the concepts of shape, form, and substance. It can be described as conscious light that uses various energy forms for its expression, communication, evolution, and exploration. The biological body and the more ethereal forms, such as the astral and thought energy forms, are all used by soul as vehicles of expression throughout the multidimensional universe.

We possess no inherent shape or form. Soul uses temporary biological forms as vehicles of expression in the dense outer world of matter. Humanoid forms are one of countless different forms used by consciousness for expression and to enhance its evolution.

We are multidimensional beings. We are far more complex than body, mind, and spirit. We possess and function with multiple energy bodies. Each energy body functions as a vehicle of soul in the various dimensions of the universe. Each subtle energy body acts as an essential transformer and conduit of consciousness. The high frequency energy of soul is progressively stepped down through the various energy bodies so that soul can interact in the dense outer world of matter.

Soul creates the many realities throughout the universe through the use of the various energy bodies. Soul has the innate ability to operate multiple energy bodies (physical and nonphysical) simultaneously. The purpose is to expand our learning and evolution opportunities.

The brain is neither the origin nor the home of consciousness. It is essentially a temporary data storage device that consciousness implements while visiting matter.

During sleep we move out of phase with our biological body by several inches. The common falling and jerk awake phenomena is caused by the rapid reorientation of the two energy bodies.

We are a multidimensional microcosm of the universe.

As we prolong our out-of-body experiences, we rapidly lose our humanoid outer form. We revert to our true self: formless consciousness.

The soul transmits information to the brain by various methods, including dreams, thoughts, visions, inspiration, and out-of-body experiences.

A relatively small percentage of soul energy or consciousness is focused upon the maintaining and operation of the physical body.

We are evolving into a fully conscious multidimensional being capable of interdimensional awareness, travel, and knowledge. The concept of ascension is derived from this process.

The biblical silver cord is an interactive nonphysical connection between the biological body and the densest or first energy body. In large mammals such as humans this cord is approximately one inch in diameter. The connecting cord of small mammals such as dogs and cats is observed as thin connecting strands. The cord is only observed when experiencing the densest nonphysical body of soul.

We can communicate with past loved ones, our guides, and experience our past lives during an out-of-body adventure.

REINCARNATION AND EVOLUTION

Reincarnation is a universal reality. It is a highly effective method used by soul for the purpose of learning and evolution. We evolve by and through personal experience. The most effective method to truly know something is to become it, to live it. We actually become that which we wish to learn.

Many entering the human state become addicted to the unending dramas and intense emotions experienced within matter. The continuation of reincarnation is sustained by the attractions and addictions to matter and emotion.

Reincarnation is a universal method of evolution. Based on out-of-body exploration there is a missing element that few recognize. Many beings never enter the physical dimension during their evolutionary journey. They shift their consciousness from the higher vibrational levels of the universe to the relatively dense worlds of thought and emotion commonly referred to as the astral. They experience some of the trials, dramas, and emotions of form without entering the density of matter. It appears that many nonphysical residents consider the physical world too extreme to enter. It is viewed as an intense hologram or virtual-reality game that you cannot terminate at will.

The density of matter creates the ideal training ground for developing consciousness. It provides a slowed thought-responsive environment where souls can learn and develop their creative abilities.

Soul selects the entry point into matter (our mother) based on the potential lessons and knowledge we desire to obtain. This entry is selected based on specific inner qualities (such as courage, selflessness, humility, love) soul plans to experience and develop during its temporary visit into matter.

Every entry into matter is an opportunity for personal growth.

We incarnate in different cultures, races, time lines, and planetary systems to diversify our lessons, experience, and the resulting wisdom.

Soul enters the fetus at different times during pregnancy.

Dependence upon the five physical senses and unchallenged beliefs severely impede the evolution of humanity.

Out-of-body, near-death, transcendental states of consciousness, and alien contact are all the direct result of the expansion, expression, and evolution of consciousness.

Unconditional love is the universal expression of God.

The early prophets and founders of today's great religions were often out-of-body explorers. The early spiritual explorers related their nonphysical experiences according to their religious and cultural perceptions of reality.

Many of the early biblical prophets are with us today assisting the evolution of consciousness in various ways.

All physical forms are vehicles and tools of reality. All manifestations of form—physical, emotional, and thought—are the creations of consciousness. They are the vehicles and expression of reality, not reality itself.

OUT-OF-BODY EXPLORATION AND EVOLUTION

The key to our personal evolution is our ability to recognize and fully experience our multidimensional nature and our spiritual essence.

Self-initiated out-of-body exploration is a direct and powerful method to experience our true spiritual essence. It is an effective method to accelerate our personal growth and evolution. In addition, it helps to prepare us for the transition of death by removing our fear and expanding our experience.

We have the ability to obtain the answers to our existence and break free from the shackles of belief and matter. This is achieved by personal spiritual experience and exploration beyond the physical limits.

The key to permanent personal freedom from matter and physical incarnations is the conscious ability to experience our true self while still immersed in the denseness of matter.

The reality that we perceive when out of body is relative to the vibrational state (density) of the observer.

THE TRANSITION OF DEATH

Death is a grand illusion. Death is simply the transition of consciousness from one dimension to another. No one dies—we simply discard the outer remnants of soul.

Countless people at their death accept the form-based dimensions, such as the astral, as their heavenly home instead of seeking the "higher realities."

NONPHYSICAL AND ALIEN CONTACT

Countless forms of intelligent life, both physical and nonphysical, exist throughout the universe. Humanoid form is only one of the infinite expressions of consciousness.

A significant percentage of the reported alien contact and abduction phenomena are actually misinterpreted out-of-body experiences and contact with nonphysical beings.

A truly advanced species can and will travel and explore interdimensionally. Physical starships are relatively primitive and unnecessary for a truly evolved species.

All forms of physical and nonphysical life are expressions of soul.

EVOLUTION AND SOUL GROUPS

We evolve through the interaction of soul groups. This is essentially an established group of souls that are interacting with one another as they grow and evolve. During out-of-body experiences we often encounter fellow members of our individual group. Each soul group varies in size; however, the reported size is usually seven to thirty. It is common for our parents, children, and siblings to be integral members of our soul group.

Evolution is the internal process of consciousness fully awakening to and directing its creative multidimensional nature and abilities. True evolution is the spiritual awakening process of consciousness.

The principle of karma, or cause and effect, is an effective learning tool for soul. Evolution is enhanced by the self-created lessons.

We create our reality by the way we direct and focus our thoughts. We are the producer, director, and actor of our lives. One of the primary lessons we are learning within the physical dimension is our personal creative ability and responsibility.

Creation continues now.

Glossary

Affirmations. Repeated positive statements placed in the present tense. They can be verbal, nonverbal, or written. (Example: "Now I'm out of body!")

Alpha state. The brain-wave state associated with meditation, daydreams, and light sleep. (See also *Beta state, Delta state,* and *Theta state.*)

Apparitions. Nonphysical inhabitants who have lowered the personal frequency of their energy body and are temporarily visible within the physical world.

Astral body. The subtle vehicle of consciousness, or energy body, experienced on the astral plane. Also called the *light body, emotional body, starry body,* or the *body of light.*

Astral plane. The closest major energy dimension to the physical in density and vibration rate. This dimension is an ethereal parallel to matter and consists of countless different realities and environments.

Aura. The energy field emanating from all life-forms.

Aura interference. The energy-field disruption of two or more people in close proximity. Generally experienced during sleep or meditation.

Bardo body. The Tibetan phrase for the densest spiritual body of man. Today it is commonly called the astral or etheric body.

Beta state. The brain-wave state associated with normal waking consciousness.

Black and white holes. Interactive energy conduits between the physical and nonphysical dimensions; interdimensional portals between the various energy levels of the universe.

Chakras. Energy centers located in the densest or first nonphysical body. These energy centers function as inner channels and adjustable gates for the subtle inner energy to flow from the higher vibration of soul to the denser energy bodies. Seven primary and more than one hundred secondary or minor chakras are believed to exist.

Cluster experiences. Multiple out-of-body experiences occurring in a series. They are commonly reported during periods of physical illness or when physical death is close.

Collective consciousness. The ethereal archives of human thought as it has existed throughout history. This massive database exists in the subtle dimensions beyond the astral and can be accessed during deep meditation and conscious out-of-body journeys.

Conscious transition. The spiritual act of fully conscious and self-directed death. As the transition of death approaches, you focus and direct your undivided attention upon the act of experiencing your true spiritual essence. This is achieved by the use of powerful affirmations, mantras, and the complete focus of spiritual intention.

Consciousness continuum. The spectrum of consciousness from the spiritual source of all life and energy throughout the entire multidimensional universe.

Consensus environments. Areas of the universe created and sustained by the group consciousness of a large number of nonphysical inhabitants. These environments are resistant to individual thought energy.

Delta state. The brain-wave state associated with very deep sleep and unconsciousness.

Dream awakening. The act of becoming fully aware and conscious while in a dream state. Also sometimes called dream lucidity or dream awareness.

Dream conversion. The act of changing any kind of dream state into a fully conscious out-of-body experience.

Dual consciousness. Being aware and conscious within two different energy bodies simultaneously.

Energy body. A general term referring to the nonphysical or spiritual form we experience when out of body. Energy bodies are necessary for the consciousness (i.e., the soul) to function within the different frequencies existing within the universe.

Energy dimensions. Distinct and stable energy systems or frequencies of the universe. Each is a separate universe of energy existing at a stable and defined frequency rate. They are separated from one another by their individual and unique vibrational frequencies. For example, the physical universe is a single energy dimension.

Energy environment. A general term used to describe a specific nonphysical or spiritual area within a dimension. Countless different energy environments can exist within a single dimension.

Energy membrane. The convergence point of two different energy systems (i.e., frequencies of energy); the energy border or barrier separating two different energy dimensions or systems.

First energy body. The nonphysical or spiritual form often experienced during out-of-body experiences. This energy form, though invisible to current technology, exists closest in density and frequency to the physical body. Commonly referred to as the *astral body* or *etheric body* in traditional metaphysical literature.

Higher self. A broad term referring to our higher spiritual nature, essence, or mind. Many use the term as a substitute for soul or a direct connection to soul.

Human radiation. A distinct feeling of energy emanating from a nonphysical human when out of body.

Hypnagogic state. The subtle state of consciousness experienced between waking awareness and sleep; a creative state in which mental imagery is especially vivid. We pass through this state every time we go to sleep.

Kundalini. The unseen energy channel or stream that flows from the root chakra along the center of the back to the crown chakra.

Lucid dream. A dream in which a degree or percentage of awareness is present.

Mantra. (From Sanskrit, meaning "a hymn of praise") A personal chant or phrase used to focus the mind and induce a meditative or altered state of consciousness.

Multidimensional universe. The entire universe seen and unseen; a continuum of energy consisting of an unknown number of energy frequencies or levels. As we explore inwardly away from matter, the inner nonphysical energy dimensions become progressively less dense and increasingly thought responsive. The visible physical universe is the dense outer molecular crust of the entire universe.

Natural energy environments. Unformed energy areas currently unaffected by thought. Easily manipulated by conscious and subconscious thought energy.

Near-death experience. An experience reported by millions of people who are declared clinically "dead" and then resuscitated. During the experience they often report a separation from their physical body, movement through a tunnel leading to a bright light, and a new environment.

Night terrors. An intense wave of fear experienced during sleep. This is often the direct result of vibrational-state phenomena such as paralysis, rushes of energy, loud sounds, voices, and so forth. The inner energy effects of the vibrational state that are experienced during sleep are often sudden, shocking, and unexplained by modern science. This energy phenomenon is the direct result of a rapid and extensive openings of one or more chakras during sleep. The massive inner energy flow creates the strange and frightening sensations and sounds that initiate night terrors.

Nonconsensus environments. Nonphysical areas of the universe that appear formed and developed but are currently not sustained and supported by conscious energy. They readily respond to individual focused thought.

Nonhuman radiation. Unique and distinctive energy emanations originating from nonphysical beings who have never had a physical human experience.

Nonphysical inhabitants. Any living being existing within the nonphysical or spiritual dimensions without a current physical body.

Out-of-body experience (OBE or, less frequently, OOBE). A general term for the separation of consciousness from its temporary biological vehicle. Also commonly called *astral projection, etheric projection, mental projection,* and *soul travel.*

Past-life regression. The process of obtaining information, impressions, or visions about previous incarnations. This can spontaneously occur during trance, meditative, and out-of-body states of consciousness.

Physical dimension/Physical universe. The visible universe; the dense outer crust of the complete multidimensional universe. The entire physical dimension makes up but a small fraction of the entire universe—less than 1 percent.

Physical life-forms. The temporary cellular vehicles used by the consciousness (i.e., the soul) for expression within the dense outer dimension of the universe. Physical vehicles are required in order to experience, explore, and interact within the physical dimension, just as nonphysical vehicles are required to experience and explore within the nonphysical dimensions.

Reincarnation. The evolution of soul through the use of multiple births into the physical dimension; the continuing evolution of consciousness through personal experience.

REM sleep. The "rapid eye movement" that occurs during dreams.

Remote viewing. The practice of extending consciousness beyond the physical body and observing a distant physical location or event.

Second energy body. The second energy form, less dense than the first. This energy form exists at a higher (finer) frequency than the first nonphysical body. Its internal frequency corresponds to the second inner energy dimension.

Shaman. (From an ancient Tungus term meaning "between the worlds") Traditionally, a man or a woman who acted as the intermediary or conduit for a tribe between the physical world and the unseen dimensions. The shaman functioned as a healer, priest, and spiritual leader, and provided communication between the living and the dead. Much of the shaman's work was accomplished in an altered state of consciousness.

Silver cord. The traditional term for the nonphysical connection between the first inner energy body and the biological body. In many aspects it is similar to an energy umbilical cord capable of stretching across immense distances. It is reported to take several different forms such as a cordlike structure about one inch in diameter or a ribbon shape, and is also observed as many thin, fibrous filaments connecting the biological body to its densest nonphysical counterpart, the first energy body.

Sleep paralysis. The experience of being unable to move the physical body during trance, sleep, or deep meditative states of consciousness. This is often experienced immediately before and during separation and sometimes during the return to the physical body. It is a temporary condition resulting from our subtle energy body being out of phase with the physical body. Physical sensations generally return within a minute or less.

Soul. Pure consciousness existing independent of all energy bodies, shapes, or forms; the pure essence of all life-forms. Soul exists beyond all form and substance as we know it and uses various vehicles of energy for its expression in the denser regions (dimensions) of the universe. Our current physical body is one of these temporary energy bodies or vehicles used by the soul to experience, explore, and perceive within this dense outer dimension of the universe.

Soul group. Each individual soul is part of an evolving group. This group has chosen to learn and grow together through many different incarnations. We essentially evolve together with a group of established spiritual friends instead of with complete strangers.

Spirit guides. A general term used for nonphysical beings that provide assistance or guidance to spiritual seekers. There exists a wide variety of expertise, knowledge, and spiritual ability of different guides. Many spiritual guides are experts in specific areas of the soul's education and evolution.

Spiritual healing. The act of healing a person from the unseen dimensions of reality; an internal energy adjustment or the removal of an energy block that occurs within one or more of the spiritual bodies. The end result is manifested as a physical healing.

Theta state. The brain-wave state associated with deep meditation and sleep.

Thought forms. Nonphysical energy formed by thought. These forms may appear as any form or shape that can be imagined and are often responsive to focused thought energy. They often appear to those out of body as ground-level clouds with varying degrees of density and structure.

Thought transference. The universal communication method used within the nonphysical dimensions. This communication is commonly experienced as an internal recognition of a progression of vivid images or thoughts entering your mind. These images can convey emotions and thought simultaneously.

Time distortion. Since linear time as we perceive it does not exist beyond the physical dimension time, distortions such as missing or slowed time are commonly reported during out-of-body experiences, altered states, and abduction experiences.

Tunnel or portal experience. The temporary opening of an energy membrane. This energy opening is often reported during a near-death experience.

Vibrational rate. The unique vibrational frequency and resulting density that all existence and life-forms generate. The universe consists of a wide spectrum of vibrational frequencies ranging from the unseen, extremely subtle vibration of soul to the coarse vibrations of matter.

Vibrational state. Internal vibrations and sounds often reported during the preliminary stages of an out-of-body experience. Buzzing and humming sounds accompanied by electrical-like vibrations, numbness, and catalepsy (i.e., sleep paralysis) are commonly reported.

Visualization. The process of creating mental imagery for a specific purpose. This mental process affects and molds the subtle energies of the inner dimensions. Thought forms that exist around a person are often the result of their conscious and unconscious visualizations.

Acknowledgments

My thanks to all of those talented and creative people who contributed to this book. I truly appreciate all that you have given, whether an idea, a shared experience, or insight. Although not all of you are named here, be assured that your efforts have not gone unnoticed.

I would like to thank you, Tom Carey, my Webmaster and friend. Your patience and creativity have kept the Web site innovative and meaningful. And in your studio, Mach 1 Audio, our ideas for video and audio projects have become a product line for which we can both be proud.

Marie Carlson, your artistic talents were especially appreciated; you have taken cover art to a new level. Your dramatic artwork on the cover of the Past Life Exploration Course and on the Out-of-Body music CD is outstanding. The graphics in this book are due in part to a fine artist, Justin Morrow. Thank you, Justin, for your time and talent.

Thank you, Art Roffey and Gail Danto, for your workshop support, for sharing your knowledge of shamanism and Peruvian culture, but most of all for your friendship. You are truly unique and I am honored to be your friend.

For arranging radio and personal appearances that advanced the study of out-of-body travel, Ken Elliott, I appreciate your professional assistance and friendship. Your help with workshops and radio shows is invaluable

Brian Paulson, I would like to thank you as an exceptionally talented musician. I am very pleased to have some of your musical creations in my audio programs.

As always, thank you, Nat Sobel, my agent, for your continued belief in my work. And David Hennessy, your patience and understanding as my editor were truly valued.

Special thanks to all of my workshop and lecture sponsors, including the Learning Annex, the Marion Institute, the UFO Congress, Inner Voyage, Great Lakes Retreat, Journeys Beyond, Bob Provasoli, and Brian and Tina Myers.

I truly appreciate Art Bell, Mike Siegel, and Whitley Streiber, hosts of Coast to Coast Radio and also Jeff Rense, host of *Sightings*. They and many other radio show hosts are to be recognized for bringing this information to listeners around the world.

But most of all my extreme gratitude goes to those of you who have answered the out-of-body survey, participated in my Web-site activities, responded to radio shows, attended my workshops, and in any other way shared your experiences. The information you have provided will be of benefit to many people all over the world.

For more information about the author's workshops, lectures, and audio products, please write to:

William Buhlman
P.O. Box 515
Bel Air, Maryland 21014

Or visit his Web site: www.out-of-body.com.

Index

Grateful acknowledgment is made for permission to reprint material copyrighted by the following authors or publishers:

From *Abduction* by John E. Mack (New York: Ballantine Books, 1995). Reprinted by permission of Ballantine. From *The Bridge Across Forever* by Richard Bach (New York: William Morrow, 1977). Reprinted by permission of HarperCollins Publishers. From *A Farewell to Arms* by Ernest Hemingway (New York: Simon & Schuster, 1929). Reprinted by permission of Simon & Schuster. From *The Light Beyond* by Raymond Moody (New York: Bantam Doubleday Dell, 1989). Reprinted by permission of BDD. From *Mindsight* by Kenneth Ring (Palo Alto, CA: William James Center for Consciousness Studies at The Institute for Transpersonal Psychology, 1999). Reprinted by permission of The Institute for Transpersonal Psychology. From "The Out-of-Body Experience Phenomenology" by Stuart Twemlow, Glen O. Gabbard, and Fowler C. Jones (a paper presented at the annual meeting of the American Psychiatric Association, San Francisco, May 5–9, 1980). Reprinted by permission of the authors. From *The Spirit of St. Louis* by Charles A. Lindbergh (New York: Charles Scribner & Sons, 1953). Reprinted by permission of Simon and Schuster, Inc. From *Theories of the Chakras* by Hiroshi Motoyama (Pasadena, CA: Theosophical Publishing, 1989). Reprinted by permission of Theosophical Publishing House. From *The Tibetan Book of the Dead* by Evans-Wentz, W. Y. (London: Oxford University Press, 1936). Reprinted by permission of OUP. From *True Christian Religion* by Emanuel Swedenborg (West Chester, PA: Swedenborg Foundation, 1996). Reprinted by permission of the Swedenborg Foundation.